Hope and Despair

Paul B. Rich has taught at the universities of Bristol, Warwick and Melbourne and is editor of the journal Small Wars and Insurgencies. He has published several books and articles on race, imperialism and South African politics including Race and Empire in British Politics (1986), Hope and Despair: English Speaking Intellectuals and South African Politics (1993) and State Power and Black Politics in South Africa,1912-51 (1996). More recently he has been working in the area of insurgency, counter-insurgency and terrorism and co-edited the collection The Routledge Handbook of Insurgency and Counterinsurgency. in 2012. In 2018 he published Cinema and Unconventional Warfare. and is currently working on a study of insurgent movements in modern world history.

Hope and Despair

English-Speaking Intellectuals and South African Politics 1896–1976

Paul B. Rich

BLOOMSBURY ACADEMIC
LONDON • NEW YORK • OXFORD • NEW DELHI • SYDNEY

To my wife Isabel and daughters
Alexa and Frederica

BLOOMSBURY ACADEMIC
Bloomsbury Publishing Plc
50 Bedford Square, London, WC1B 3DP, UK
1385 Broadway, New York, NY 10018, USA
29 Earlsfort Terrace, Dublin 2, Ireland

BLOOMSBURY, BLOOMSBURY ACADEMIC and the Diana logo
are trademarks of Bloomsbury Publishing Plc

First published in Great Britain by British Academic Press 1993
An imprint of I.B. Tauris
Paperback edition published by Bloomsbury Academic 2021

Copyright © Paul B. Rich, 1993

Paul B. Rich has asserted his right under the Copyright,
Designs and Patents Act, 1988, to be identified as Author of this work.

All rights reserved. No part of this publication may be reproduced or
transmitted in any form or by any means, electronic or mechanical,
including photocopying, recording, or any information storage or retrieval
system, without prior permission in writing from the publishers.

Bloomsbury Publishing Plc does not have any control over, or responsibility for,
any third-party websites referred to or in this book. All internet addresses given
in this book were correct at the time of going to press. The author and publisher
regret any inconvenience caused if addresses have changed or sites have
ceased to exist, but can accept no responsibility for any such changes.

A catalogue record for this book is available from the British Library.

A catalog record for this book is available from the Library of Congress.

ISBN: HB: 978-1-8504-3489-4
        PB: 978-1-3501-8455-8

To find out more about our authors and books visit
www.bloomsbury.com and sign up for our newsletters.

CONTENTS

	Preface	vi
	Introduction	1
1	Science and White Supremacy	13
2	R. F. A. Hoernle and Liberal Idealism	40
3	Edgar Brookes and the "Lie in the Soul" of Segregation	66
4	Liberals, Radicals and the Politics of Black Consciousness	90
5	Liberal Realism in South African Fiction	119
6	Laurens van der Post: The Noble Savage and the Romantic Image of Africa	146
7	The Decline of the Idea of Civilization	169
	Conclusion	200
	Notes	213
	Bibliography	249
	Index	261

PREFACE

This volume has been written in order to explore the nature and role of English-speaking intellectuals in South African politics from the late nineteenth century to the Soweto crisis of 1976. Most of it was written while I lectured in the Department of Politics at the University of Bristol before moving to the University of Melbourne in September 1990. It forms in part a sequel to my previous book, *White Power and the Liberal Conscience: Racial Segregation and South African Liberalism, 1921–1960* published in 1984 by Manchester University Press and Ravan Press in Johannesburg. That study was a historical examination of liberalism in South Africa before the massive repressions of the 1960s and 1970s.

The present study is not intended to be simply an examination of English-speaking liberalism. The English intelligentsia in South Africa has a deeply conservative strand which has helped sustain the ideology of racial segregation in the course of the twentieth century. Liberalism has always seemed a slender plant in South African politics, though it has also served as the moral conscience of the English-speaking intelligentsia.

The study of ideas in South African politics has an increasing relevance at a time when a new constitution appears to be in the offing. The new post-apartheid state is likely to have a constitutional structure heavily shaped by the liberal democratic political tradition of the advanced industrial societies of the West. At the same time, it is important to have an understanding of the ways that previous generations of scholars and intellectuals tried to apply these ideas to the specific conditions of South Africa. I intend to extend this study through further research and analysis of the political debate among the black political elite and educated class in the years before and after the Second World War.

The sources for a theme such as this are extensive. A considerable number of collections of private papers as well as those of organizations have become available in recent years. In some cases, the absence of these collections reflects the traumas of South African politics over the last few decades. One of the most notable and tragic of these omissions is undoubtedly the destruction of the papers of Edgar Brookes. Since Brookes was himself a historian, this vandalism seems even more inexplicable, though it very probably reflects the deep pessimism he felt in the last years of his life, like so many liberals of his generation. The renewed emphasis upon human rights and ideals of freedom and democracy in more recent years in the aftermath of the cold war suggests that many of the aims of this earlier generation may not be so irrelevant to South African politics as many analysts imagined in the 1970s and early 1980s.

I am grateful to a large number of people for helping to make this book possible. In particular, I should like to thank Christopher Saunders and Stanley Uys for reading and commenting on the manuscript. I should also like to thank my colleagues at the University of Bristol for helpful comments, especially William Beinart, Michael Lee, Nicholas Rengger and Vernon Hewitt. I am grateful too to Rodney Davenport, Iain Smith, Saul Dubow, Marcia Leveson, Tom Lodge, David Maughan Brown, Bruce Murray, Peter Vale for various comments and suggestions. I also thank the Leverhulme Trust, the British Academy, the Nuffield Foundation and the Drakensberg Trust for grants and financial assistance that made the research and writing of this study possible. I would like to mention as well Mrs Anna Cunningham and her supporting staff at the Church of the Province Archives, University of the Witwatersrand, for her great and invaluable help as well as the librarians at the Universities of Bristol and Sussex, The Jagger Library, University of Cape Town, Rhodes House, Oxford, the South African

Institute of International Affairs, the Killie Campbell Library and the Union Archives in Pretoria.

University of Melbourne,

INTRODUCTION

This volume examines the role of English-speaking writers and intellectuals in twentieth-century South African politics. Intellectuals are usually a disparate group of people in any society, though broadly speaking they can be identified by the fact that they infuse into the wider population what Edward Shils has termed a "perceptiveness and an imagery" which would be otherwise lacking.[1] Intellectuals are important for being close to the symbols that can motivate or reorganize social and political activity. Their roots are sacred in that they emerged within medieval Europe from the clerical estate and they frequently have pretensions to acting as a clerisy in modern society if social, cultural and political conditions permit.

The category of "English-speaking" South African intellectuals is a broad one, since it transcends any simple ethnic categorization of South African society. The English language was historically introduced into South Africa as a result of the intrusion of British commercial, missionary and imperial forces in the late eighteenth and nineteenth centuries. While for radical Afrikaner nationalists and some contemporary African nationalists English has been seen as a language of domination, it has succeeded in spreading far beyond the white English-speaking South African population. It has been aided in this process by the fact that in the course of the nineteenth and twentieth centuries English became a major world language stretching far beyond the communities established by British imperial expansion. The language is spreading in importance in South African society and culture as Afrikaner ethnic domination of the South African polity diminishes and the society moves away from apartheid. H. L. Watts estimates that English is spreading among whites, Coloureds and Asians faster than Afrikaans while only among Africans is the growth rate of 3·62 per cent less than the 4·98 per cent growth for Afrikaans.[2]

The term "English-speaking South Africans" will in this book be used to refer to a range of figures that include the British-born white liberal Edgar Brookes, Afrikaners such as E. G. Malherbe and Laurens van der Post and African political leaders such as Z. K. Matthews, D. D. T. Jabavu and Alfred Xuma. The key influence that brings these different South Africans together is their general usage of the English language, though in many cases they often spoke and wrote in a second language such as Afrikaans, Sotho or Zulu.

Writers and intellectuals have employed English in South Africa for varying reasons. For many, such as those whites that have been most commonly identified as "English-speaking South Africans" like Edgar Brookes, it was the language that they were born with. It was for these individuals an apparently "natural" language of communication during a period when South Africa was part of a wider British Empire-Commonwealth. For others, the use of English was as a result of either colonial domination and missionary education or of deliberate choice.

Many black South African political and educational leaders used English as a result of contact with local mission stations. The American Zulu mission in Natal was instrumental in helping to establish a class of educated Zulu *kholwa* who became the leaders of their local communities such as the Luthulis in Groutville.[3] Similarly in the Eastern Cape a number of African political leaders like John Tengo Jabavu and his son D. D. T. Jabavu, who had been educated in such missions as Lovedale and Healdtown, used English in newspapers such as *Imvo Zabantsundu* from the latter part of the nineteenth century. English became the main language of communication for a number of black political movements by the early twentieth century. It was reinforced by the educational and cultural contacts of a number of black South Africans with both Britain and the United States over the following decades, often as a result of overseas missionary connections.[4]

In the case of Afrikaner writers and intellectuals, on the other hand, the use of English was frequently a more controversial issue in the face of an increasingly exclusive ethnic nationalism in the years after the Anglo-Boer War of 1899–1902. In the nineteenth century, early Afrikaner nationalists such as "Onze Jan" Hofmeyr in the Cape had championed a bilingual policy which was by no means intolerant towards the use of English.[5] Similarly, in the Transvaal the government of Paul Kruger was willing to accept the general incorporation of the English-speaking *uitlanders*, who had come to settle on the Witwatersrand in the wake of the opening up of gold mining in 1886, into a common society outside British imperial control.[6] It was only in the early twentieth century after the Anglo-Boer War of 1899–1902 that a more exclusive form of Afrikaner nationalism began to acquire a popular political base. As separate Afrikaans-speaking schools and universities began to be established, Afrikaner writers increasingly risked isolation and even active ostracism from their own people if they chose to write in English. A writer like Laurens van der Post, as chapter 6 seeks to show, became in some degree estranged from his Afrikaner background by his adopting the identity of an English-speaking writer in South Africa, especially as this became combined with a critical attitude towards the entrenchment of apartheid. Others, such as the educationalist E. G. Malherbe, tried, as is shown in chapter 1, to bridge the two communities, though this became difficult in the wake of the victory for Afrikaner ethnic exclusivism in the election of 1948.

In the years up to the 1948 Nationalist election victory the use of English in South Africa was strongly sustained by the former British imperial connection. The creation of a white-dominated Dominion in South Africa with the Act of Union in 1910 meant that South Africa became a member of the emerging British "Commonwealth of Nations". Over the following decades an English-speaking liberal "establishment" began to emerge, based on the English-language press such as the Johannesburg *Star* and the *Rand Daily Mail*, whose first editor was the British thriller-writer Edgar Wallace. The development of new universities such as the University of the Witwatersrand in the 1920s further helped sustain the cultural and educational connections with Britain.[7] The churches, too, were an additional influence, though by World War Two some churchmen were becoming increasingly opposed to the drift of the government's segregation policy.

English-language writers and intellectuals felt themselves to be increasingly on the defensive after the advent of apartheid. Externally, Britain was declining as an imperial power, though the use of English was boosted by the rise of the United States to superpower status. Internally, the nationalist government proceeded to make Afrikaans the main language of government, though it was not strong enough to make it the dominant language throughout the rest of the society. English remained the dominant language in business and commerce and it was fostered in English-speaking schools and by cohesive English-language white communities in such provinces as Natal and the Cape. As chapter 5 points out, a number of South African English writers continued to hope during the 1950s that English would progressively spread in South African society, enabling the English language group to act as a bridge-builder between the two rival "ethnic" groups of Afrikaners and Africans. On this basis a new "multi-racial" South African national culture, it was hoped, would eventually emerge.

This project of a number of English-language intellectuals in the 1950s – men such as Jack Cope and Alan Paton – remained dogged by the moves of the South African government to institutionalize ethnic compartmentalization under apartheid. Growing ethnic and class polarizations within South African society produced conditions in which it became increasingly impossible for English-language writers and intellectuals to develop into a cohesive national "intelligentsia". Intellectual life in South Africa as a consequence has remained fragmented and disjointed.

The term "intelligentsia" is a critical one in the South African context. It was a term which had a different meaning to that of "intellectuals", though the two words have become intertwined in popular parlance. Originally it was a Russian word that was coined in the nineteenth century and has since come to acquire a wide-ranging significance. Isaiah Berlin has argued that for an intelligentsia to exist its members must think of themselves as a group united by more than a mere interest in ideas for they must conceive themselves as being a "dedicated order, almost a secular priesthood, devoted to the spreading of a specific attitude to life, something like a gospel".[8]

Some social scientists have distinguished between an older "classical" intelligentsia, such as that of nineteenth-century Russia, and a more modern "working" intelligentsia. The classical intelligentsia became a social stratum and tried to perform moral and intellectual leadership in the society in which it was formed, as far as possible free from any specific class links. This conception of an intelligentsia, certainly as far as Eastern Europe was concerned, really began to collapse after the First World War. Its charismatic role began to be overtaken by the newer force of the machinery of single party domination, whether it be fascist or communist.[9] In its place there has emerged a less grandiose notion of the intelligentsia which is no longer seen as occupying a specific social stratum but is now much more allied to various social and class groups in the form of teachers, religious and political leaders, and artists and cultural workers. It is in these latter roles that intellectuals have increasingly acted in modern South African politics.

Intellectuals and the South African Crisis

Given this picture of the origins and nature of intellectuals and the intelligentsia, it is probably more correct to speak of a series of sub-national South African intelligentsias, frequently drawn together by ethnic and language identification, than one dominant national intelligentsia. This partly explains the continual issue in South African intellectual and cultural life of there being no apparently authentic "South Africans" since there has been no cohesive intellectual class able to formulate a set of national symbols and images that can command widespread consent.[10] This is not a uniquely South African problem, for other states in the English-speaking world – Canada, for example – have also faced a crisis of national identity. The South African case, however, is compounded by a far-reaching political crisis of a ruling white minority regime which has progressively lost its ideological legitimacy in the years since World War Two as it became accused of resisting the general drift towards decolonization and the end of European imperial domination.

It is this dimension of crisis which makes the nature and role of intellectuals and the various "intelligentsias" so important in understanding South African politics. As Randolph Starn has pointed out, periods of historical "crisis" in societies tend to be of an ambiguous nature since they allow for both continuity and change. The idea of "crisis" implies, Starn has argued, the "continuity of organic processes but not steady equilibrium, decisive conflict but not 'total' revolution".[11] It is possible for a revolutionary situation rooted in an alliance of popular forces to emerge out of a crisis situation, but so too can one of reaction in which the power of a ruling class becomes reorganized and consolidated. In such situations the role of ideas becomes immensely heightened as does that of intellectuals generally.

Intelligentsias, then, tend to develop in periods of social crisis. They do this because they usually inhabit a niche in the social structure between what Aleksander Galla has termed the "power establishment", on the one hand, and various class groupings on the other.[12] In a situation of mounting political polarization, the pretensions of these intelligentsias to being neutral and "free floating", as the sociologist Karl Mannheim hoped, become rapidly undermined.[13] As chapter 4 of this volume endeavours to show in the case of the English-language intellectuals organized around the South African Institute of Race Relations, the pretensions to mediation became undermined in the course of the mid 1940s and the African boycott of the system of "natives representation". A number of English-language intellectuals began trying to reformulate a role for themselves in the context of a society that began to be established on apartheid lines, but this too proved a difficult task.

A major aspect of the situation in South Africa confronting English-language intellectuals is the attempt to rework themes brought from the British imperial metropolis in order to fit them to the South African context. This is an aspect of South African intellectual history which has been rather submerged by the upsurge in research in social history since the mid 1970s. The history of ideas has fallen under suspicion both in South Africa and internationally for allegedly dealing only with debate at the elite level and for being preoccupied with the grand ideas of a few great men or women.

The growth in interest by students in the social history of South Africa has undoubtedly been important for demonstrating the significance of popular movements at the local level. Too excessive a preoccupation with this form of historiography, however, devalues the importance of intellectual and political history at the national level. Gertrude Himmelfarb has pointed out that to the extent to which social history devalues the political realm, it ends up devaluing history itself, since it renders meaningless those aspects of the past which "serious and influential contemporaries thought most meaningful". It also makes meaningless the struggle over political authority and "the very idea of legitimate political authority", since it ends up destroying all idea of political rule that is not merely a euphemism for "social control". Political ideas can often end up simply being interpreted as the "hegemony" of a ruling class.[14]

It is important for historians to understand the way that political power and authority has been conceptualized in the past, and here intellectual history has an importance in historical study over and beyond being a mere appendage to social history. Ideas in history have an autonomy and importance of their own and they need to be understood outside the matrix of social history, which tends to look only to those ideas and ideologies which had a major social impact rather than ideas which "lost out" in the market place of political debate.[15] Historians generally can benefit from a broad understanding of how the general climate of political debate was conducted in a society, and the various intellectual atmospheres that fed into it. Intellectual history is a means of unravelling patterns of ideas among intellectuals and intellectual groupings that make up what Dominick Lacapra has termed a "community of discourse". Such a community acts as a reference group on the basis of a network of shared associations and common objectives and shapes the way that intellectual inquiry is conducted by its component members.[16] In varying degrees, boundaries are maintained around different intellectual communities, whose cohesion will depend on the wider political structure and dominant ideological conceptions within the wider society.

The Methods of Intellectual History

Intellectual history has traditionally been faced with a problem in terms of the method of analysis to be adopted in understanding the evolution and development of ideas over time. One *internalist* approach is simply to look at ideas as a set of abstractions, and examine these in isolation from the rest of the social and political process. This might be of interest to a narrow range of scholars interested in ideas for their own sake, but it is generally a bloodless enterprise. As John Dunn has remarked, "It is a tale to be told by clever and subtle men [sic], and it signifies much but in it there is neither sound nor fury".[17]

An alternative *externalist* approach is to look at ideas generated by real men and women and to see them as a product of their social and economic surroundings. This second method resembles what might be termed a "social history of ideas" and has much to commend it and will be, to a considerable degree, adopted in this book. But a purely contextualist approach has weaknesses as well since it is a fallacy to assume that a thinker or organizer of ideas acts simply as a result of economic or political pressure. Clearly thinkers also act in response to the pressure or force of intellectual argument as well, and so the historian of ideas needs to pay some respect to the role of intellectual tradition in looking at why some ideas have more attraction than others. One solution to this question is to adopt a "person and ideas" approach in which the ideas of particular intellectuals are investigated in their own terms as well as put into a wider social and political setting.[18]

One key element in the evolution of South African intellectual debate is the emergence of a series of professional intelligentsias organized around universities and scholarly research. Chapter 1 of this volume examines the growing importance of university-educated intellectuals in the debate on race and the processes of academic closure which operated on the nature and direction of ideas. In this process certain key individuals – what Gramscian analysts might term "organic intellectuals" – emerge in the role of "gate-keepers" behind this closure. Alternative lines of argument become either screened out altogether or else modified and adapted to fit the dominant ethos of the academic or professional milieu concerned. For individuals unable or unwilling to fit into such a milieu, only a few courses of action are open: the establishment of a rival orthodoxy to that from which he or she has been excluded or else the joining of rival professional or intellectual grouping. The third possibility is simply retreat into intellectual exile, either physically by leaving the country, or else by continuing the enterprise of writing and disseminating ideas in lonely isolation.

English-Speaking Culture in South Africa

These latter alternatives have faced a number of figures in the English-language tradition in South Africa. In a society so sharply divided by political ideology the scope for intellectual consensus has been minimized, especially in the years since 1948. Intellectuals have been faced with a clashing set of reference points in the formulation of their ideas. The colonial inheritance of the society meant that at the time of Union in 1910 one of the chief reference points was

English intellectual culture anchored in the public schools and Oxford and Cambridge. This culture continued to exert a considerable impact on the ideas of such figures as R. F. A. Hoernle, Edgar Brookes and Laurens van der Post, as this volume seeks to show.

This English intellectual heritage, however, had by the inter-war years increasingly come under challenge from a more ethnically exclusive Afrikaner nationalism. The arrival too of a number of Jewish intellectuals from Eastern Europe began to challenge the parochialism of the mainstream English-speaking intellectual establishment by the inter-war years. Much of this debate took place at one remove from central imperatives of policy-making as there was a general reluctance of the English-speaking South African community to engage in the political process at the national level. Allister Sparks has recently argued that the white English-speaking South African population remained without any major political leader of its own after the death of Cecil Rhodes in 1900, though the Jewish businessman Harry Oppenheimer has begun to emerge as a kind of spokesman for conservatively-inclined English-speaking business interests in more recent years.[19] The English-speaking population has come to number some 1,720,000 out of a total white population of 4,900,000. It has traditionally been eclipsed politically by the larger Afrikaner population. Alfred Milner's hope after the Anglo-Boer War of 1899–1902 of settling large numbers of English-speakers in the new South African Dominion and so swamping the Afrikaners failed to come to fruition. Politically English-speakers found themselves progressively marginalized from government, and all prime ministers and the one president since 1910 have been Afrikaners.

White English-speaking South Africans have thus maintained only a weak form of group identity. They have not engaged in the same intense form of politicized ethnicity as Afrikaner nationalists. Their input into South African political and ideological debate has been a more cosmopolitan one, based on continuing economic, cultural and ideological ties overseas with Britain and the United States. This has made the development of a rigid set of ethnic mythologies hard to achieve and one that English-language opinion-leaders have been anxious to avoid. The writer Guy Butler, for instance, declared at a conference in 1974 on English-speaking South Africans at the newly opened 1820 Settlers National Monument in Grahamstown in the Eastern Cape that its purpose was not "an attempt to turn the laconic

English-speaking South African into an Ulsterman".[20] The proponents of English-speaking culture in South Africa have been increasingly driven on to the defensive and have failed to stimulate an alternative nationalism to that of their political rivals as strong cultural ties continue to be maintained with Britain as the former imperial "mother country".

English-speaking culture in South Africa has had an uncertain quality as its intellectual leaders increasingly lacked a sense of political mission. The very term "English-speaking South Africans" only came into use in the period since Union, for before then most English speakers were known as "British South Africans".[21] The attenuation of the imperial connection, however, has revealed efforts to stake some form of claim in the country's heritage, but one that is mainly confined to the cultural and intellectual rather than political realms.

It has been mainly at the level of ideology and literary culture that the English-speaking presence has been felt in South Africa, though this has not always been of a particularly liberal kind. Some of the origins of South African "native policy" lay in the tentative experiments in racial segregation in nineteenth-century colonial Natal, especially in the policies of Theophilus Shepstone.[22] As chapter 1 shows, English race theorists after Union continued to exert a considerable impact on the discussion on segregation. They also became involved in experiments in intelligence-testing to explain racial differences, though at the same time a number of English anthropologists and psychologists began to criticize these by the 1930s. But some of this work underpinned the later racism of the Afrikaner theorists of apartheid.

Similarly, a number of English-speaking writers adapted older forms of imperial popular romances in the vein of Rider Haggard and John Buchan, as is exemplified in chapter 7's discussion of Laurens van der Post. The dominant strand in English-speaking political discourse in South Africa until at least the 1940s remained an imperial one and so became subject to pronounced shocks following the British decision to relinquish colonial possessions in the 1950s and early 1960s. Some of the more conservative elements within the English-speaking population moved towards the National Party government in the course of the 1960s and 1970s as older ethnic antagonisms were forgotten in a common urge to protect white rule. On the other hand, a smaller group of liberal and radical opinion-leaders have begun to drift towards an alliance with black nationalism as a cultural crisis began to surface in the English-speaking South African literary tradition.

English-speaking intellectuals and opinion-leaders have found themselves in a situation similar to other parts of the former Empire where the energy in stimulating new developments in English-language culture has moved away from the former imperial metropolis to the post-imperial periphery. The cultural roots of this cosmopolitan process can no longer be seen in terms of a Christian ideal of a civilizing mission rooted in European imperial expansion. Indeed, its basic terms of discourse, as chapter 7 shows, are no longer those of a classical culture but rather of post-Second World War social science.

English-speaking South African culture is thus in an acute dilemma as the South African crisis heightens. It faces a number of different political avenues in the drift towards a post-apartheid state. The different sorts of possibilities have been examined and investigated by a number of English-language intellectuals over the years and the debates that they instigated is the substance of what follows. Chapter 1 evaluates the role of English-speakers in the debate on segregation before and after Union, while chapters 2 and 3 look at the contrasting thought of two prominent liberal intellectuals, R. F. A. Hoernle and Edgar Brookes. Chapter 4 surveys the developments in liberal thought in the years after World War Two and the differing responses to the rise of black consciousness in the 1970s. Chapter 5 examines the literary crisis in English-language writing in the 1950s and 1960s as the mainstream tradition of liberally-inclined realism became progressively undermined, while chapter 6 discusses the more conventional forms of imperial-adventure fiction of the writer Laurens van der Post. The final chapter evaluates the changing meanings behind the notion of "civilization" in South African political discourse, which was originally one of the main anchoring points of English-speaking imperial doctrine before it became appropriated by other groups, including some black leaders as well as Afrikaner nationalists.

The chapters in this volume seek to begin an analysis of a vast topic which, it is to be hoped, more detailed monographs will develop in subsequent years. The theme of English-speaking South Africans is one that may well develop in historiography as attention is increasingly focused on the transmission of political and cultural ideas, and there is a growing revival of interest in ethnicity in South African politics. Earlier obsessions with "modernization" and "development" by liberal analysts or with "class struggle" by Marxist social historians have diverted attention away from the significance of cultural and ethnic groupings.[23] At the same time, an inward-looking parochialism in some of this historiography has led to a neglect of the impact of international movements of ideas and cultural values on South African politics and society. It is as part of an effort to rectify this that the present volume has been written.

1
SCIENCE AND WHITE SUPREMACY

Ideas of race in South African history have usually been seen in the context of the rise of white nationalism and apartheid. This has led to a focus upon the internal dynamics of Afrikaner political mobilization organized by such bodies as the Dutch Reformed churches, the Broederbond and the National Party.[1] More recently, scholars have begun to examine the role of British racial ideas in South African politics. Leonard Thompson has shown, in a study of historical mythology in the development of apartheid ideology, that some British notions of Social Darwinism and race fitness became taken up in South Africa by both English- and Afrikaans-speaking race ideologues in the early years of the twentieth century.[2] Thompson's book did not pursue in any detailed manner the influence of British and United States racial ideology on the emergence of white South African racism, which was mainly seen through the development of Afrikaner nationalist consciousness.

Radical scholars have also begun to stress the importance of ideas generated in the imperial metropolis seeping through into South African political debate before and after Union in 1910. In the 1970s Martin Legassick began a reassessment of the British ideological impact at the time of the reconstruction in the Transvaal after the Anglo-Boer War. Legassick emphasized the role of class rather than ethnic divisions in white politics as an ideology of segregation began to be mobilized in defence of white settler power. He saw racial ideas as important in transcending Afrikaner–British divisions since they underpinned a segregationist ideology that was an instrument of white mining interests bent on mobilizing cheap black labour.³ In a series of unpublished seminar papers, Legassick's work directed attention to the role of English race theorists in systematizing a doctrine of racial segregation as a means of rationalizing a policy of perpetuating pre-capitalist economies in the African reserves. The research was strongly influenced by the sociological model of Harold Wolpe, which saw the transition from segregation to apartheid in South Africa as a result of the collapse of the subsistence base of the reserves. Migrant labour was seen as undermining the rural peasant economy that had, in its initial phases, artificially subsidized African wage rates in the urban areas.⁴

More recently, Saul Dubow has re-examined this structural explanation for segregation by the revisionist school, pointing out that some of the English-speaking apologists for segregation in the early years of this century were not so much concerned with cheap African labour migrating from the reserves but with more general issues of social discipline and social control over the African work force.⁵ Segregation for Dubow appears more as an extension of Victorian fears of the "dangerous classes". The ideology was constructed to maintain social order as well as social and moral hygiene, which became a powerful metaphorical image in the drive for urban segregation in South Africa in the early twentieth century.⁶ It was also evident from an analysis of the role of the administrative class in the South African state – the Native Affairs Department, for example – that there was an independent bureaucratic rationale for segregation in terms of a desire to consolidate the department's control through such legislation as the 1927 Native Administration Act.⁷ According to this view it is inadequate to see segregationist ideology as the mere rationalization of capitalist class interests in South Africa's industrializing society.

These efforts at refining historical knowledge on the nature and trajectory of South African segregationist ideology indicate that it has to be taken far more seriously in its impact on South African political economy than many historians of an earlier liberal generation have imagined. Segregation was not simply the atavistic product of a pre-industrial frontier but was part of a wider pattern of modernization of South African society. To this extent, segregation can be seen, as John Cell has pointed out, as an extremely adaptive and protean ideology that focused a drive towards the "highest stage of white supremacy" with logic and consistency.[8] As part of this drive, there was a desire to incorporate modern and "scientific" modes of discourse within the segregationist lexicon. This chapter argues that this was for a period an important part of the South African debate on race before the emergence of apartheid. It became superseded in the 1930s by a language that was influenced by an anthropology emphasizing cultural rather than racial differences – themes which will be discussed more fully in susbequent chapters on R. F. A. Hoernle and Edgar Brookes.

Race and the Drive for "Scientific" Segregation

The theorists involved in the South African debate on segregation after the Anglo-Boer War were small interlocking groups of political activists, racist doctrinaires and amateur anthropologists, some of whom came from missionary backgrounds. Much of their reading was second hand and, until the rise of anthropological research in the 1920s and 1930s, there was little attempt to back up propositions with systematic evidence. Argument often fell back upon well-worn stereotypes, though this did not preclude a strong determination among many of them to try and develop a "scientific" vocabulary to justify segregation.

The appeal of science lay in the rapidly growing connections in the international scientific community by the early twentieth century. Scientific discourses began rapidly penetrating new subject areas at this time – geography, anthropology and psychology. The prominent missionary role in the discussion of race issues was beginning to be undermined by this new secular interest from ostensibly neutral "experts" who appeared to be gaining allies from within a new professional intelligentsia in efforts to influence policy at the level of the state. But the newer scientific discourse ended up largely perpetuating older conceptions of African society inherited from nineteenth-century travellers and missionaries in a new guise. The scientific popularizers of race looked for tendencies described by Philip Curtin as "diversificationism" that emphasized aspects of human difference rather than similarity. Behind much of their thinking was the assumption that there was some form of order and hierarchy in human races in which the white, Anglo-Saxon race occupied the topmost position.[9]

Political debate in South Africa raged as elsewhere on the possible future outcome of the relationship forged by colonial conquest between blacks and whites. C. T. Loram, a prominent educationalist from Natal, identified three schools of thought on the issue: "repressionists", "equalists" and "segregationists". The latter school of segregationists Loram saw as holding the middle ground between the first school that wanted to return to the tough-minded policies of the old Boer republics and the second school's hope for racial assimilation on the model of the qualified African franchise of the nineteenth-century Cape.[10] "Scientific" evidence to buttress the arguments of the segregationists was open-ended, since it could be used to support a variety of predictions regarding the future. Few Social Darwinists in South Africa held that Africans would completely die out in the face of advancing white colonial settlement, in contrast to some contemporary exponents of this view in the United States.[11] The demographic balance in South Africa, in which whites numbered some one million in the 1904 census compared to three and a half million Africans, ensured that even the most ardent of white racists had to accept the permanence of African occupation in a "white man's country".

Territorial segregationist ideology, as in the popular novel of the Milner Kindergarten member, John Buchan's *Prester John* (1910), tended to be perceived in the early twentieth century in terms of different geographical regions of white and black land settlement. Cities and urban areas and the temperate high veld regions were considered the abodes of whites while the low veld areas and regions of dense African peasant settlement such as Transkei and Zululand were the terrain of Africans.[12] It was hoped that in time the rural peasant economies would undergo an internal evolutionary adaptation towards the white model of agriculture.

From the mid 1880s, a progressive erosion occurred in the Cape liberal impulse based on the idea of a civilizing mission that would progressively accommodate educated Africans into a single colonial society.[13] It is possible to see in this period many of the roots of later segregationist ideology that developed after the Anglo-Boer War during the reconstruction in the Transvaal under the British colonial administration of Lord Milner. A number of scholars have pointed to the long-term importance of the South African Native Affairs Commission (SANAC) of 1903–5 under the Secretary of Native Affairs in the Transvaal, Sir Godfrey Lagden. Though the

Commission never specifically referred to "segregation" as such, it certainly envisaged the separate holding of land by whites and Africans.[14] Legassick has argued that the Commission represented a synthesis of local ideas current in South Africa rather than of those from the British metropolis.[15] This was due in part to the fact that opinion in colonial circles in Whitehall was unclear over the long-term direction of "native policy". There was a general preference for preserving indigenous African institutions in the belief that Africans did not like being pressurized into accepting too hasty a pace of change. But what theorizing there was tended to be of an academic kind that had little direct relationship to the actual situation on the ground in Africa.[16]

Some of the British officials in South Africa after the Anglo-Boer War also shared this political scepticism. Lagden began to doubt as early as 1903 whether the Commission's work would lead to clear policies and considered that "we can do little more than generalize our conclusions".[17] As Secretary of Native Affairs between 1901 and 1905, Lagden was anxious to deal with the "black peril" scares and fears of attacks on whites by the large black servant population on the Witwatersrand.[18] He was keen that the "native question" would be debated in a "non political" manner so that it could at least appear respectable to an external audience of liberal-minded critics outside South Africa in Britain. As he wrote in some notes of 1903 the main "fear" came not from "South African opinion, nor that of intelligent men of the world, nor the forfeiture of our pledges, but the screamings of loose philanthropy and academic arguments".[19]

SANAC was in many respects part of a holding operation by the colonial establishment in the Transvaal against pressures for a more overtly racist interpretation of South African politics that frequently resorted to a pseudo-scientific Darwinism. *The Transvaal Leader* articulated a more virulent white racism prevalent in some quarters of white society on the Witwatersrand. It campaigned strongly against the extension of the qualified Cape African franchise to the Transvaal and pointed to "disgraceful scenes" that had occurred in the 1904 Cape elections where white candidates had been "begging and manoeuvring for the votes of black men". It drew the moral:

> ... we can say with scientific certainty that the process of evolution must be so prolonged as to deprive any speculations based on it of present political interest or importance, even

were the negro or negroid races of an ethnological equality with the people of Aryan or Caucasian descent. That, however, is a position that no one yet maintains. The very formation of the negro skull is so antagonistic to the theory, recalling as it does the Neanderthal head, which is admittedly a member of the European race which existed many thousands of years before the dawn of history.[20]

In the face of such populist attacks, the governing establishment in the Transvaal tried as far as possible to lead white political opinion and reduce the influence of the racial extremists, who threatened to stir up feelings at a time when there were mounting demands for self-government. Lagden saw the arrival of the British Association for the Advancement of Science in South Africa in 1905 for its annual meeting as an important opportunity for expert backing for a moderate position on the "native question". He declined an invitation to give a paper to the gathering himself, but asked Howard Pim to address it. He assisted Pim in visiting Basutoland (Lesotho) as part of his research for the paper, as this appeared to be a working model of a self-sufficient peasant reserve in Southern Africa – the model so favoured by the segregationists.[21]

Pim had made a favourable impression on Lagden in 1903 when he had argued in a paper to the Transvaal Philosophical Society that there was a need for an agreed policy on "native policy" in the effort to build a united South African state. He warned against direct methods of forcing Africans out into the labour market and saw the value of the reserve economies less as a means of promoting cheap migrant labour for the mines than as a mechanism of social control.[22] He shared the view of James Bryce that black and white would be unable to live side by side, though he was concerned to pursue a humanitarian ideal through the logic of the free market. This meant championing the ideals of De Tocqueville in his work *Democracy in America*, for "if the Natives in this country work voluntarily as free men in the open market, we need not fear the degradation of the white man".[23]

In 1905, Pim also began urging a closer comparison between the situation in South Africa and that of the US South since the apparently similar tendencies in both societies "must be due to racial difference of a fundamental nature, and for this reason must receive the closest attention and be treated with the greatest respect".[24]

During this period, liberal humanitarians internationally were not averse to trying to link a code of humanitarian ethics with what appeared to be self-evident race differences. By the late 1920s and 1930s, however, many liberal intellectuals in Britain and the United States started to question the idea that there were valid scientific criteria for measuring race differences.[25]

There was in some black political circles already a feeling of despondency by the time that Lagden left South Africa at the end of 1905. The Cape paper *Izwi Labantu* complained that Lagden had "lost the sympathy of the intelligent native", for his opinions were "simply theories thrown out as capitalist kisses to bolster up a policy which as far as his conduct of Native Affairs goes has been discreditable to the country and the credit of the British government".[26] The black elite in the Cape felt increasingly betrayed by the British colonial administration in the Transvaal. They saw the Milner administration as failing to make a strong stand against the white settler interests on the Witwatersrand who opposed the extension of the qualified Cape African franchise to the rest of South Africa.

This despondency grew in the following few years as there was mounting pressure for a "native policy" in South Africa with an "element of finality in it".[27] The attainment of "Responsible Government" in the Transvaal following the victory of the Het Volk Party of General Botha and General Smuts in 1907 provided a political focus for an attack upon the cautious trusteeship of the previous Milner administration. As the question of "Closer Union" in South Africa began to loom on the horizon, the issue of a coherent native policy for the new state increasingly permeated political debate.

This became evident with the founding in 1908 of the Transvaal Native Affairs Society "for the study and discussion of the South African native question, with a view to enunciating and advocating a liberal, consistent and practical Native policy throughout South Africa".[28] The Society soon proved less than liberal in refusing to admit Africans as members. It tended to represent English-speaking commercial and professional interests on the Witwatersrand. In March 1908, Howard Pim was elected chairman and David Pollock secretary, and it met on the premises of one of its members, a baker J. W. Quinn.[29] The colonial establishment in the Transvaal tended to avoid the body; the High Anglican Bishop of Pretoria, Michael Furse, dropped out of it, while the Governor of the Transvaal, Lord Selborne, refused to become Honorary President. At Pim's inaugural address as president only sixty people were present.[30]

Despite its tiny size, the Transvaal Native Affairs Society was a significant catalyst of ideas on racial segregation which had up until that time been debated in more elite circles of missionaries or groups of colonial administrators such as the Fortnightly Club founded by members of the Milner Kindergarten.[31] The Society was notable for discussing the ideas on industrial education which had been strongly influenced by the experiments of Booker T. Washington at Tuskegee in Alabama.[32] In the course of 1909, however, a split emerged between moderates and the hardliners led by an insurance broker F. W. Bell. The Bell faction secured the support of a British anthropologist visiting South Africa, A. H. Keane, author of a number of anthropological works and a former Vice President of the Royal Anthropological Institute. Keane was drawn to the South African debate as a virulent racist who dismissed Africans as of low intellectual capacity. A figure from the Victorian anthropological tradition, he had become marginalized from British anthropology by the early twentieth century through his refusal to accept the general enthusiasm for anthropometric measurement of skulls in preference to discovering racial differences through the study of language.[33]

Keane addressed the Transvaal Native Affairs Society in September 1909 and declared that Africans had "ceased to evolve" and were "incapable of development". He cited the work of the US racist R. W. Schufeldt, a physician from Virginia, whose work *The Negro: A Menace to Civilisation* had become popular among Southern segregationists.[34] Such "scientific" support was welcome to the Bell faction who were sceptical of Pim's humanitarianism and support for a trusteeship role for whites in the subcontinent.[35] Bell succeeded Pim as President in 1909 and in a series of pamphlets urged a programme of radical segregation that would make the Africans "like fish out of water" in the urban areas. He strongly attacked the evolutionary arguments of Lord Selborne on the grounds that they would lead to the disappearance of the white race in South Africa.[36]

This emergence of racial extremism on the Witwatersrand occurred at a time when there was little formal anthropological research in South Africa. In Britain, "Africa experts" such as Harry Johnstone urged that there should be far more interest in investigating the nature of African societies in South Africa.[37] This was a view that was echoed by Howard Pim in his retiring address as President of the Transvaal Native Affairs Society when he claimed that the "most obvious want of data sufficiently well established" made it hard to "justify our founding upon them a rational policy towards the native races of this country".[38] By the time of Union in 1910 segregation was still viewed by a number of observers as a rather dangerous experiment that had little sound scientific or empirical base on which to ground rational government policies.

Segregation, furthermore, appeared to be a strategy that contained the implicit danger of cutting South Africa from the ethical basis of statecraft that was generally considered to underlie the government in Britain. To some of the supporters of Bell – men such as H. J. Crocker, for example – this was not considered an especially serious problem. Restating the Darwinian view that the "ascendancy" of Western peoples was "physical and intellectual" rather than "moral and spiritual", Crocker argued that white rule in South Africa depended upon "some important modification of the ethical system upon which it is founded".[39] Other writers and opinion-formers at this time took a different view and were anxious for South African policy to rest upon a more universal ethical basis. "Self preservation" wrote Edward Dallas in 1909, was "not a matter of mere military dominance" for "the preservation of our moral status is as important. We hold almost as dear as life itself the mode of civilisation which is the expression of our national development – the organisation of social and public life in which the ideals of the race have found embodiment".[40] This anxiety found expression in some political speeches at the time, and in 1909 General Smuts warned an audience at Troyeville in Johannesburg that "if they wanted to push the ideal of segregation further they must be prepared for the gravest trouble that South Africa had faced in the course of its whole history".[41]

In the period after Union there seemed to be an increasingly favourable climate for segregationists to impress their ideas on political decision-makers. "Instinctively I feel the native problem cannot be longer shelved," Bell wrote to General J. B. M. Hertzog, the Union Minister of Native Affairs in 1911. "If you tackle the problem you will need all the help possible from those whose heart is fired."[42] Segregationist ideology began slowly to permeate the administrative echelons of government, though sections of the Native Affairs Department (NAD), especially from the Cape and Transkei, remained hostile to it for a considerable number of years. The Cape NAD was particularly suspicious of the extensive resettlement of the African population that would be required if segregation was to be successfully implemented. This was felt likely to lead to disruption and the erosion of the more paternalistic structures of control which the Department had been able to build up through its system of Native Magistrates.[43]

Hertzog's espousal of segregationist ideas also alarmed Cape politicians such as John X. Merriman who considered that "if it means trying to bottle the Natives up body and soul then we may as well pack up our portmanteaux, for the European race will perish".[44] The appeal of segregation to many white opinion-formers and political leaders lay in its apparent ability to guarantee the whites a place in a future South Africa. Even Bell was driven to confess that South Africa could never be a complete "white man's country", though he felt sure that "certain large areas may be preserved for each race once the desirability and the principle of segregation be recognised".[45]

The problem lay in being able to demonstrate the scientific validity of the segregationist idea to an audience that remained doubtful about both its morality and practicability. To a section of the South African professional class that was emerging at this time, the best way to justify it lay in the area of scientific evidence proving the essential differences of whites and blacks. Attention began to turn to the sociological and psychological aspects in which Africans were adjusting to the challenges of urbanization and industrialization in South Africa.

The Measurement of African Personality

In the years after Union, segregation in South Africa gained a number of adherents among the small South African professional intelligentsia, as it took on a form that appeared politically feasible and morally acceptable, despite the doubts of earlier critics. In Natal, Maurice Evans became a popular exponent of the segregationist ideal. Addressing the Durban Native Affairs Reform Club in 1912 he drew on parallels with the US South following a visit there the previous year. Like Pim, he was concerned with maintaining the cohesion of African peasant society in the face of advancing industrialization and was sceptical about the long-term prospects of an African urban population being able to survive. The point was to "protect, advise, assist, control, study to give the black man in our midst, not an individual opportunity but a racial opportunity".[46]

Racial differences were a basic reality of South African life for Evans. Despite his acknowledgment that "zoologically we are of the same species", he exhibited a strain of neo-Lamarckian thought when he emphasized that races were different through the inheritance of acquired characteristics:

> Through countless generations we have diverged, and the physical differences which are so plain to us are the outward and visible signs of mental and spiritual differences, and ... no change or treatment and environment will within any time available to us, make the black man's mind and spirit, any more than a black man's body, that of a white man.[47]

It appeared increasingly necessary to undertake some form of scientific measurement of what these supposed inherited differences really were. Evans's books, *Black and White in South East Africa* (1911) and *Black and White in the Southern States* (1913), indicated the growing importance of American ideas on industrial training and the rustication of black peasant communities on South African race thinking.[48] This was to be taken a step further when some analysts began to approach the question of intelligence-testing. By the First World War there was a growing popularity of biological and psychological theories of heredity in the British and US scientific communities. Craniological and anthropometric measurements appeared increasingly unreliable indices of race differences, and analysts were drawn to intelligence tests as a more accurate way of assessing the educational potential of different racial and ethnic groups. The tests, as Stephen Jay Gould has pointed out, were generally based upon the fallacy that the percentage variation of individuals with each group could also explain differences between groups, especially whites and blacks.[49]

The scientific community in South Africa, though small, was quick to respond to these methodological developments. The South African Association for the Advancement of Science (SAAAS), which had been founded in 1903, exhibited a continuing interest in the ideas and approaches of the scientific communities in Britain and the US, from where a number of its members were recruited. The meetings of the SAAAS also had a strong symbolic importance since they demonstrated in a tangible form the inclusion of the new Dominion of South Africa in the British Empire-Commonwealth. Members of the Association grew from 547 in 1915 to 770 in 1939, indicating the slow professionalization of science-teaching in schools and universities. The Association's meetings acted as an important forum for a variety of groups, who in the early years included a number of missionaries and educationalists as well as civil servants. The Association enjoyed a fairly close relationship with the South African state, aided by the personal interests during the inter-war years of a number of prominent politicians such as General Smuts and Jan H. Hofmeyr.[50]

The Association's proceedings from the First World War included a Section F on social and anthropological issues, and these became dominated by the capacity of Africans to "adapt" and "evolve" towards the standards of "Western civilization". The participants in these proceedings usually avoided the earlier forms of anthropometric measurement and moved rapidly towards intelligence tests modelled on those developed by Alfred Binet and Theodore Simon in France and Henry H. Goddard, Lewis A. Terman and R. M. Yerkes in the United States. One early South African analyst, Stephen Gottheid Rich, though, confessed to severe doubts in 1917 as to the applicability of the tests to Africans, following a test conducted on 170 African children and students between six and twenty-two years of age at the Amanzimtoti and Adams primary schools in Natal. The Simon-Binet tests seemed to "test as much cultural conditions as of mental ability" and there were problems in establishing what was "normal progress" among Africans. Mission-educated Africans were not necessarily "typical" either and the problem remained of establishing a valid test to assess the kind of educational curriculum that would "fit" Africans.[51]

The same year as this presentation, C. T. Loram published a book entitled *The Education of the South African Native*. This work was to have a considerable impact for a number of years on the debate on African educability. Loram was interested in the subject of "racial psychology" and the book was originally a doctoral dissertation submitted to the Teachers College at Columbia University where intelligence-testing had been developed through the work of Edward Lee Thorndike.[52]

Loram was a strong advocate of segregation at the time of writing the book, for he felt that the education of Africans should be geared towards industrial and agricultural rather than "literary and bookish" training.[53] He attacked what he saw as the "assimilationist" principles of the Cape system and stressed the differential patterns of mental development of whites and blacks on the basis of comparative tests of school children. In the case of arithmetic, for instance, he reported that African children were 30–100 per cent slower than white children and less accurate. The "slowness" of Africans was, he claimed, "proverbial" and "until we realise that our educational programme must be based upon the peculiar characteristics of the people we are doomed to disappointment".[54]

Loram doubted whether these "peculiar characteristics" were rooted in a firm pattern of "arrested development" since a eugenic programme involving "the spread of civilisation, selective breeding, improved environment, and better teaching" would in time "lessen the mental differences between Europeans and Natives".[55] The work blurred the distinction between heredity and environment and urged that both biological and social engineering were needed in South African "race relations" as it was being increasingly termed.[56]

The discussions in the SAAAS reflected this growing interest in the importance of both heredity and environment in the years after World War One. This was a period in which there was mounting anxiety in white political circles over the possible threat to white racial "purity" through sexual "miscegenation" with black Africans. Sarah Gertrude Millin's novels of this period such as *Dark Water* (1921) and *God's Stepchildren* (1924) exemplify this preoccupation with interracial sexual liaisons and the emergence of a supposedly degenerate "half caste" progeny.[57] In 1927, the Immorality Act, outlawing sexual relationships across the colour line, was passed by the South African Parliament.

In academic circles, there was a similar interest in issues of heredity. The same year as Loram's book was published, H. B. Fantham took up the post of the first professor of comparative anatomy at the newly established University of the Witwatersrand in Johannesburg. Fantham brought considerable prestige to the post, having graduated from Cambridge (Christ's College) and University College, London, where he had been gold medalist in zoology and a Derby research scholar. A passionate eugenicist, Fantham established a school of research at Wits and also served on the university's senate as well as being dean of the science faculty. He urged in a number of public lectures the need for sociologists to become "thoroughly versed in biological science" and outlined the basic precepts of eugenics and race fitness in terms of a Darwinian pattern of evolutionary development.[58]

Fantham was sceptical of Lamarckian ideas on the inheritance of acquired characteristics. He emphasized, in contrast to the rather more open-ended approach of such figures as Evans and Loram, the notion of an ineradicable heredity. His ideas were strongly shaped by the germ plasm theory of the German scientist August Weismann, who claimed that human heredity was shaped by an ineradicable "germ plasm" inherited from the earliest beginnings of *homo sapiens*. The influence of heredity was, Fantham claimed, "ineradicable, certain and immediate". This meant that in the study of human sociology "sentiment must be curbed or kept in bounds in accordance with scientific knowledge", since the goal of human improvement could only work in the context of a more basic set of hereditarian limits. Fantham warned of a general rise in the black birth rate and supported the banning of inter-racial marriages and sexual contact. The mentally unfit, he also recommended, should be sterilized. Such policies were necessary as part of a campaign for what Fantham termed a "eugenic conscience" in South Africa and he became active in establishing in the SAAAS a series of committees on genetics and eugenics.[59]

Fantham's emphasis on the centrality of heredity did not go unchallenged in SAAAS circles. In a paper at the 1926 meeting of the Association, the professor of zoology at Rhodes University in the Eastern Cape, J. E. Duerden, attacked the "force" of heredity and the idea that "the germ plasm contains within itself something which must necessarily express itself in a certain fashion in the completed body". Duerden accepted that there were limits on the extent to which heredity could be malleable. In the case of experiments on improving the quality of ostrich feathers in South Africa, for instance, it was found that "with all our selection of germ plasm in the ostrich, interacting with the best of feeding and management, we have never been able to produce a plume beyond a certain length, or a certain width, or a certain lustre and grace of form".[60] The critics of the extreme hereditarian argument tended to work within the basic assumptions of the germ plasm theory, though Duerden doubted the contemporary stress on the "rising tide of colour" as it had been described in the United States and Britain in the writings of such racists as Lothrop Stoddard and Putnam Weale. Duerden emphasized the importance of "Bantu Studies" in the training of "experts", for in

South Africa the "problem" was "no longer racial in the strict sense, not between white and black, but industrial and economic, though with peculiar features compared with other countries".[61]

Duerden's attack on the hereditarians reflected a growing realization in some quarters of the SAAAS that if the organization was to have any impact politically it had to be geared to current debate on policy, especially in the area of rescue work for "poor whites" and African educability. The Association had been considerably marginalized during the 1920s by the emergence of rival bodies formed to discuss and formulate policy on "the native question". In particular the Native Affairs Commission was established in the 1920s as a result of the Native Affairs Act, and during the early 1920s succeeded in creating a significant role for itself in debate on racial issues. Loram became a prominent member of the Commission and at the 1921 meeting of the SAAAS urged greater support for "experts" on the "native question", including political scientists, economists, psychologists and sociologists.[62]

In the course of the 1920s a number of liberals began to question the hereditarian orthodoxies of the eugenicists. One work that was especially important in this counter-attack was the book written by a former Rhodesian magistrate, Peter Nielsen, entitled *The Black Man's Place in South Africa*, published in 1922. This was critical of the craniological classification of races and debunked the mythology of skull measurements that was still finding support in some SAAAS papers at this time.[63] Nielsen also attacked the notion of "arrested development" at puberty among Africans as being "another popular notion for which a sort of pseudo scientific authority may be quoted from encyclopedias and old books of travel".[64] The work dismissed the idea that there was a distinct "native mind" intrinsically different to that of whites, and it developed the Lamarckian argument that there could be inheritance of acquired characteristics.[65] Nielsen was one of the most important early South African critics of the gamut of images and popular mythologies inherited from the phase of European colonization of the African continent. He rejected the Darwinian assumption that human ethics were subordinate to the imperatives of natural selection and emphasized instead the importance of human intelligence in transcending the laws of biological struggle. White "superiority" was not based, he argued, upon longer exposure to education, for "now that Western civilisation is spreading over the land the difference in the moral outlook of the two peoples tends to decrease; with the savage vices go the savage virtues, and soon there will be no difference at all."[66]

Nielsen's book represented a landmark within local South African debate over the nature and direction of supposed racial differences. While many of its arguments were already becoming familiar at this time in liberal circles in Britain and the US, it was a significant rejection within South Africa of many of the basic assumptions of "diversificationism" in most of the contemporary race thinking in the country. The book had an appeal to a number of the English-speaking liberals organized around the Joint Council movement in South Africa in the 1920s and 1930s. Edgar Brookes, as chapter 3 points out, saw Nielsen's book as a major challenge to the idea that there was a distinct African "mind" which could be explored through various forms of "scientific" intelligence-testing. This was a view that came to be shared by the Joint Council organizer, J. D. Rheinallt Jones, who publicly rejected in an SAAAS paper in 1926 the ideas of a "primitive mentality" based on the theories of the French anthropologist Lucien Levy-Bruhl.[67]

This did not prevent some of the English-speaking liberals becoming involved in various efforts at intelligence-testing, especially those concerning the attainments of "poor white" children. The professor of philosophy at the University of the Witwatersrand, R. F. A. Hoernle, started conducting such tests in 1926 on behalf of the Transvaal Education Department, though his conclusions were bitterly attacked in the Afrikaner nationalist paper *Die Burger* for alleged bias.[68] Hoernle acknowledged that the results were "experimental and provisional" in nature, though he lectured on the tests to the YMCA in Johannesburg as well as to the East Rand Teachers Association.[69] There was a considerable fund of interest in intelligence-testing at this time among both welfare and educational circles in South Africa, as the testing was seen as representing a "scientific" approach to the question of tackling the "poor white" issue. As the next chapter shows, Hoernle was keen to mobilize more extensive academic support behind this objective from his colleagues and he became influential in the 1930s in developing it as part of more general applied social research at the University of the Witwatersrand.

Intelligence tests also began to be examined with some interest in government circles in the course of the 1920s as a means of gathering evidence to tackle the "poor white" issue. Differences between different groups of "white" children were usually interpreted in terms of environmental differences, while those between whites and blacks were perceived in hereditarian terms. In 1923 the Commissioner for Mental Disorders, J. T. Dunstan, delivered the Presidential Address to Section F of the SAAAS and made a comparison between "retarded" and "defective" white children. In comparison with the good prospects for educating the "retarded" white children, there was, Dunstan claimed, "such a deficiency of brain cells" among Africans that "neither education, nor environment, nor any other factor except a mutation, can lead to their rising to the level of advancement of the higher races".[70] This interest in intelligence-testing continued throughout the 1920s, and in 1928 the psychologist I. D. MacCrone published some early research in social psychology (which he later disclaimed) examining the comparative scores of African girls in Rosettenville, Johannesburg, and those of London school children collected by the educationalist Cyril Burt. He concluded that there was an apparent peak in the average level of performance around eleven to twelve years for the African children and thirteen to fourteen years for the white children. This appeared to demonstrate the phenomenon of "arrested development".[71]

By the late 1920s, there were pressures to put this kind of research on to a more organized footing, especially with the onset of the depression and the growing political importance of "poor white" issues in South African politics. In 1929, E. G. Malherbe, was appointed Director of the newly established National Bureau for Education and Social Research. Malherbe had been strongly influenced in his early approach to educational issues by C. T. Loram who pressed him to go into a similar field as himself on "race relations".[72] Like Loram, Malherbe had studied at Teachers College in the US where he kept close links with its academic teaching staff. However, a period of teaching in the newly formed Department of Education under the British educationalist Fred Clark at the University of Cape Town in the early 1920s had impressed on him the need to avoid areas of too great political controversy.[73] Loram himself had fallen out of favour with the Union Minister of Native Affairs, E. G. Jansen, in the late 1920s and was forced to resign from the Native Affairs Commission in 1929. The following year he opted out of South African issues in a state of some bitternes and took a post as Professor of Race Relations at Yale.

Malherbe was determined not to fall into the same trap as Loram.

In a paper to the SAAAS he focused upon the economic dimensions of the "poor white" issue, which he saw, on the basis of W. M. Macmillan's 1919 study, *The South African Agrarian Problem*, as one of transition from an agrarian to an industrial society. He condemned the "colour bar" as a barrier that checked the "natural growth of the native" and broadly supported the aims of industrial education for Africans.[74] During the following decade he began to direct the research of the National Bureau towards what he perceived to be the policy needs of the government. He tried to influence official thinking towards alleviating the hardship of poor white families and breaking a cycle of pathology that was generally believed, on the pattern of studies (now widely condemned as unscientific) of the Jukes and Kallikak families in the United States, to run through several generations.[75] Malherbe was particularly keen as part of this educational proselytization to establish links with the mainstream white liberal establishment that was organized, after 1929, around the South African Institute of Race Relations.[76]

The National Bureau tried to act as a forum for debate on African educability and provided the base for further intelligence-testing by the psychologist of the Department of the Interior, M. L. Fick. This had involved the testing of individuals through the model of the Simon-Binet tests and group tests modelled on the Army Beta test devised by R. M. Yerkes in the US during the First World War. The findings of Fick's study were based on 10,000 white, 817 Coloured, 762 Indian and 293 African children. Fick challenged the findings of Loram in his 1915–16 study by arguing that the scores showed significantly different levels of ability between white and African children. Even the mission-educated African children, he declared, did not grow up with pictures or diagrams and he suggested that African children "may have a different type of intelligence". There appeared to be among the African children "a complete lack of power of working as a group", though the school teaching methods were found to be based on learning by rote such that "when the child is faced with a novel situation that requires some initiative or independent activity, as in the intelligence test, it is confused and at a loss".[77] The "poor white" children, on the other hand, were tested on government-funded "indigent settlements". Two farms were tested before and after the introduction of a feeding scheme lasting for a period of eighteen months. Though there was no significant increase in intelligence levels, "greater alertness and application" were noted in the school children and it was suggested that if the results were "corroborated by a longer period of feeding and stricter control, they hold out great possibilities for overcoming the apathy, lack of application and of initiative – qualities which appear to be the greatest obstacles in rehabilitating the majority of the poor whites".[78]

The impact of the research on intelligence testing on government education policy in the 1930s appears to have been limited. The research that Fick initially reported on at the 1929 meeting of the SAAAS became rather eclipsed in professional circles by the debate surrounding the report of the Native Economic Commission in 1932, which advocated the "adaptation" of African societies in the reserves towards those of white settler society in South Africa. This represented a middle course between the Cape ideal of assimilationism on the one hand and "repression" on the other. While segregationist in its acceptance of the idea of separate African land ownership in South Africa, it was concerned as far as possible to persuade and convince the African political leadership of the just nature of the segregationist programme.[79] It was going to be difficult to do this if it was seen as resting upon the premiss that Africans were permanently inferior to whites in their capacity for education.

The role of black opinion in the issue of African educability also became an additional important element in debate in the 1930s. An informed class of black opinion-leaders had emerged in South Africa by the 1920s whose political views became sharpened by the trajectory of segregation policy. In the Cape, D. D. T. Jabavu at the University College of Fort Hare was a strong exponent of Cape liberal ideals and a passionate defender of the colour blind franchise threatened by the proposed legislation of the Pact Government of J. B. M. Hertzog. In 1929 he challenged Fick's assertions concerning African mental inferiority at the SAAAS meeting, maintaining that the differences were culturally induced. Jabavu backed up this assertion by pointing out that over the previous twenty years sixty black South Africans had obtained higher degrees outside the country, while at the University College of Fort Hare a further seventy-seven had passed the university matriculation and ten had graduated in the University of South Africa.[80]

The development of an articulate black intellectual opposition to the claims of the hereditarians helped to buttress the opposition of the white liberal establishment to the continuing trajectory of segregation in South Africa. Jabavu became a member of the

Committee of the South African Institute of Race Relations and during the 1930s many white liberals established much closer connections with members of the black political and educational elite. This black liberal opposition represented a generation of what Shingler has termed African educational modernizers who avoided nationalist ideals in favour of remodelling African society around norms of Christianity and industry and the creation of a black assimilationist elite.[81] Not all black leaders in South Africa unanimously accepted such goals, but the black input into the education debate proved important for the emerging group of white liberal critics of segregation in the early 1930s who were anxious to shift the debate away from race towards cultural attributes. Black leaders and intellectuals, however, still remained junior partners to the white liberals in this enterprise in the 1930s.[82] Z. K. Matthews, a colleague of Jabavu's at Fort Hare teaching anthropology, hoped to establish discussion groups of black leaders in order for Africans to debate issues on race in a manner similar to the SAAAS. But this scheme failed to get established in the pre-war period leaving black leadership generally beholden to the mainstream bodies of the white liberal establishment.[83]

New Departures

By 1930 a number of white South African liberals such as Edgar Brookes, James Henderson and R. F. A. Hoernle had visited the United States and observed the progress of US blacks in comparison to black South Africans.[84] To some of this group, the older ideals of segregation began to appear increasingly wanting in that they failed to allow for the creation of a Westernized urban black elite that could be incorporated into a common industrial society. Many liberals saw themselves as cultural intermediaries between what they termed "Western civilisation" and a proletarianizing black African society.[85] They managed to exert some influence on the political debate on black education in South Africa in the 1930s. The Report of the Inter-Departmental Committee on Native Education in 1935 showed signs of the new thinking on race differences in that it avoided any supposedly "scientific" evidence of inferior African educability. It opposed the idea that education should be aimed at keeping Africans in segregated reserves.[86] It was impressed by the evidence of a number of witnesses, including Edgar Brookes, that there was no difference philosophically in the ultimate aim of education but only of "method", since "the education of the White child prepares him for life in a dominant society and the education of a Black child for a subordinate society".[87] Official ideology in South Africa by the 1930s tended to fall back on justifying the present social order through the previous historical legacy of colonial conquest rather than resorting to an argument for permanent black racial inferiority. This related to its interest in gearing education to a changing economic pattern in which growing numbers of Africans were envisaged as leaving the reserve economies and coming into "contact with European economic life".[88]

Such a policy entailed the emergence of a more skilled or semi-skilled African work-force, though there was also a continuing emphasis upon the need to maintain social cohesion. A number of new theoretical approaches began to be developed from both psychology and social anthropology to reinforce this shift away from race towards a cultural analysis of South African political and economic divisions. The ideas of the social anthropology school of Malinowski in Britain as well as US anthropologists such as Franz Boas began to permeate the thinking of South African liberal discourse in the early 1930s in the wake of the 1932 Native Economic Commission Report. The school of social anthropology rejected supposedly "scientific" determinants of racial difference in favour of a social model rooted in concepts of cultural change. Winifred Hoernle, the wife of R. F. A. Hoernle, who taught anthropology at the University of the Witwatersrand, ardently defended this view in a presidential address to the Section E of the SAAAS at its 1933 meeting. In the process, she shifted the emphasis away from the historical study of African cultures towards an inductive study of their functioning components. She described social anthropology as emerging as a discipline that was no longer simply concerned with "lower cultures" but with more general issues of "culture contact" as African societies began a process of social transition towards a Western style industrial order. This approach was to have a considerable impact on anthropological research in both South Africa and Britain in the course of the 1930s.[89]

In the case of psychology, too, there was a shift away from intelligence-testing towards a wider study of inter-group relations. I. D. MacCrone stressed the need in 1932 for social psychologists to reach agreement on the criteria for measuring both personality traits and social attitudes and to begin tackling the question of "inter-racial attitudes".[90] By the mid 1930s this approach began to have some impact on liberal attitudes towards "race relations" in South Africa. MacCrone felt that race differences as such were a "pseudo-problem" and that what was far more important was a study of the group psychology that underlay racial cleavages which were of a perceptual kind. MacCrone drew upon North American studies which showed that supposed differences between children in schools in northern and southern states were due to selective migration. He felt compelled to agree with the American scholar Otto Klineberg that these differences would disappear as the black "environment" more nearly approximated that of whites. What was far more significant than any supposedly innate racial differences were group contacts and the way that group psychology was formed.[91] MacCrone's ideas had an immediate impact on J. D. Rheinallt Jones, the director of the South African Institute of Race Relations, who reported to the annual SAIRR meeting in Durban a series of tests on English and Afrikaner perceptions of each other in the South African context.[92] MacCrone's work was vital for adding a psychological dimension to the "frontier thesis" in South African historical debate. His *Race Attitudes in South Africa* (1937) advanced the idea that contemporary racial aversion in South Africa was a product of racial attitudes generated in the pre-industrial frontier setting and which had survived into the era of industrialization.[93]

This shift away from hereditary explanations for intelligence differences also became evident in the important 1934 conference in South Africa, organized by E. G. Malherbe and entitled *Educational Adaptations in a Changing Society*. Here R. F. A. Hoernle attacked Fick's conclusions on African educability on the grounds that there was no clear scientific evidence for a distinct African "race psychology" and that any differences were culturally induced. This might still nevertheless lead, Hoernle acknowledged, to conclusions similar to the segregationists in that "Europeanization" of Africans might be opposed on the grounds that it threatened their cultural unity but it could not be based on any hereditarian evidence. Citing the work of Nielsen, Hoernle argued that it "would be a gain for the discussion to be switched from attempts to demonstrate the inherent congenital inferiority of the Bantu to an examination of their disabilities under White rule or of the positive values inherent in traditional Bantu culture".[94]

The advocates of the unity of the human species ended up winning a limited victory in South African political debate in the 1930s. They were able to shift the intellectual ground towards a discussion of cultural rather than racial attributes in African educability. This shift did not become immediately apparent to all those involved in research on intelligence. The official psychologist of the South African government, Oswald Black, expressed interest in 1935 in establishing an investigation on children's mental development in the belief that both Loram and Fick's research showed that African intelligence was "arrested" at the age of twelve or thirteen.[95]

Nevertheless, the shift in perspective from race to culture began to exert an impact by the late 1930s on Afrikaner anthropologists and educationalists. Even Nationalist advocates of Christian National Education started to avoid overtly "scientific" arguments of African inferior educability. In 1939, Dr W. W. M. Eiselen, Professor of Volkekunde at the University of Stellenbosch and later Secretary of Native Affairs under Dr Verwoerd in the 1950s, wrote a non-commital foreword to Fick's study, *The Educability of the South African Native*. Grading based on intelligence tests could "hardly be accepted as reliable," Eiselen wrote, "unless it shows a distinct superiority in comparison with that based on Class achievement." Fick's data confirmed for Eiselen that "the Native" was not "educable in precisely the same way as the European", though there was still a need for more data on the subject.[96]

In the period up to the outbreak of World War Two there were signs of an emerging consensus among English-speaking liberals and Afrikaner nationalist intellectuals on the centrality of culture rather than race in South African debate. This did not prevent markedly contrasting emphases upon the *degree* of the cultural differences involved and the form that state policy in South Africa should take to deal with them. But "scientific" arguments for biological race difference had a diminishing impact on the debate and were to become further marginalized once the war itself had begun. The bogus claims of National Socialism in Germany made scientific racism increasingly unacceptable intellectually. Malherbe wrote acerbically in his private notebook sometime during World War Two of the embarrassing memory of some of the claims made at SAAAS meetings. It was an "amazing spectacle", he felt, "that men of science will come together annually in solemn conclave and pass upon [condone] results of measurement inaccurate the like of which they wd never have tolerated in their own scientific work".[97] Such an outlook indicated a more aggressive mood among many liberally inclined scholars.

Fick's research came in for particularly strong attack in the early 1940s. Though serving in the Royal Air Force in Britain, the young researcher Simon Biesheuvel managed in 1943 to publish through the South African Institute of Race Relations a monograph, *African Intelligence*, that systematically investigated the fraudulent assumptions behind *The Educability of the South African Native*. Biesheuvel thanked Hoernle in the preface for the "scientific and spiritual heritage" which he had bequeathed to South Africa.[98] He went on to develop in the book a detailed analysis of approaches to measuring intelligence. It was extremely doubtful, he concluded, that it would be possible to select two representative examples of "African" and "European" races. African intelligence was influenced by a variety of sociological forces and "the manner of living of the Union African population" had, as a result of contact with "Western civilization", become "so diversified that it would not be correct to speak of one cultural milieu common to them all".[99] The quality of schooling and general home environment had some influence on the intelligence levels, as did other basic qualities – such as, for example, the nutrition of children. Biesheuvel considered it highly likely that intelligence could be impaired by malnutrition so that straight comparisons between white and black children were hardly likely to be valid.[100]

Given these basic problems, Biesheuvel considered that Fick's research did not meet any basic scientific criteria. A representative sample of Africans would have to consist of at least 2000 subjects of both sexes ranging from one to twenty years old, whereas Fick's sample had been just 180 with no clear criteria for their urban or rural origin.[101] The tests themselves were also accused of being culture-bound. The Porteus Form and Assembling test, for instance, consisted of pictorial representations of a wheelbarrow with a hammer and head and a coffee pot with a body which would very probably be unfamiliar to considerable numbers of African children.[102] It would thus be highly dubious to conclude that there was any innate tendency towards "arrested development" among African children as Fick presumed.

Biesheuvel's work was in many respects a landmark in South African psychological research, despite the fact that many of its notions would be now considered old-fashioned. The influence of

SCIENCE AND WHITE SUPREMACY 37

the culture contact school of anthropology, particularly the work of Ellen Hellman on urban African slum yards, was important for steering Biesheuvel into a more sociological investigation of what would now be termed comparative disadvantage in terms of access to health and education of different ethnic communities.[103] The work pointed the way forward for social research in the post-war years as it steered the central line of questioning away from "race" *per se* towards social, economic and cultural factors in the make-up of South African society. This kind of research, though, did not necessarily develop in any simple or unilinear manner.

The Post-War Years

The more sociologically orientated outlook articulated in Biesheuvel's early work continued to prevail after 1945, though the contribution from English-speaking social psychology in South Africa got rather stuck in the paradigm that had been evolved in the course of the 1930s and early 1940s. I. D. MacCrone, in particular, remained a dominant figure for the following three decades. His writings tended to reinforce the perception held by many English-speaking intellectuals of a rigid Afrikaner group psychology that was strongly resistant to change. Social psychology in South Africa was steered under MacCrone's influence towards a sociological investigation of racial attitudes and group conflict. There were close similarities in this work to the post-war obsession in the United States with the sociology of "race relations", though MacCrone was notable for maintaining a historical view of the origins and development of this group conflict, which he located on the pre-industrial frontier. These roots from the eighteenth century onwards had helped sustain a rigid Calvinist dogma within Afrikanerdom which in turn was impelled by a collective urge to exert group domination over the rest of the society.[104] At the heart of what was a rather primitive variant of the "frontier thesis" in South African historiography there lay an implicit Social Darwinism in the sense that history was seen as formed by continuous group struggles with the dominant group determined to preserve its status as long as possible.

The social science study of group psychology that was fostered by MacCrone in South Africa in the post-war period was also important for laying the foundations for later debates on ethnicity which were to become fashionable in the early 1970s.[105] It established that racial attitudes along with class, religious and national attitudes were part of the same species of "group attitudes", though the structural and economic forces sustaining these were not examined in any systematic manner. Neither was there any recognition that these group identities could be in some degree contrived or manipulated by dominant political elites or classes. The typical individual that MacCrone and his students tested for the level of ethnocentric attachment appeared to be a relatively passive subject who was "in the grip of forces operating at emotionally toned and primitive levels of personality".[106] To this extent, the research appeared to be unable to develop a theory that would explain how such ethnocentric attitudinal change could occur; all it could do was to warn against the dangers of perpetuating Afrikaner domination of South African society which MacCrone considered little short of a "nightmare".

MacCrone liked to describe himself as an "old fashioned Cape liberal" and his public lectures tended to confirm the English-speaking South African folk wisdom that the ills of South African society could be put down to Afrikaner ethnocentrism and group domination of the society's politics. It was the "Calvinistic-Puritanical personality", he declared in 1958, which formed the basis of South African society's ethnocentrism and which resulted in an "uncharitable toughness" towards the "underdog, the underprivileged and the unfortunate generally".[107] There was little systematic recognition in this kind of work of how the economic system might affect racial attitudes or the degree to which changing existing racial attitudes would transform the balance of power in the wider society.

The research work fostered by MacCrone, like that of Biesheuvel, did shift attention away from the biological phenomenon of "race", while also keeping alive the liberal ideal that reason could ultimately be brought into play to resolve the society's tensions. The obsession with trying to measure intelligence, however, remained. There were pressures for the development within social psychology of more reliable indices of intelligence than those of the inter-war years, since the future of South Africa appeared to rely on the creation of a larger technical, professional and administrative elite. The earlier fascination with biological eugenic fitness of Fantham was shifted in some degree towards a more specialized and sophisticated strand of research by the 1950s, concerned with discovering more accurate and reliable indices of intelligence among school children. The work of Simon Biesheuvel after World War Two for the National Institute for

Personnel Research, for instance, avoided the earlier emphasis on the social and economic background of the different groups of subjects studied. It became more concerned with developing methods for testing intelligence which were divorced from the old-fashioned IQ tests and concentrated instead on measuring aptitude. The point should be to measure *probabilities* of success in order to predict the likely numbers who would be able to qualify in vocational training courses or the proportion of men and women in semi-skilled jobs who could train for more skilled occupations.[108] The main focus became manpower, or more specifically personpower, and planning that would relate the resources available for training to the likely numbers available. This kind of research tended to reflect the needs of industrialists rather than racial ideologues and indicated the degree to which eugenics and intelligence-testing had developed from the pre-war years. At its heart was a belief that social progress could be facilitated by an enlightened and rational elite. Whether, though, this trend would necessarily lead in a society like South Africa in a more "liberal" direction was a philosophical rather than a psychological question. It was not one to which liberals responded with large degrees of optimism as the following chapter on R. F. A. Hoernle indicates.

2
R. F. A. HOERNLE AND LIBERAL IDEALISM

R. F. A. Hoernle is a major figure in the intellectual formulation of modern South African liberalism. His ideas helped define the aims of the generation of liberals that emerged in South African politics during the inter-war years. They also continued to exert a considerable influence on later political thinking long after his death in 1943.

The political dimension of these ideas has been rather neglected by the school of South African social historians. Martin Legassick has argued that Hoernle's idealist thought was significant for its stress upon social cohesion and for reinforcing what many neo-Marxist historians have perceived to be a liberal role in South African politics, acting as "agents of social control" and managers of class conflict.[1]

On the other hand, Richard Elphick, in a more sympathetic assessment, has emphasized Hoernle's political realism and recognition of the obstacles confronting liberals in South African politics. Unlike other liberals of the inter-war period, Elphick has argued, Hoernle was notable for subjecting the intellectual assumptions of the South African liberal tradition to a systematic critique, for it was no longer enough simply to rely on the traditional Christian hope that better things would eventually come. Hoernle thus recognized the difficulties in making liberal institutions in an ethnically divided society like South Africa politically durable.[2]

Both these themes of social control and political realism are important in Hoernle's thought and have continued to exert considerable influence in liberal discourse in the decades since Hoernle's death. A single-minded focus upon them detracts from other important features of Hoernle's life and work. Hoernle's thought was not always systematic, revealing ambiguities and a leaning, on occasions, to an opportunism of the moment. From a long-term standpoint, however, he exerted an important intellectual impact on South African politics for two main reasons. Firstly, he contributed to the undermining of the classical liberal tradition inherited from Britain in the nineteenth century by stressing the predominance of group over individual identities in South African politics. Secondly his overwhelming keenness to establish a dialogue with a segregationist state led to a serious erosion in the credibility of liberal precepts in the eyes of a later generation of black political activists. This has helped create a situation where "liberal" has become almost a term of political opprobrium in many contemporary black political circles in South Africa.

Hoernle, unlike many South African liberals, was not from the Cape but Germany, where he was born in Bonn in 1880. His family had been for two generations missionaries in India and were British subjects. His father A. F. Rudolph Hoernle was a leading scholar of Sanskrit and the first five years of his life were spent in Britain before the family moved to Germany.

The young Hoernle was educated at a Protestant *Landschule* at Pforte before going in 1898 to Balliol College, Oxford, to read Greats. He originally intended entering the Indian Civil Service but became drawn to philosophy, strongly influenced by the late nineteenth-century liberal idealism of T. H. Green and Bernard Bosanquet. His academic record at Oxford was impressive and he was elected to the Jenkyns Exhibition at Balliol and the John Locke Scholarship in Mental Philosophy. The following year he secured election to the Senior Demyship at Magdalen College.

In 1905, Hoernle took his first lectureship at the University of St Andrews, where Bosanquet was professor, before moving to the South African College in Cape Town in 1908. In 1912 he moved to Armstrong College, Newcastle-upon-Tyne (then part of the University of Durham), followed by Harvard in the summer of 1914, where he became considerably influenced by the absolute idealism of such philosophers as R. B. Perry and W. E. Hocking. After spending six years at Harvard, Hoernle returned to Armstrong College in 1920.

By this time he had married a South African anthropologist, Agnes Winifred Tucker. His wife's poor health encouraged him in 1923 to accept the offer from the Principal of the newly established University of the Witwatersrand, Jan H. Hofmeyr, of the chair of philosophy.[3] In Johannesburg Hoernle became increasingly involved in university administration as well as in the South African Institute of Race Relations after its establishment there in 1929. He became president of the Institute on the death of Howard Pim in 1934 and remained so until his own death in 1943.

The Intellectual Background

Hoernle tried to apply liberal idealist concepts to South African politics and society and his work is interesting for its development of a conservative strand of Greenian idealism that was expounded by his mentor Bosanquet. Green's liberal Hegelian idealism represented a secularized version of a Broad Church philosophy of social duty. It questioned the mid-Victorian obsession with ideas of enlightened self-interest and the utilitarian ideal of the greatest happiness of the greatest number. Green tried to link these to a more positive conception of duties that needed to be performed through the state in the interest of the public good. He rejected the idea that humanity was driven merely by impulses and instincts. He also saw individuals as being motivated by freedom of choice and a conscious mind that could pursue ends that were not merely *caused* but *posited*.

The Greenian doctrine shared the utilitarian rejection of resting political rights on a priori natural rights. The very notion of natural rights seemed to Green to be a contradiction in terms, since rights could only be exercised in society and not outside it. Political ends for Green needed to be located in the Kantian conception of ideal ends since it was by such means that the action of the individual could be linked to the wider common good.

Green strove to redefine the ends of liberalism, making them more favourable to the actions of the state, which earlier liberals had treated with suspicion. He saw the state's role as one that did not simply co-ordinate the actions of self-interested individuals but also pursued the organic notion of the collective common good. In the process it was hoped a moral transformation in the outlook of the state's citizens would occur, since Green saw *will* and not *force* as the basis of state power. Such ideas contributed in the late nineteenth century to the shift towards a more collectivist idea of a benevolent state whose objectives were the securing of social and political reform.[4]

The Greenian legacy in England filtered into a number of philosophical streams after his death in 1882: towards a "new liberalism" espoused by social reformers such as L. T. Hobhouse, J. A. Hobson and J. B. Haldane; towards Fabian socialism as espoused by Graham Wallas and the Webbs; and towards a more conservatively inclined social imperialism and campaign for "national efficiency" favoured by the Milnerites in the years after the Anglo-Boer War. In some cases these groups formed alliances, such as that of the Milnerites and Fabians through the Coefficients Club in Edwardian England. But these contrasting approaches contained different social and political ideals.[5]

The latter variant of conservative social imperialism was the one strain of liberal idealism that had some influence on Hoernle through the work of his colleague Bernard Bosanquet at St Andrews. Bosanquet took Greenian idealism into a more conservative direction as he played down Green's notion of common citizenship rights at the heart of the conception of the public good. Bosanquet reinterpreted Greenian liberalism in rather illiberal terms by abandoning the stress on the moral development of individuals and the notion of liberty as a personal value.[6]

Bosanquet recognized only a limited space for democratic choice by the individual citizen. In an 1895 essay, "The Duties of Citizenship", he saw citizenship located in the classical model of the Greek city state where a small community presented no institutional barriers between the individual and his fellow-citizens. Small communities ensured that the only association the citizen was compelled to belong to was the state itself in which politics was a necessary part of the citizen's life. Otherwise, the interests of the citizen could be pursued outside the formal political arena in such bodies as the family, the neighbourhood, the trade union or the professional association.[7] This minimalist definition of political action in the modern state returned in some ways to an older conception of politics in the mid-Victorian era, in which the pursuit of what Macaulay termed "things political" was mainly the preserve of an educated and interested elite.[8]

The Development of Hoernle's Thought

A similar outlook pervaded Hoernle's early thinking on the nature of citizenship. In a lecture to the Institute of Bankers in Cape Town in 1908 he emphasized the role of the cash nexus rather than political activity in fostering the notion of citizenship. The psychological dimension of the use of money, he declared, "may, without exaggeration, be described as one of the most striking symbols of citizenship".[9] The cash nexus could be used as a major instrument of social reform through encouragement of home ownership rather than "the street or the public house".[10] Hoernle showed a strong predilection to link ethical change with economic prosperity, though he avoided too outright an identification with Whiggish economic liberalism. The significance of Bosanquet's ideas, he pointed out, lay in the development of "strong, self reliant, enterprising individuals, ready to shoulder their responsibilities and to meet with courage and self control whatever fortune may bring".[11]

Similarly on the "native question" Hoernle had similar views to those of the liberal segregationists in the period before World War One such as Howard Pim, Patrick Duncan, Philip Kerr and Richard Rose Innes. To Hoernle the issue revolved round the incorporation of wage-earning Africans into the "social organism" without at the same time creating a "corrupt, discontented and dangerous industrial proletariat". Rhodes's Glen Grey Act of 1894 was one possible solution since it served as a *via media* between the "maintenance of the primitive tribe outside the white state, where the native is a danger to civilisation because he is savage" and, on the other hand, the "creation of a native proletariat inside the white state, where the native is a danger because he is only half civilised".[12] Hoernle viewed race issues through Victorian spectacles of civilization counterposed to barbarism; and though his thinking grew in sophistication, this basic outlook remained.

Hoernle also imagined a future South African state rooted in a local civil patriotism similar to the ideal of Bosanquet. He urged the teaching of history and classics in the school curriculum as a means of realizing this end and hoped that the white "civilization" being established in South Africa would embody the classical humanism that lay at the heart of much of the Victorian notion of civilization.[13] As chapter 7 shows, such ideas had a considerable impact on South African liberals in the early twentieth century in fostering the notion of a new classical "civilization" in the new white settler state.

Hoernle acknowledged, though, that the state was not a monolithic organism and there were rights which the individual had against it. After the First World War there was an intellectual reaction in Britain to late Victorian Hegelian idealism. Philosophers such as J. N. Figgis, G. D. H. Cole and Harold Laski were progressively drawn towards ideas of pluralism that emphasized the role of corporate groups between the individual and the state.[14] In his inaugural lecture as Professor of Philosophy at the University of the Witwatersrand, Hoernle stressed the significance of pluralism as a means of reducing the authority of the state as well as increasing its duties and responsibilities. Citing Laski's argument in his book *The Foundations of Sovereignty* that it was "morally inadequate" to have a "unified sovereignty" which was also efficient, Hoernle argued that the best defence of the state lay in decentralizing power away from it. He was doubtful of the guild socialist ideas of G. D. H. Cole which enjoyed some popularity at that time in sections of the Labour Party in Britain. Bodies such as the guilds would, Hoernle considered, gather to themselves the same sort of antagonism and loyalties as the state they sought to replace.[15]

Hoernle recognized that the state would perform a central role in managing class conflict in societies undergoing industrialization. He was careful not to go so far as reifying the state as the embodiment of the social whole and the guardian of its biological and eugenic fitness, a view propounded by General Jan Smuts in *Holism and Evolution* (1927) when he tried to extend the Darwinist notion of natural selection into a more organic notion of "holistic" social development.[16]

Hoernle also tried to shift idealist metaphysics away from Bosanquet's notion of God as an absolute to a less divine concept of "nature". He remained a religious agnostic and tried to respond to criticisms from the philosopher A. N. Whitehead in the 1920s that his ideas were out of touch with developments in modern science. Hoernle's understanding of "nature", though, was rather vague for he considered it was "what we think her to be, subject only to the proviso that bad thinking can be corrected by better".[17] He never really freed himself from a mystical notion of mind, which he saw as "manifestly a quality of power which admits of infinite degrees and variations".[18]

Whitehead argued in *Science and the Modern World* (1926) that the idealistic schools of philosophy had "conspicuously failed to connect, in any organic fashion, the fact of nature with their idealistic philosophies", especially in the light of developments in modern behavioural psychology where human subjects could be manipulated to perceive illusory objects.[19] By the mid 1920s Hoernle's idealism appeared to be out of tune with developments in science and from this time on he began to reorientate his interests towards experimentation in both psychology and anthropology. As chapter 1 showed, both these subjects were beginning to entrench themselves in South African universities at this time, and in July 1925 Hoernle wrote to Smuts that "the opportunities for scientific research here in SA are so manifold that there are times when I feel tempted to regret that I chose philosophy instead of science".[20]

In a paper to the SAAAS the following year, Hoernle suggested that there were two rival approaches to the study of mind: the "naturalistic and psychological", on the one hand, and "logical and metaphysical analysis" on the other. He suggested that they could still work side by side, though this idea would be effectively destroyed within ten years with the rise of logical positivism following the publication in 1936 of A. J. Ayer's *Language, Truth and Logic*. From the mid 1920s Hoernle was drawn into experimentation in the area of mental testing as a means of trying to test the metaphysical speculation of his idealist training. He was encouraged in this following a visit to Harvard in 1927 to address the 6th International Congress of Philosophy. Over the next few years he tested some 20,000 children on the Witwatersrand and in Pretoria, the biggest experiments of their kind in the British Commonwealth.[21]

Hoernle's lectures in the 1920s indicate this growing interest in the training of mind and psychology. In a lecture on Graham Wallas's *Our Social Heritage* in 1921 he argued that instincts could be capable of being educated through sublimation. Reason and intelligence had a major role to play in this sublimation since they were essential to humankind's ascent to moral freedom. The moral heritage of the past was not final for it too stood in need of criticism by means of "conscience", which Hoernle understood in terms of "one will learning by experience" and the " 'self righting' tendency of the instincts in their search for satisfaction".[22] Hoernle tried to preserve as far as possible a philosophical justification for the autonomy of mind and human reason as it was confronted with the growth of scientific interest in apparently irrational psychological forces threatening to disrupt the stability of Western civilization.

The issue became especially heightened in the context of racial relationships in South Africa. Hoernle saw the differences between white and black as a result of "social heritage" rather than of "constitution or capacity". Like the novelist Laurens van der Post, whose ideas will be examined in chapter 6, he was considerably influenced by the work of the French ethnologist Lucien Levy-Bruhl. He was drawn in particular to the argument in Bruhl's book *How Natives Think* (1923) that black African cultures were driven by a "pre-logical mentality".[23] Hoernle rejected any simple equation between whites as an adult society and Africans a childlike one. He recognized a difference between "civilized" and "savage" though he now realized that this difference had been "seriously misconceived by being compared with that between an adult and a child.... For the native is not a child, but an adult with a culture of his own. The white child has no culture except that which it is being trained to assimilate". The issue boiled down to one of the cultural reconstruction of African society in the face of white colonial intrusion:

> A primitive people, when it comes into contact with white civilisation, experiences a more or less rapid, and more or less complete, disintegration of its culture, and its problem is to build out of the ruins of the old and the fragmentary acquisition of the new, a set of beliefs and behaviour patterns by which adults can successfully meet the problems of their adult lives.[24]

By the late 1920s Hoernle began to become aware, like a number of white South African liberals at this time, of the emergence of a black American urban culture. The American black experience appeared to offer some form of comparative yardstick by which to evaluate trends in South Africa. In some notes in his copy of Alain Locke's edited collection *The New Negro* (1925), which explored these developments in the United States, he wrote that "race problems" were more interesting even than contemporary international issues such as those between France and Germany. They invoked, indeed, a "supreme test in Christian ideals" while on the "cultural side" they posed the "problem of the enrichment of European civilisation by minds steeped in other traditions".[25]

Hoernle doubted whether South African race relations would replicate those of the United States, since genetic fusion would not take place in South Africa on the scale that it had in the United States. Like the chairman of the 1932 Native Economic Commission, John Holloway, he thought South African "native policy" should aim for the "accommodation" rather than the "assimilation" of blacks and whites. The "American evidence" indicated for Hoernle that "the real problem" was "how to secure the benefits of Western civilisation for all, whilst maintaining by common consent such group differentiation and even barriers, as experience shows to be necessary to the harmonious living together of the various groups as members of the same political, social, economic organism".[26]

The Issue of Race in South Africa

Hoernle discussed racial issues in South Africa in the late 1920s and early 1930s when the popular African protest and strike wave after the First World War had declined. Located in Johannesburg he had little direct familiarity with conditions at the local level in the towns and rural areas of South Africa and made no extensive investigation of black rural areas like the historian W. M. Macmillan at Herschel in the Eastern Cape.[27]

Hoernle confronted issues of black–white relationships at a time when the small African political elite on the Witwatersrand appeared to lack political direction in the depression years of the early 1930s. The return of Pixley Seme as President of the ANC marked a timidly conservative trend in the organization's political outlook which only began to change under the leadership of Alfred Xuma in the 1940s.

In March 1931, Hoernle discussed the question of how far black Americans had been able to make economic and political advances in the United States at a meeting of the African discussion group *The Gamma Sigma Club*, which had been founded in the early 1930s in Johannesburg by the American Board missionary Ray Phillips. The African traditions amongst South African blacks, he argued, would survive longer than those of blacks in America.[28] The line of argument appeared to justify some form of cultural separation of white and black in South Africa. This was a view that was not at the time unpopular among the Club's black members and the following month a motion that segregation was "not in the best interests of the Bantu People" was defeated.[29]

It appeared to Hoernle in the 1930s that segregation was a major political creed in South African politics that had to be taken seriously and one to which liberals had to adapt. The outlook was partly inspired by the shift towards "Bantu Studies" in the English-speaking universities. At the University of the Witwatersrand the departure of W. M. Macmillan early in 1933 left a vacuum in the area of research in economic history which was not really made up until the late 1960s.[30]

Hoernle was keen for the development of empirical research in the social sciences. In July 1933 he submitted a memorandum to the University of the Witwatersrand on the urgent need for developing the "scientific study of social problems". The English-speaking universities in South Africa, he warned, could only neglect this at their peril. Hitherto such work had been mainly conducted outside the academic arena by church and charity societies, but he saw that a new interest was developing in the Afrikaner economic community in the wake of the reports of the Carnegie Commission on the poor white issue. He urged the university to consider the issue of "human engineering" and suggested two new appointments in the field of applied psychology and social work.[31] A special committee of the University considered the proposal and agreed that training in this area should not be *ad hoc* but concerned with the "fundamental principles of the social and related sciences". As a result of the meeting a Board of Social Sciences was established which began slowly to develop social science research in the years up to World War Two.[32]

Hoernle's family background in the Berlin Missionary Society also enabled him to recognize the intellectual importance of *Volkekunde* in Afrikaans-speaking universities. This ethnological study of African cultures had been inspired by the work of German missionaries. One of them, Gustav Warneck, argued in a book *Evangelische Missionslehre* (1902) that people should be studied in terms of ethnic units.[33] One of the most important academic exponents of *Volkekunde* was Professor W. W. M. Eiselen at the University of Stellenbosch. Eiselen was himself the son of Ernst Ludwig Gustav Eiselen, a missionary in the Berlin Missionary Society. As a fluent Afrikaans speaker, Hoernle saw himself as a bridge between the Afrikaans- and English-speaking academic communities. In the course of the 1930s he paid increasing attention to the debates on racial segregation in the nationalist-minded Afrikaner universities.

The same year that Hoernle became president of the South

African Institute of Race Relations in 1934 a militant Afrikaans-speaking body was established to study race issues, entitled the *Rasserverhoudingsbond van Afrikaners*. The body drew upon a considerable fund of support from the Dutch Reformed churches and proclaimed the central issue in South African politics to be the rival principles of equality between races ("Die Gelykstellingsidee"), which it traced back to eighteenth-century European rationalism, and the separationist idea ("Die Afskeidsidee") which it traced back to the doctrine proclaimed in Article 9 of the 1858 Transvaal constitution that there should be no equality between black and white in church and state.[34] The *Rasserverhoudingsbond* was a reflection of a movement towards racial separation that had been developing in the DRCs since earlier in the century under the influence of a number of German missionaries organized through the Berlin Missionary Society. A similar influence came through the teaching of *Volkekunde* in the Afrikaans-speaking universities. In a lecture in 1929 Professor W. W. M. Eiselen supported racial segregation as a means of fostering separate African religious and linguistic identities.[35]

The sources of this segregationism in Afrikaner political thought were in the 1930s still heavily influenced by religious doctrine. In the English-speaking tradition in the early 1930s, on the other hand, many missionaries began to abandon the earlier commitment to philanthrophic segregationism as they came under growing pressure from secular intellectuals in both South Africa and overseas. As a consequence many began to move towards a progressive process of racial integration.[36] The links with overseas missionary groups in the English-speaking world – a nexus that Richard Elphick has termed a "benevolent empire" – ensured that it was becoming increasingly difficult for English-speaking South African liberals to isolate themselves from wider discussions on race issues.[37] For the Afrikaner ethnologists, however, there were not the same pressures in this period impelling them towards a commonly understood code of international respectability on race. This isolation was encouraged by the domestic forces mobilized behind Afrikaner nationalism.

Afrikaner nationalist populism in the 1930s was stimulated by the breaking away in 1934 of the Purified National Party under D. F. Malan from the United Party government of Generals Hertzog and Smuts. Leonard Thompson has argued that before the capture of state power by Afrikaner nationalism in 1948 the anti-imperial element took precedence over racism, which could be by and large assumed rather than elaborated, given that similar views existed externally in Britain and America. It was thus the struggle against British imperial dominance which still gripped the imaginations of Afrikaner nationalist politicians and intellectuals.[38] Nevertheless, the celebration of Afrikaner historical myth, such as the centenary of the Great Trek in 1938, when men grew beards and re-enacted the ox-wagon trek, encouraged a view of innate African savagery and the essential differences between African "tribal" culture and "Western civilization".

The *Rasserverhoudingsbond* was part of this populistand racist challenge to liberal values in South African society and politics. It was a body that the fledgling Institute of Race Relations could not afford to ignore if it were to make headway beyond the English-speaking section of the South African white population. In June 1935, Hoernle attended a conference of the *Rasserverhoudingsbond* where demands were made for the state control of African education in order to remove Africans from the "interference" of English missionaries. Speakers also attacked schemes of "industrial training" that were developing in some of the English-speaking missions at Lovedale on lines similar to the Tuskegee Institute in Alabama which, it was alleged, were educating Africans to compete with white workers.[39]

Hoernle stressed that these attacks had to be taken seriously by English-speaking liberals. In a talk "The Future of the Natives in South Africa" he began exploring the idea of some form of ideological consensus between the rival ideals of segregationism and that of assimilationism based on the model of Cape liberalism. He accepted that total racial separation was economically and politically impracticable but hoped that it would be possible to shift mainstream white South African opinion towards accepting a doctrine of a "separate but equal" system of segregation on the pattern of the American South. Eventually, it was hoped, reasonableness and humanity might emerge from such a process for "once we take the principle of racial segregation to be firmly established by mutual agreement, we can afford to relax some forms of social segregation on which, from fear of racial-mixture, we now insist". It might then be possible to establish a pattern of segregation which African leadership would be willing to accept:

> Our line of action should not be to abolish or abandon social segregation in principle, but to take the sting of its functioning

out of it by providing equivalent and parallel opportunities for all. On that condition, we shall gain the willing support of all thoughtful non-Europeans – for, after all, all of [us?] are like the proverb holds: birds of a feather flock together. Social segregation should not be used as an instrument for the domination of one group by another.[40]

Within this conception of segregation Hoernle envisaged Africans as being able to develop their own culture free from paternalistic white supervision. There were, he wrote in 1935, two senses in which something was the Africans' "own": it could be seen as being simply "different" from anything of the whites in South Africa and it could be seen as something which Africans could actively "*make their own*, and indeed *must* make theirs, if they are to survive at all under the conditions which European conquest and overlordship, economic and political, impose upon them".[41]

This meant for Hoernle far more than Africans simply "developing upon their own lines" (as common political parlance at the time often had it) since African society had been inextricably drawn into the "orbit of western civilisation". There would be a gradual process of cultural accommodation to dominant Western values in which what "they [the Africans] will retain of their traditional past will colour what they acquire from western civilisation, just as the folkways of the different peoples of Europe are now but instances within the general type of a uniform civilisation".[42] This was a view that gained fairly wide assent among the English-speaking liberals. The prominent Cape liberal James Rose Innes thought the article's conclusion was "unassailable" for "the Natives know no other than western civilisation under the tremendous impact of which they have been for many years. And they want no other".[43]

Hoernle was anxious that the English-speaking liberal establishment should not become politically isolated by rejecting root and branch the 1936 Bills on land and the Cape African franchise. After some initial scepticism in which he felt that Hertzog was bluffing, he came round to the idea that there was some "merit" in the Prime Minister's proposals.[44] It was possible that a new political atmosphere would be created by the legislation, for it would allow new approaches to be made to the "liberal Dutch" so as to create a political consensus that would isolate the Afrikaner nationalist extremists.[45]

During this period there was some confusion in Hoernle's outlook on inter-racial "miscegenation". In 1934 he attacked Peter Nielsen for failing to be more specific on what policy the government should promote on inter-racial "mixture". Biological assimilation might in fact become inescapable.[46] In another article the same year "Race Mixture and Native policy", though, he argued that the existing legislative barrier on inter-racial sexual intercourse in the form of the 1927 Immorality Act could well be preserved "so that we need not be deterred from a liberal native policy by the fear that race-mixture throughout the community will be the inevitable result".[47] Hoernle to some degree remained confused on the whole issue.

It was by no means evident in fact that Hoernle always managed to argue on the basis of the "synoptic method" in philosophy, in which a "problem", in I. D. MacCrone's words, was examined "from the point of view not of any single group but of all the groups concerned".[48] When tackled, for instance, on the issue of "race mixture" by an Afrikaner district surgeon from Springbok in Namaqualand in the Northern Cape Province where there was a large "Coloured" community, Hoernle confessed that he was personally opposed to "miscegenation" and had "spoken and written consistently against it". It was doubtful whether the "mixed breed" was "invariably inferior to the pure breed", and Hoernle cited in support of this the study of the German ethnologist Eugen Fischer of the Rehoboth Bastards. But it was still the case that such groups were "generally more or less outcasts from the society of purer stocks and suffer from many discriminations and handicaps, social, economic and political, which tend to keep them back and even make for actual demoralisation and degeneration".[49]

Hoernle's view of mixed race communities usually being culturally if not biologically degenerate was by no means unusual amongst professional opinion in the 1930s in Britain and America as well as South Africa.[50] His language was a reflection of a discourse on race that had not as yet been redefined through research in genetics. He still spoke of "purer stocks" and linked different races with specific cultural characteristics. Most South African liberals had similar views at this time, though J. D. Rheinallt Jones began to move to a more sophisticated position by the late 1930s: his lecture notes from his teaching of "Bantu Studies" indicate doubts about being able to establish any satisfactory criteria by which to identify different races, for such features as colour, hair, shape of nose and head and face differed significantly within each group.[51] By the war years Hoernle too appeared to have shifted his ground on the issue as he wrote to Alexander Kerr, the Principal of Lovedale, that though humanitarians might think it better not to advocate inter-racial marriages so as not to "endanger other parts of the humanitarian programme", they still believed that "racial assimilation by inter-marriage must come in the end; that it is the inevitable destiny of multi-racial societies".[52]

Hoernle was an important strategic theorist of South African liberalism during a period when it was entering a major phase of political retreat before the advancing programme of racial segregation. Some leading English-speaking politicians, such as the former Kindergarten member Patrick Duncan, did not consider that segregation had any philosophical basis.[53] Hoernle, however, was keen to engage some of the leading advocates of segregation, such as the ideologically zealous chairman of the Native Affairs Commission, George Heaton Nicholls, in political debate. He tried to convince Nicholls in the late 1930s that segregation was unrealistic economically if it meant trying to drive Africans back into the reserves in order to revive peasant agriculture there.[54] But in the years up to 1939 there was an increasingly pessimistic tone in Hoernle's writing that was to lead him into trying to rethink the whole purpose of what he termed the "liberal spirit" in South African politics.

Growing Pessimism

By the late 1930s when Hoernle wrote his important Phelps Stokes lectures, *South African Native Policy and the Liberal Spirit*, he became anxious that race differences in South African society were in danger of being fixed into rigid caste gradients. His Indian missionary childhood was undoubtedly an important influence in the shaping of his outlook in this regard, while the comparative success of Gandhi's campaign of *satyagraha* against the Raj in India appeared to throw into sharper relief the general state of demoralization of South African blacks. "How can one confidently predict," he wrote in 1939, "when, if, they [the Africans] will be ready for the use of such a weapon, which makes such exceptional demands on its users?" The "day of a native Gandhi" was not yet, though he envisaged the South African Indian population providing the leadership for a passive resistance campaign by a "united non-European front".[55]

Hoernle's poor assessment of the black South African potential to resist encroaching white state power led him into a generally gloomy analysis of South African politics. There appeared to be, he wrote to a correspondent in 1938, only two really feasible ways out of this caste-like society. He started out by rejecting the possibility of racial *assimilation* which he regarded as politically impossible given the general state of white political opposition to it. This left only two alternative courses. The first was racial segregation modelled on that of Booker T. Washington in the US South. This meant in effect *parallel development* by two separate societies. The other possibility was total separation on a territorial basis as though whites and blacks were two *separate nations*. Both alternatives left white overlordship intact since Hoernle recognized – long before the creation of Homelands – that any artificially created black state would be subject to white control.[56]

Hoernle's lectures *South African Native Policy and the Liberal Spirit* developed this line of thinking by showing that South African society was characterized by a multiple set of techniques to ensure continued white domination. Though a firm believer in the ideals of the British Commonwealth, Hoernle was forced to conclude that the doctrine of trusteeship based on classical nineteenth-century liberalism had to be "ruled out as impracticable in the present state of racial feeling".[57] It was essential for South African liberals to think out an alternative set of formulas for a convincing liberal agenda in South African politics.

Hoernle aimed his book at a wider audience than his fellow South African liberals and pointed out that the South African predicament had ramifications for other multi-racial societies in the Commonwealth. The important point was to try and relate what he termed the "liberal spirit" to the realities of the modern world in which the vision of the American president, Woodrow Wilson, in 1919 at the Versailles Peace Conference, of a liberal world order based upon self-governing nation states had begun to break down.[58] Hoernle's thinking reflected a wider mood of pessimism in the aftermath of Neville Chamberlain's capitulation to Hitler at Munich in 1938 and the failure of appeasement to halt the tide of fascism in Europe.

At points *South African Native Policy and the Liberal Spirit* invoked the spirit of the Victorian public-school ethos, as it called on liberals to recognize that liberty could only be exercised in situations where there was "muscular strength and trained bodily skill and efficiency". Moreover, there had to be the "social control of the use of power". Liberty could never be absolute and its reapplication in South Africa needed to be conditioned by the recognition of the power of social groups as well as individuals.[59]

The lectures have often been seen as the genesis of the group-based approach to South African politics, and indeed Hoernle had himself favoured pluralism when debating newer modes of political organization at Harvard during and after World War One. However, his focus upon what he termed the "racial caste" nature of South African society led him to doubt whether it was accurate to describe it as "plural". In a letter to the British scholar Margery Perham in 1942 he argued that South Africa was essentially a *Herrenvolk* democracy "even if tempered in varying degrees by trusteeship and paternalism" and he doubted whether the term "plural" was expressive enough. It was possible for "plural" societies such as the Soviet Union to be "equalitarian" in their aims and very different from the "inequalitarianism" of South Africa. The *Herrenvolk* outlook of the Union appeared to be "deep-seated", such that "a more outspoken outlook" was "called for".[60]

Hoernle's dislike of "pluralism" was motivated by a desire to point out to Margery Perham the increasingly different political trajectories of British and South African "native policies". He realized that while the old imperial relationships in Asia and the Far East had been dealt a mortal blow by the War against Japan, the same could not necessarily be said at this stage for Africa where colonial rule looked like surviving for a good deal longer. It did not appear that Britain would have the energy after the war was over to direct any liberalizing aims against South Africa and Hoernle feared that segregation might be able to extend itself northwards to other territories of white settlement in East and Central Africa. From the vantage point of the late 1930s and early 1940s it did not seem likely to Hoernle that there could be a strong enough liberal conscience internationally to be mobilized against South Africa. To this extent, like many liberals of his generation in South Africa, he underestimated the capacity for anti-colonial opinion in Britain to mobilize in opposition to imperial policies in Africa in the post-war years – policies led by such bodies as the Africa Bureau and the Movement for Colonial Freedom.[61]

Hoernle tended therefore to look primarily to the South African government in Pretoria as the embodiment of real power in the southern African region. He doubted whether Britain could play any major role in promoting trusteeship by encouraging the social and economic development of the Protectorate territories of Bechuanaland,

Swaziland and Basutoland, as some South African liberals like William and Margaret Ballinger argued during the 1930s.[62] Like the Ballingers, Hoernle opposed the incorporation of the Protectorates into the Union, but this was mainly because trusteeship could not be seen to work without the "willing" consent of the African "wards". It would be highly undesirable for South Africa to have additional large blocs of "disaffected" African people who would make the country's "native problem, already difficult enough, quite unmanageable except by machine guns, aeroplanes and poison gas".[63] In 1941, he urged caution on the British High Commissioner in Pretoria, Lord Harlech, who was keen to see Swaziland transferred to South Africa at an early date as a result of the obstinate refusal of King Sobhuza to accept reforms in administration in the territory. Hoernle recognized that a large proportion of the chiefs and people in Swaziland were opposed to any such transfer and it was "of the utmost importance that they should be given no shadow of excuse for thinking that Great Britain is scheming to shuffle out of her agreements with them".[64] Hoernle retained a limited faith in the idea of British trusteeship up to the end of his life, though he had become despondent about the continuation of this doctrine in South African "native policy".

Hoernle was generally pessimistic that the humanitarian ideals of the liberal tradition inherited from Europe could easily permeate a society gripped by segregationist ideology. In effect he had a rather low expectation for humanitarian ideals in the twentieth century compared to the nineteenth-century upsurge of humanitarianism during the campaign against slavery. As Thomas Haskell has pointed out, this humanitarianism gave an edge to the anti-slavery impulse and extended it beyond mere capitalist self-interest by establishing the idea that the individual in the free market had a set of rights as a human being over and above his rights to own property or sell his labour. This humanitarianism, Haskell has pointed out, varied in intensity in different times and places.[65] Hoernle, with a pessimism partly derived from the pressures of domestic South African politics, and partly from the events occurring in Central Europe after Hitler's rise to power, did not consider it likely it would have the same political or intellectual impact on South African society, which appeared successfully to have resisted its appeals.

Hoernle placed some hope in the ideals of the British Commonwealth. He attended the Second British Commonwealth Relations Conference in Sydney, Australia, in September 1938 and, on his return, in a lecture to the South African Association of University Women, he spoke in glowing terms of the Commonwealth being the possible nucleus for an "inclusive World Order" that would entail the rebuilding of the League of Nations. This idealism, which resembled that of General Smuts, was typical of many inter-war liberal idealists in international relations who tended to underestimate the power of sovereign nation states. Hoernle failed to call for drastic action to try and rectify this state of affairs. South Africa was not at this stage seen as a polecat state that demanded international action to end its domestic structure of white minority rule.[66]

Hoernle did recognize, though, that the "liberal spirit" ran into conflict with the working of South Africa's caste society. He saw a need to develop both a "short-range" and a "long-range" liberal programme in South Africa. The "short-range" programme would be concerned with pressing "constantly for a liberal interpretation of trusteeship and to use the elasticities of the present system, such as they are, to insert into it as much of the liberal spirit as [they] can". The "long-range programme", on the other hand, was directed towards formulating an alternative to the present system in South Africa. On this count Hoernle saw only three possibilities presenting themselves: *parallelism*, *assimilation* and *separation*. Assimilation had, he acknowledged, occurred in a number of areas of South African economic life, but it was resisted by strong forces favouring segregation. To this extent, his views were somewhat different from those of the advocates of the "frontier thesis" in South African historiography – men such as Eric Walker and C. W. de Kiewiet, who saw segregation as a product of the pre-industrial frontier, logically opposed to the whole trend of modern capitalist industrialization.[67]

There seemed to Hoernle to be powerful forces in South African political and economic life sustaining segregation. The option of parallelism might have helped to "create a liberal atmosphere" but it had been ineffective as a "real force for the reconstruction of race relations in multi-racial societies".[68] It appeared that only the alternative option of total racial separation offered any possibility of maintaining the liberal spirit for this meant nothing less than the "sundering or dissociation so complete as to destroy the very possibility of effective domination". The creation of separate communities of whites and blacks on the basis of "territorial segregation" would be the only way of ending the caste system and allaying whites' fears of "miscegenation".[69]

Hoernle's argument offered up a model for the decolonization of South African society before the advent of popular African nationalism. He recognized that there was a colonial dimension to South African society, perhaps in part as a result of the debates in the Communist International in the late 1920s and early 1930s when South Africa had been perceived as a case of "colonialism of a special type".[70] Hoernle had been aware since at least the mid 1930s of radical criticism of the piecemeal work of the SAIRR. In 1934, Rheinallt Jones passed on to him a letter from a Communist writer George Findlay pointing out the consistent aim behind government legislation of forcing Africans into the service of whites. Findlay accused the Institute of failing to explore "unpalatable major issues in order to get a hearing". This left the "major issues untouched in the minds of the antis, indeed almost seems to do lip-service to such untenable objectives, and accordingly fails to interest the pros as being trifling and unanalytic".[71] Hoernle acknowledged the force of such arguments by drawing the conclusion that since race relations was dealing with attitudes of mind, most people usually acted from unreasoning habit. The important point was that "the momentum of habit may resist better knowledge of principles, esp. if supported by fear of consequence of social non-conformity".[72]

It was the desire to expose the underlying principles before his fellow-liberals that motivated Hoernle's 1939 Phelps-Stokes lectures. Hoernle was performing the role of what Gramsci has termed an organic intellectual amongst the class of South African English-language professionals. He tried in effect to awaken them to the underlying realities of their political situation.

Hoernle failed to offer any politically feasible solution that could command widespread credibility amongst both white and black liberal activists. He recognized this when admitting that the "will" to realize the separationist ideal would not be forthcoming. There was, in short, no "ultimate hope" for the liberal spirit in South Africa.[73]

Hoernle confessed to Edgar Brookes that he did not expect much public interest in his book, given the general preoccupation with the war.[74] He hoped that it would make an impact in British discussion on colonial policy, especially as regards the possible return of the Protectorates to South Africa.[75] One flattering analogy was made by Bishop Paget in Southern Rhodesia to Arnold Toynbee's *Study of History*. Hoernle drew on Toynbee's observation that successive civilizations throughout history have generally decayed through a dominant minority excluding a subject majority from the privileges that it enjoys.[76]

Reviewers in South Africa were generally sceptical about Hoernle's arguments. For those on the left, such as Findlay, Hoernle had failed to realize the degree to which the country had been welded into one economic whole through the power of black labour. In a materialist critique of Hoernle's idealism, Findlay accused Hoernle of "ignoring the pyramid of production and its essential character" in order to focus on psychological attitudes. The important point was that "men's minds must and inevitably will come into correlation with the facts outside them, and that the mind cannot influence real developments".[77]

In a series of seminars at the University of the Witwatersrand, a number of liberals also criticized the book for being directed at only white opinion. Hoernle's long-term programme for liberals was considered impractical politically, especially as it could not be made consistent with the short-term policy of trying to alleviate the harshness of the existing segregation policy. The general view was that liberals needed to be willing to adapt to changing political circumstances and not maintain an unqualified pessimism.[78] One of the more favourable reviews in the liberal press came, rather curiously, from the African anthropologist and political leader Z. K. Matthews in the SAIRR journal, *Race Relations*. Though sceptical that Hoernle's idea of "separation" was any different from existing segregation, Matthews still considered that it deserved "the serious attention of all those who are interested in the development, here in South Africa, of stable 'areas of freedom' for all the racial groups in the population".[79]

Hoernle had challenged his fellow-liberals to rethink their position in South African politics, especially those who placed most faith in the efficacies of the government's "trusteeship" policy. To fail to rethink the application of liberal principles in a "multi-racial society" in the name of "faith" or "confidence" was, he charged, to "continue to take an intellectual holiday".[80] There were both liberal and illiberal tendencies within the trusteeship policy and the small progress which was sometimes made often occurred at the expense of asking what the overall direction of the policy was. When the question did start to be asked a conflict of principle occurred which liberals were bound to lose.[81]

Hoernle, in the last three years of his life, did take some comfort from limited gains that were made at the level of the short-range programme. As a result of pressure he exerted on the University of the Witwatersrand, it was decided to admit African students to dentistry and medicine, though Hoernle remained worried that the South African medical profession might still remain deeply segregationist.[82]

In the early 1940s Hoernle also served as chairman of the Alexandra Health Committee during a period when there was strong pressure from the United Party council of Johannesburg to get the African township redeclared a white urban area. The area of Alexandra Township had originally been proclaimed in 1905 and consisted of 1588 lots, of which 2135 were held by African and Coloured property-owners in May 1940. The total population of the township was estimated at between 40,000 and 50,000 and conditions of gross overcrowding prevailed in a rapidly growing urban slum where an estimated 22 people lived on each stand.

Hoernle attempted to drive a *via media* between the African property-owners in the township, who sought to preserve the rights to their properties, and the surrounding white suburban property-owners organized in the North East District Protection League. At a conference of the various parties involved in the issue in October 1942 at the Union Buildings in Pretoria, Hoernle professed himself not to be against abolition of the township as such, though this would have to be with the consent of the inhabitants. Hoernle supported increased public expenditure on the township involving a one-third contribution from the City Council, one-third from the Transvaal Administration and one-third from the government. There should, he maintained, be a national policy for all townships.[83] This could have meant the national government having to spend £3 million to secure the removal of the township and Hoernle engaged in a lobbying campaign to persuade the property-owners to accept favourable terms. "Personally I can tell you," he wrote to Douglas Smit, the Union Secretary of Native Affairs,

> that my appeal to effect abolition by offering to the inhabitants terms so favourable that only a fool would reject them appears, from all I hear, to be resulting in the elaboration of a scheme which comes as near to being heaven on earth for urban natives as conceivable.[84]

Smit himself came out in favour of abolition, which he estimated would cost £2,430,000. But he was reluctant to get the government involved in this, fearing that it would lead to a spate of other claims from all over the Union.[85] At the time of Hoernle's death, the matter remained suspended as the government was preoccupied with the war, and Alexandra Township continued to survive despite the hostile response of the surrounding white property-owners in the Johannesburg northern suburbs.

The experience of working on the Alexandra Health Committee led Hoernle to become increasingly sceptical of the idea of total racial separation given the rate of African urbanization. In 1942 in a pamphlet on urban Africans he urged policy-makers to make "detribalization" the initiation into a "fuller life and the realisation of a finer humanity in African men and women than any which their traditional tribal ways afforded them". This required increased wages and social services for an urbanized African proletariat and the provision of a rudimentary welfare state organized around the principle that the first charge on national income should be a general minimum standard of life "whatever higher standards the society may allow to those of its members whose superior capacity enables them to render superior service".[86]

But Hoernle remained at heart pessimistic regarding the long-term transformation of the South African "caste society" since he saw neither the will nor vision for effecting any major change. It was, he charged, only complacency or delusion for liberals to believe otherwise and "the changes which will come will be forced upon us by world forces and world events over which humanity has little conscious control".[87]

Hoernle's Legacy

There was ultimately a strong element of resignation in Hoernle's understanding of how the South African political conflict could be resolved. He became critical of the reformist assumptions of many liberals and castigated the idea that "ambulance work" could do much to reverse the general direction of segregation policy given the entrenched nature of the "racial caste society" in South Africa.[88]

Hoernle's idea that racial separation might be compatible with liberalism did not find much favour internationally. The wartime climate engendered a democratic mood that saw the real issue in South African politics as no longer one of ethnic group antagonism between British, Boers and Africans but as a struggle between a democratic and authoritarian mode of government. On occasions this seeped through into such journals as *The Democrat*, *Trek* and *The Forum*. The latter periodical pointed out to its readers in 1941, for example, the necessity of building a new order. This involved a simple choice between the "violence, dogmatism, racialism and ignorance of the Nazi new order" or a "revised conception of our social and economic conditions, our ethical and religious system and the idea (already becoming obsolete) of the state as 'sovereign' in its independence".[89] A similar approach was articulated by Alexander Campbell in his book *Smuts and Swastika*.[90]

This democratic approach appealed to only a section of South African English-speaking liberal opinion. Others saw Hoernle as confirming the view that it was pointless to strive for a single South African society and that it was better simply to concentrate upon equal citizenship rights in a "multi-racial" society of multiple social groups. Many too were doubtless attracted by his shift of attention away from class interests towards ethnic group identities or what were then termed "racial" differences.

Hoernle also reinforced intellectually a mood among many English-speaking liberal activists that it was pointless to ask questions about the long-term future in South Africa of liberal ideals, which could only be resolved by larger-scale forces operating outside the narrow parameters of South African national politics. The anthropologist Ellen Hellman, for example, concluded in a review of Hoernle's writings in 1946, that "in the long run, the answer will not be fashioned within the brains of men, even though they be emancipated from blind emotion and motivated rationally, but by the compulsion of developing economic forces – forces generated on a world scale, the moulding pressure of which SA will not be able to withstand."[91]

By the post-war years, Hoernle's ideas contributed to a growing dependence of many South African liberals on economic change eroding and destroying the apparently anachronistic ideology of segregation or apartheid. At the same time, some Afrikaner intellectuals such as Professor W. W. M. Eiselen were intellectually indebted to Hoernle for the apartheid conception. Eiselen quoted Hoernle's conception of "total separation" with approval and argued that apartheid was itself a "long range programme" which would not lead to economic breakdowns.[92] While it is by no means clear that

Hoernle, if he were alive, would have approved of the way his ideas were used, they were symptomatic of the dialogue he had tried to cultivate with Afrikaner nationalists like Eiselen during the 1930s.[93]

Hoernle's general outlook was one, though, that more radically inclined liberals by the 1950s found hard to accept. Writing in 1956, Patrick Duncan attacked Hoernle for his pessimism regarding the ultimate defeat of segregation and for envisaging that racial groups would remain a permanent phenomenon in South African society. "The Liberals that matter today," he urged, "are those that have seen the vision of a new South Africa, now being so painfully born, which has forgotten race, and which fosters those things which unite all South Africans and which puts aside those things which divide us." Only then, he concluded, would it be possible to establish a democracy.[94]

Further doubts from liberals came at the end of the 1950s when Donald Molteno gave a Presidential Address to the SAIRR in January 1959 entitled *Towards a Democratic South Africa*. Molteno had been active in politics as a "natives representative" in the House of Assembly before his resignation in 1948. He came from a prominent Cape liberal family and served as a major spokesperson for the South African liberal conscience. Molteno was concerned to ally liberal ideals of freedom under law to a pressure for progressive democratization of South African society. He reflected the increasingly democratic mood in liberal debate at the time. Molteno saw Hoernle's three a priori theoretical objectives of parallellism, separation and assimilation as being of marginal use, since even Hoernle had recognized that they were politically impracticable. He considered that a democratic strategy should be developed by asking the question *why* these objectives were impracticable.[95] Molteno did not spell out the political conditions behind such a democratic strategy. He appeared to consider it a continuation of the existing approach of seeking piecemeal reforms rather than a political alliance with African nationalism. Nevertheless, he considered that Hoernle's address did serve as a half-hearted recognition of the need to talk the language of democracy.

The most serious criticism came from the radical political activist Jack Simons who wrote in the left-wing journal *Liberation* in 1959 that if anyone could lay claim to inventing the actual idea of apartheid it was Hoernle. Simons argued this for two reasons. Firstly, Hoernle's writing was important for stressing the word *separation* rather than the more conventional term *segregation* in the political discourse of the period. This directly translated into Afrikaans as *apartheid*. Secondly, Simons considered that Hoernle pointed a way forward for those intellectuals who "recognised the injustice and impermanence of White domination" by his stress on the creation of "separate areas of liberty for separate racial groups" as the only solution to the problems of a "racial caste society".[96] Simons's criticisms were significant for pointing out how Hoernle had contributed towards making the "separation" concept intellectually respectable in both English and Afrikaans-speaking intellectual circles in the 1940s. However, he rather overstressed Hoernle's role in actually inventing the apartheid concept which owed far more to an input from Afrikaner intellectuals such as those involved in the *Afrikanerbond vir Rassetudie* and in teaching *Volkekunde* as well as the group who came to form the South African Bureau of Racial Affairs in the late 1940s. It is also not clear, had he lived, whether Hoernle would have accepted the conception of apartheid since his attitude towards the idea of complete racial separation had been ambiguous and to a considerable degree uncertain.

Hoernle's thinking nevertheless did exert a considerable impact on a number of English-speaking intellectuals after World War Two. To this extent it reflected a continuing resistance within these circles to demands for popular democracy. In the course of his life Hoernle had moved some way towards these ideals, whilst also recognizing the entrenched nature of ethnic antagonism in South African politics. This latter outlook was seen by some liberals to be moving some way away from the Christian precept of love behind the liberal tradition. A considerably different vision of ultimate aims in South African politics was articulated by Edgar Brookes, who is the subject of chapter 3.

3

EDGAR BROOKES AND THE "LIE IN THE SOUL" OF SEGREGATION

Edgar Brookes was, like Hoernle, a liberal who began his career with a firm belief in racial segregation as a means of providing a just solution to the "native problem". Unlike Hoernle, though, he moved increasingly away from this idea in the years before the Second World War. Brookes is an interesting figure for his growing awareness of changing attitudes internationally on race issues and of the need for liberals in South Africa to try to stay abreast of opinion outside the country's borders.

Brookes was born in Birmingham in 1897 at the high point of British imperial self-confidence. His family background was not a wealthy one and in 1901 his parents moved to Pietermaritzburg in Natal where his father became an NCO in the 64th North Staffordshire Regiment. His Welsh mother was a formative influence, instilling a strong sense of ambition he later viewed with considerable reserve.

Brookes's education in Natal was in a strongly Victorian mould with a heavy dose of classics through the teaching of the classical scholar Alexander Petrie, to whom Brookes later dedicated his *History of the University of Natal* in 1966. Petrie's influence was important for instilling a conception of history governed by the rise and fall of imperial civilizations, an ideal that frequently lay at the root of British ideas of imperialism as can be seen in chapter 7.[1] It was a theme Brookes would turn to in the 1950s when he examined the political thought of St Augustine.

It was not possible for Brookes to obtain sufficient funding for a continuous university education. Between 1913 and 1920 he worked in the Customs Department with a year of war service in Pretoria in 1914–15. Here he picked up the many of values of public administration which at this time in South Africa was still shaped by the ethos of the British Civil Service. This experience encouraged him to try to link academic scholarship with more immediate political tasks. He became keen to employ academic research towards influencing public policy as well as infusing political decision-making with ethical ideals.

During his short period in Pretoria, Brookes's Christian convictions became awakened by Dean Gordon of the Cathedral of St Albans. His upbringing had originally been Methodist, but he was attracted to Anglicanism by its emphasis upon duty and service. The Anglican Church of the Province was at this time broadly in favour of a segregation policy in South Africa, though not uncritically. At the Diocesan Synod in 1915 Bishop Furse of Pretoria urged the establishment of a council of "experts" to deal with the "native question", an idea taken up by General Smuts's Native Affairs Act in 1920 when it established the Native Affairs Commission.[2]

Brookes started to get involved in South African politics after his appointment as lecturer in Political Science at the Transvaal University College (a forerunner of the University of Pretoria) in 1920. To many liberals of Brookes's generation the ideal of racial segregation still appeared both politically and economically feasible as well as being an apparently just "solution" to rising racial antagonism in South African society. White progressives viewed the urbanization of African peasants with considerable alarm, though Brookes gained a better insight than many into the issues involved through his work as Secretary of the Pretoria Native Welfare Association. The Association began to co-opt a number of African members at the end of 1921 including I. Bud Mbelle and S. R. Makgatho, the President of the Transvaal African Congress.[3] Brookes had a fairly free hand in the Association and used it to widen his contacts with the organizers of the Joint Council movement on the Witwatersrand. In 1923 he was one of the Association's two representatives to the conference convened by the Federal Council of the Dutch Reformed churches on European and Bantu. This proved in some respects to be a watershed in the emerging consensus amongst English- and Afrikaans-speaking intellectuals on segregation.[4]

The Appeal of Segregation

The conference served as Brookes's debut in this political debate. His paper linked segregation with the notion of "differential development" which he felt likely to appeal to a conference "searching for a formula of cautious and moderate liberalism which it might commend to educated African opinion". Brookes hoped that both white and black "culture" could be allowed to flourish separately through this policy which allowed African territories their own marketing outlets. He did not consider it likely that it would be possible to achieve any early resolution of the question of land.

Brookes's views differed in some respects from those of earlier liberals such as Howard Pim and Maurice Evans. These theorists had been attracted to segregationist ideology as a means of maintaining social control over African society during South African industrialization by reinforcing as far as possible the coherence of tribal society and chiefly authority. Brookes was rather more concerned that too much social engineering might lead to a violent African political reaction. He wrote, for example:

> To double existing locations will not produce the simple results that segregationists predict. South Africa will still be a living chessboard of black and white squares. Blacks would have constantly to be crossing white areas and vice versa. Unless an expensive and harassing police system guarded the borders of black and white areas, the scheme would undoubtedly break down in a generation. On the other hand, the provision of large black areas would, on my computation, involve the moving of from 45% to 55% of the tribes from their existing locations. Everybody knows the objection which the tribal Native has to being shifted from his ancestral home. Tribes are apt to resist such transference passively or actively. Do we not recollect the Bullhoek incident? It must be left to imagination what the effect would be of wholesale moving of Natives in the manner suggested all over South Africa, whether in one mad catastrophic revolution, or spread over a series of unsettled and angry years. It is like playing bowls with live bombs.[5]

Brookes had an instinctively conservative distrust of too much state interference with social processes. His sense of the potential hazards of a far-reaching strategy of segregationist social engineering was only shared by a small number of liberal critics at a time when state planning was becoming increasingly fashionable in reformist circles in Britain and the United States. A similar view, though, was made by R. A. Lehfeldt, Professor of economics at the University of the Witwatersrand, who warned that segregation would "revolutionise the country" since Africans were already thoroughly incorporated into its industries.[6] Similarly, the historian and liberal critic W. M. Macmillan, while suggesting that the reserves be maintained as the "barracks" for African migrant workers, opposed the idea of "transplanting" whole African families to the urban areas and urged a radical policy of rural development.[7] Brookes can therefore be seen as part of a group of liberals in the early 1920s who were becoming sceptical of the idea that segregation would be an adequate strategy for social control of the African proletariat.

Brookes's early ideas on segregation were considerably shaped by his admiration for Afrikaner nationalism and his support for the creation of a South African republic that would end its links with the British Empire. He developed these sympathies while teaching at the Transvaal University College in Pretoria and they rather isolated him from the other English-speaking liberals on the Witwatersrand. As a result of this love affair with what he later termed "the Afrikaner legend" he learned Afrikaans and fell under the spell of the romantic nationalist poetry of Celiers, Totius and Leipoldt.[8]

But the growing suspicion at this time in English-speaking South African circles towards Afrikaner nationalism meant that he was unable to serve as a mediator between Afrikaner nationalists and English-speaking South African liberals. None of the English publishers in South Africa would agree to publish his doctoral thesis entitled *History of Native Policy in South Africa* and he was forced to turn to the Afrikaner Nationalist leader, General J. B. M. Hertzog, for assistance. The book came out in 1924 at an opportune time as a general election was pending. Hertzog saw in Brookes's work historical justification for segregationism in South African "native policy" and agreed to get Die Nasionale Pers to publish it.[9]

Brookes's *History of Native Policy* expounded at much greater length the 1923 conference paper. The book argued for a middle course of "differentiation" between "subordination", epitomized by the policy of the Orange Free State, and "identity" represented by the Cape policy of assimilation. Brookes favoured a policy of guided African "self-government" modelled on that of Theophilus Shepstone in nineteenth-century Natal. Brookes's *History* maintained that the Shepstone legacy in South African "native policy" had not adapted sufficiently to changing circumstances, though he felt that a policy of "differentiation" could be achieved through a cautious programme of legislation.[10] He had considerable faith in the officials of the Native Affairs Department and urged that the Transkeian system – "the most successful Native Administration in South African history"[11] – be developed as the nucleus of a separate system of African government. The Cape African franchise would then fall away by default while a "Native national Council" could be established containing both elected representatives as well as nominated chiefs, together with the Minister of Native Affairs, the Native Affairs Commission and the chief magistrates. He hoped that the democratic element would be progressively increased.[12]

Brookes envisaged in 1924 that a system of "possessory segregation", meaning segregation based on separate areas of territorial ownership, would gain the progressive acceptance of African political leaders. He hoped that Hertzog's Pact Government that was elected in 1924 would be able to initiate major reforms, especially as Hertzog warmly welcomed the publication of Brookes's *History* and ensured that its publishers receive a grant from National Party funds of £360 for 1000 copies.[13] For a period Brookes became a propagandist for the nationalists and claimed on the basis of "good authority" that segregation would not entail the immediate territorial division of the country, but rather the addition of "neutral" areas to existing black and white areas.[14] This optimism was not shared by most black leaders. Selby Msimang warned that Hertzog's policy of increasing the allocation of land to Africans would meet increasing resistance from white farming interests.[15]

Brookes's *History of Native Policy* was cautiously received in the Native Affairs Department. The years after the First World War were marked by a growing uncertainty in the Department over the direction of policy following a number of retrenchments and retirements. Many of the older Cape liberal officials were coming under pressure from segregationist influences in the Department of Justice, and it was in response to this that the Department eventually produced the segregationist Native Administration Bill in 1927 that considerably increased the powers of the central government in the administration of the reserves.[16]

A History of Native Policy in South Africa was critical of the conservatism of the Cape officials who were accused of delaying legislation in the interest of preserving the Cape African franchise. The Chief Native Commissioner for the Cape, T. C. Norton, in response to a request from Hertzog, generally praised the book and used it to attack the procedure whereby the Department had to work "though men of another Department even with consultation before appointment. This must, in a majority of cases, result in compromises which is to the advantage of neither Department."[17] Norton favoured reforming the NAD on lines similar to the Indian Civil Service and interchanging personnel from different provinces in order to break down provincial boundaries. He urged, though, a limitation on the powers of the Native Affairs Commission and opposed Brookes's suggestions for an extension of local African councils under the 1920 Native Affairs Act.[18]

Norton's comments reflected a strong paternalism in the NAD that lived uneasily with the more ardent designs of the segregationist social engineers. For the latter group, Brookes's book represented a major defence of segregationism, despite Brookes's own doubts about extensive legislation. Copies went out to most of the ministers in the Pact government and Thomas Boydell, the Labour Minister of Transport, considered that the book "could be regarded as the standard work on the native question in South Africa".[19]

The relatively fluid period in the early years of the Pact government was short-lived. The government came under pressure from its segregationist supporters for a clarification of its policy, and doubts were expressed over Hertzog's Smithfield speech in November 1925, outlining a policy based upon increased territorial allocations to Africans and a measure of African political representation on a Union-wide basis. Arthur Barlow, a Pact representative from Hertzog's own domain of the Orange Free State, warned that there would be a "storm of opposition" if the proposals led to an extension of the African franchise to the province.[20] The Pact's ability to win qualified support from some English-speaking liberal groups such as the Joint Councils appeared to be threatening its more traditional bases of support.[21]

By 1926, Hertzog's interest in Brookes's ideas began to decline. The government pressed ahead with its Colour Bar Bill, entrenching job segregation, and published its four Native Bills that provided for an end to the Cape African franchise in return for seven white "natives representatives" in the Senate and House of Assembly. Brookes failed to receive any major appointment from the government, such as to the Native Affairs Commission, though in 1927 he was sent as the South African representative to the League of Nations at Geneva. The Natal liberal C. T. Loram felt optimistically by September 1926 that Brookes was developing "splendidly" and had "great hopes of him now that he knows that is not going to get the job just yet".[22]

The second edition of Brookes's *The History of South African Native Policy*, which appeared in 1927, indicated a progressive rift with the Pact. While the 1924 edition had considered the Cape African franchise "indefensible from any point of view" the 1927 edition considered the only alternative to it to be "repression".[23] The 1926 Colour Bar Act was condemned as an unnecessary legislative enforcement of legislation and a 1924 passage was excised – a passage stating that "... the growth of the Bantu into a nation clamouring for some form of autonomy is a process as sure as the circlings of the planets, a process which we may direct with ease, but dam only at our peril".[24]

Brookes became concerned that the development of nationalism appeared to conflict with the pursuit of liberal principles. His exposure to the debates at the League probably underlined this consideration. In a 1927 essay *The Political Future of South Africa* he warned of the dangers of mobilizing "yellow perils" or "black perils" and cautioned that behind both there lay a "great unity of humanity". He refused to countenance any "lesser vision" and urged the establishment of a Liberal party in South Africa in order to further a "consistent and aggressive liberalism". It was now, he declared, a "semi religious dogma" rather than a "reasoned conclusion" to imagine that a "white South Africa" could stand apart from the "great world movements".[25] Territorial segregation was impossible in the Transvaal or the Cape and the main goal to aim for should be at least common political participation if not common citizenship. "We are in South Africa not to govern the non-European races," he wrote, "but to teach them, first to govern themselves, and next to cooperate with us in the government of the common fatherland."[26]

By 1927, Brookes was gaining a broader intellectual perspective on South African politics, though his *History* was still suspicious of

"American negro propaganda" on South African blacks.[27] He was particularly critical of the "slavish imitation" of British political institutions and was receptive to alternative liberal political models. Whilst travelling to Geneva he visited Britain and attended Harold Laski's lectures at the London School of Economics, though avoided more radical critics of African colonial policy such as Norman Leys and Sydney Olivier.[28]

What proved to be especially significant in the development of Brookes's thinking was a visit he made in 1927 to the United States. The North American pattern of "race relations" proved to be a considerable stimulus to his outlook on racial issues, as it was for a number of South African liberals and missionaries at this time.[29]

Brookes considered the US visit to be "a great turning point" in his career since it exposed him to new ideas in the emergent subject of "race relations" at the University of North Carolina at Chapel Hill as well as the usual *locus classicus* of Black American advancement, the Tuskegee Institute in Alabama founded by Booker T. Washington. Brookes drew "the salutary lesson that the black man was capable of considerable achievement in the milieu of white civilisation". The experience of seeing black American economic and educational advancement at first hand confirmed his existing doubts on the trajectory of South African segregationist policy. Booker Washington's ideas at Tuskegee appeared to Brookes "so reasonable, so convincing, so safe".[30] Like Hoernle, he was impressed by the work edited by the black American sociologist Alain Locke, *The New Negro* (1925), which emphasized that the old negro of folklore was mainly a fabrication of the white imagination, though many blacks had themselves played up to this as a "protective social mimicry".[31]

In the aftermath of his return from the US, Brookes became an active member of liberal circles on the Witwatersrand and helped establish the South African Institute of Race Relations in 1929. He became an enthusiastic advocate of inter-racial "contacts". At the 1929 annual European-Bantu conference in Cape Town the influence of Alain Locke's ideas became apparent when he emphasized that a "new Bantu" had begun to emerge in South Africa with command of "excellent English" and able to propound arguments "just and sure in substance, restrained and dignified in expression".[32] Over the following few years Brookes moved towards the ideals of an assimilationist Cape liberalism at a time when it was itself coming under growing attack from the government. In 1930 he chose the venue of a student conference at Fort Hare to admit, before a gathering of over 150 black and white students, some of his previous errors.[33]

Recantation

By the late 1920s liberal opinion internationally was beginning to swing away from the idea of maintaining segregation as a means of "protecting" African societies from white capitalist intrusion.[34] The Fort Hare conference raised the hopes of a number of the African organizers that social and economic issues could be debated, though in the event the main agenda concentrated on more orthodox theological matters. One of the African participants, Victor Selope Thema of the Johannesburg Joint Council, even went as far as suggesting, in praising the farm schools, that conditions were improving for Africans in the Orange Free State.[35]

Brookes's paper proved to be a disappointment to the black American activist Max Yergan, then attached to the University College of Fort Hare as a social worker, who had hoped the paper would discuss economic issues.[36] Brookes kept to the theme of "personal and social Christianity" which he felt was essential if communist ideas were not to spread amongst the African leadership. He berated the "lack of honesty and speech" in South African political debate and called for clear thinking as a means to dispel "fear" on racial issues.[37]

From the early 1930s Christianity became an increasingly important aspect of Brookes's thought as he fell under the influence of the ideas of the Oxford Group, later known as Moral Rearmament. He felt a sense of divine guidance as he tried to obtain the nomination as South African Party candidate for the Cape constituency of Woodstock in August 1931, despite feeling that "it may be that I am meant to serve in other and less public spheres".[38] The shift towards the English-speaking liberal camp left him isolated from his Afrikaner colleagues at the Transvaal University College. After he failed to get the Woodstock nomination, he decided to resign his professorship in 1933. He began work as a fund-raiser of the Institute of Race Relations, of which he became president the same year, and effectively cut himself adrift from academic teaching for the next twenty years.

Christianity provided a new sense of purpose for Brookes as he severed his links with the South African academic establishment. It provided an ethical yardstick by which to evaluate the supposedly "scientific" measurement of racial attainments. Unlike Hoernle, Brookes became suspicious of intelligence-testing as well as the older craniological measurement of skulls. "Government by scientists may be a good thing," he wrote in an essay in 1929, but

> ... government by pseudo scientists would be indeed a wretched policy. Most of the infusion of "scientists" into the field of race relations is of this kind. Inaccurate craniologists, slapdash psychologists, biologists who live in the Victorian atmosphere of Herbert Spencer, statisticians who force their decimal points are but a sorry company to guide us on the difficult route which leads us to racial peace.[39]

Both editions of *The History of Native Policy in South Africa* had been uncertain over the question of whether there was complete mental equality between white and black. By 1929, Brookes was no longer prepared to leave the matter open-ended. He considered Peter Nielsen's essay *The Black Man's Place in South Africa* to be one of the best statements against what he perceived as the "tyranny of caste" and he pleaded for an educational system that would provide equal facilities for both whites and blacks.[40]

Brookes's intellectual development made him an idiosyncratic figure in the pantheon of South African liberal heroes. Whilst not moving to the Fabian left, as W. M. Macmillan did, he had nevertheless begun to challenge some of the orthodoxies of the mainstream liberal establishment in South Africa represented by the thinking of C. T. Loram, to whom he continued to pay public homage. As was seen in chapter 1, Loram considered that the "immaturity" of African mental ability necessitated rural training and the continued restraint on African urbanization. He viewed Brookes with some suspicion, especially after his 1933 Phelps-Stokes lectures entitled *Colour Problems in South Africa* and was partly instrumental in getting Brookes removed from work for the Institute of Race Relations.

Brookes's 1933 Phelps-Stokes lectures were notable for their passionate defence of a liberal idea of South African patriotism transcending individual "national" group differences. Brookes was sceptical of nationalism seeing it as inextricably wedded to segregationism. In an era when African nationalism was not yet so visible on the South African political landscape, he considered nationalism to be merely a defence of white privilege and at the same time a corruption of political morality. It was essential to return to the individualist tenets of liberalism to expose the "lie in the soul" at the heart of segregationist ideology and to "make all South Africa the goal of our endeavours". "Let us realise," he continued,

> that South Africa can only be great if the individual members of the community, be they Black, White or Brown, are great. Let us treat individuals as individuals, as persons, entitled to respect and to recognition on their merits, *not merely as members of artificially defined groups* (emphasis added).[41]

The lectures gained a number of admiring critics outside South Africa. A critic in the *Manchester Guardian* noted Brookes's "flaming sincerity and instinctively revolutionary cast of ... mind"[42] while the anthropologist Lucy Mair considered them "a courageous and stimulating criticism of a number of popular opinions".[43] On the other hand, W. W. M. Eiselen, Professor of *Volkekunde* at the University of Stellenbosch, criticized the lectures in 1935 in the Afrikaans periodical *Die Huisgenoot* for their failure to suggest any coherent programme of economic development in the African reserves and locations and their being fixed on individualism as opposed to what Eiselen perceived to be the more general trend towards national self-identification.[44]

Brookes's lectures marked a major intellectual revolt by a prominent liberal against the ideology of segregation. They reflected a growing ideological polarization in South Africa in the early 1930s which threatened to take on an ethnic dimension as liberalism became identified with English-speakers. At the same time Brookes had launched a powerful moral case against policies of ethnic social engineering that threatened to end any slender degree of influence the SAIRR might have on the course of government policy.

Rheinallt Jones and Loram considered that the role of the Institute was to impress on the government the fruits of research on African economic "development" and to humanize as far as possible the thinking behind the government's "native policy". They were prepared to work within broad parameters of the 1932 Native Economic Commission Report, which Brookes castigated as a "splendid failure" for inadequately analysing the degree of economic decline of the reserves economies.[45]

Brookes's strong moral condemnation of segregationism made him appear an uneasy ally for the Institute liberals. Loram opposed Brookes's reappointment as the Institute's main fund-raiser and suggested one of his own students, the segregationist John Kirk, as the body's representative in "South East Africa".[46] A continuing shortage of funds indicated that it would be difficult for both Brookes and the Institute's "Adviser" J. D. Rheinallt Jones to remain on the payroll. After fund-raising from July to December 1933, Brookes went to England and returned to South Africa to take up an offer of Principal of Adams College in Natal, following an invitation by J. B. McCord of the American Board of Missions. Brookes's move to Natal was a welcome one for the Witwatersrand liberals. It removed a potentially troublesome activist from mainstream Institute activities while still keeping him in welfare work in a province where there was a majority English-speaking, if conservative, white electorate.

Adams College and Election as Senator

Brookes's move to Natal came at a time when local initiatives in the province in developing African studies and race relations had been effectively quashed. In 1928 the wealthy collector of Africana in Durban, Killie Campbell, had offered to fund a chair of African Studies at the University College of Natal. The offer was turned down by a suspicious university senate. A further proposal by a lecturer at the University College, Mabel Palmer, to develop an institute to study the effects of urbanization on African society also failed to come to fruition.[47] By 1934 there appeared to be little possibility of any research with a generally liberal motivation being achieved in the province.

The welfare work of the Durban Joint Council was also viewed with suspicion by local African political leaders. The Zulu businessman and trade union organizer Allison Champion resented the paternalistic control of the Council by Mabel Palmer and rejected offers from her to reorganize the ICU Yase Natal.[48] Liberalism was generally at a low ebb in the province and this only began to change with the outbreak of World War Two and the formation of a branch of the SAIRR in Durban in 1940.[49]

Brookes's work as Principal at Adams College between 1934 and

1946 thus played an important role in its own right in stimulating new ideas on race relations. The college had initially been started as a seminary by the American Board Mission in 1853 and was located at Adams Mission south of Durban in 1865. Though there was still a rather paternalistic approach in the inter-war years, the college was probably the most racially integrated in the country. In 1924 Z. K. Matthews went on its staff as headmaster of the high school. Together with St Peter's College in Johannesburg (run by the Community of the Resurrection) Adams began to rival the old Eastern Cape institutions such as Lovedale and Fort Hare, emerging by the 1940s as one of the main innovatory centres of black education in South Africa.[50]

Brookes's work at Adams encouraged him to consider once again a career in politics. In the early 1930s, he had refused to countenance any compromise over the Cape African franchise, urging the liberal politician Jan Hofmeyr in 1932 to reject any further conciliation unless the government repudiated segregation entirely.[51] By 1935, however, he began to have second thoughts as the two bills covering land and political representation were clearly going to become law. The SAIRR leadership in Johannesburg also began to develop a conciliatory attitude.

R. F. A. Hoernle, the Institute's president, indicated to the Natal members in July 1935 that the government was favourable to a series of regional consultations with African political leaders.[52] This rather blunted the hopes of Cape African leaders such as D. D. T. Jabavu that there would be one national consultation. In Natal a number of local leaders, including Pixley Seme and John Dube, favoured the idea of the regional conferences, even though the conservatively inclined *Umteteli wa Bantu* regarded the whole idea as a strategy of divide and rule.[53]

The conferences ended up threatening the position of the "moderate" African leadership. In Pietermaritzburg the leadership led by Dube were out-voted by a more radical faction organized by the Zulu linguist Carl Faye, who was (rather surprisingly) a member of the NAD.[54] In December 1935, Brookes tried to persuade Dube to support a compromise formula whereby a Natives Representative Council (NRC) would be introduced by the legislation and the abolition of the Cape African franchise deferred. He hoped this would "save the government's face" as well as allowing it to maintain its authority over African leadership.[55]

Brookes's attempted compromise only proved acceptable to the African leaders if it was not a *quid quo pro* for the abolition of the Cape African franchise.[56] It was impossible to get the support of the seven SAP MPs in Natal at a conference organized in Durban on 11 December.[57] By February 1936, Brookes decided to support the compromise engineered on the Bills by one of the seven SAP MPs, the Durban lawyer, Leif Egeland. This entailed the abolition of the Cape African franchise in return for Senate representation on a community basis and the establishment of the NRC. "If it can bring together *con amore* men like Hofmeyr and Pirow," Brookes wrote to Egeland, "especially if Pirow is going to develop into the kind of statesman that he can be and not the negrophobe that he might be, there is much to be said for it."[58]

Brookes was quite anxious to secure election as a natives representative. He refused to support the Durban Joint Council's opposition to the "compromise", thinking that this would make them an "irresponsible minority" in the eyes of mainstream white opinion, though some liberals regretted his failure to take a stronger stand.[59] The pressures to get involved in the system of "natives representation" were building up.

Brookes was invited soon after the passage of the legislation by Chief Mshiyeni ka Dinuzulu to stand for election to the Senate. By April of 1936 Allison Champion was also approached to support his strongly Christian and anti-socialist approach to race relations.[60] With Champion's endorsement secured, Brookes built up a formidable base of support among the African electorate, winning the votes of 180,263 African taxpayers compared to 156,394 for his rival, Douglas Shepstone. There were some rumblings of discontent from Africans who were familiar with Brookes's segregationist past. W. J. Gobhozi from Esperanza on the Natal south coast considered him responsible for the loss of the Cape African vote.[61] But African political leaders in the Natal in the aftermath of the election were mainly content to consolidate their position and were unwilling to take a more radical stand.

Many African leaders in Natal initially considered the 1936 legislation would open up new channels of political influence with the central government. Champion hoped this would lead to the South African Native Trust, established under the legislation to help African business ventures.[62] Pixley Seme also speculated that the NRC would be granted autonomous legislative powers.[63]

Brookes's support for the system of "natives' representation" accorded at first with a wider climate of opinion amongst both black and white liberal circles in the late 1930s. The white "natives representatives" were able to act as a cohesive political group until the election defeat of Rheinallt Jones by the ex-communist Hyman Basner in 1942. The group resembled in some respects the parliamentary radicals in mid-Victorian Britain and it was fervently believed that through the sheer power of rational argument the desired ends would eventually be achieved. Even Smuts felt at the end of 1937 that if the NRC proved a success it might "well open a new era in our racial relations".[64]

The relationship of the natives' representatives to African leaders was one of patron and client. Champion urged Brookes in August 1937 to take up the wage issue among African workers who remained organized in Champion's union, ICU Yase Natal. Brookes only agreed if he was "consulted in advance before the union acted".[65]

Brookes's political position was supported by the revival of traditional tribal authority through the Zulu Society. This body was inaugurated in January 1938 by Chief Mshiyeni at the Bantu Men's Social Centre in Durban in front of some 3000 Zulus from all over Natal.[66] In May 1939 the secretary of the society, Charles Mpanza, wrote to Brookes stating that the society considered him their "chosen white man to speak for them to the government".[67]

The NRC proved to be a very ineffective body. To most educated councillors the Council lacked any real power to effect legislation.[68] In the early 1940s, Allison Champion began to look more to Brookes in the Senate than to the NRC members, though this meant he rather distanced himself from newer currents emerging in African politics in the form of the Congress Youth League. In the years after 1941 a fairly close personal relationship developed between the two men and Champion supported Brookes in his re-election to the Senate in 1942.[69]

In the early 1940s, a national revival began to take place in African politics. Within the NRC a radical group of councillors began to coalesce around the younger and better-educated leadership of Z. K. Matthews and Paul Mosaka. By 1943, this group began pressing for an extension of African representation in local councils.[70]

Brookes had initially seen the NRC as a body for "canalising the revolutionary activity which is inevitably to be found among the younger Bantu leaders today".[71] He praised the NRC for its "ability, dignity and restraint" and urged that reform should be brought about by the informal method of "influencing individuals and changing their point of view".[72] This was essential if there were to be any restraint on the mobilization of ethnic group consciousness.[73]

By 1943, even the most moderate members of the NRC, such as James Moroka from Thaba 'Nchu in the Orange Free State, reputedly wanted the body smashed and replaced by a system of direct African parliamentary representation.[74] Brookes failed to urge any coherent effort to meet the NRC on a regular basis and concentrated more on trying to maintain the unity among the white "natives' representatives" following Basner's election in 1942.[75] This was not always straightforward and Margaret Ballinger criticized him for acting as a "timid conservative" and failing to take a stronger stand against segregation policy. Brookes responded by pointing out that with five "natives' representatives" the Cape could afford to have a wider range of opinion than Natal. If he fell foul of the government there would be no effective channel for African interests and so this could only be done in an "extreme case".[76]

This focus upon the central loci of power tended to leave Brookes oblivious of the change in political mood in the African political leadership. The collapse of support for "natives' representation" by even the most moderate of African leaders and the suspension of the NRC after the African mine strike of September 1946 took him by surprise. Brookes urged on the ministers of the Smuts government the need to retain the political credibility of the system established ten years earlier. With some of the other natives' representatives he desperately tried to suggest proposals to reform the institutions of African representation in order to win back the support of the moderate black political leadership.

Brookes considered the 1946 resolution in the NRC for non-cooperation as containing nothing less than an "evil spirit".[77] But he recognized in a memorandum to Douglas Smit, the former Secretary of Native Affairs, that the crisis could not be "taken lightly", for it was "not so much a case of preserving dignity or saving face as of preventing developments which may lead to national disaster". He pressed that the NRC's powers be increased to make it a more credible forum. It was nothing less than "a question of 'stooping to conquer' ".[78]

Smuts had been favourable in principle to reform of the NRC before the crisis blew up, suggesting in a note to a memorandum by

E. B. Young that the Council could be doubled from its present total of sixteen African members to thirty-two.[79] These efforts at reform proved still-born. The Native Affairs Department, under its Secretary of Native Affairs, Gordon Mears, was generally favourable to reform but the hand of Smuts as Prime Minister eventually proved decisive. By the middle of 1947 Smuts decided to postpone the whole issue until after the election which he confidently expected to win. The issue appeared to be alienating the more conservative sections of the *platteland* United Party, which was already on the defensive as a result of the aggressive attacks by the Nationalist press on the mild liberalism of Jan Hofmeyr, the Deputy Prime Minister.[80]

After 1946, Brookes channelled some of his energy into trying to influence government thinking on the African reserves. As a member of the Social and Economic Planning Council he exerted a considerable impact on its important report number 9 of 1946, *The Native Reserves and their Place in the Economy of the Union of South Africa*. The report tried to think out a long-term set of policy objectives regarding the reserves. It favoured an extensive programme of reserve reclamation and sought to build on the programme that had been introduced a year previously by Douglas Smit as Secretary of Native Affairs. But it was critical of measures aimed at arbitrarily bolstering up tribalism and implicitly attacked the provisions of the 1927 Native Administration Act that gave arbitrary powers to tribal chiefs (a measure that Brookes had attacked at the time as being essentially fascist in nature). It argued that the reserves could not absorb all the African population and urged the creation of a permanent and stable labour-force, whilst at the same time suggesting the creation of a Regional Development Authority to develop the reserves, operating initially in the Transkei.[81]

This last proposal at least gained a positive response from most of the major government departments involved and one that a meeting of heads of departments in November 1947 considered a matter of high policy.[82] Though the proposal was not acted on during the period of the Smuts government it is possible to see in it the germs of the later Bantu Investment Corporation and Xhosa Investment Corporation that were established by the Nationalist government under Dr Verwoerd in the 1950s.

By the last two years of the Smuts government, Brookes became increasingly aware of the growing international hostility to South African policy. In a pamphlet, *South Africa Faces UNO*, he drew the lesson that illiberal regimes usually ended up as "unwise as well as evil".[83] His outlook reflected a general sense of liberal confidence after World War Two in the wake of the defeat of National Socialism. It was to be abruptly shattered by the shock election victory of the Nationalists in 1948 which most English-speaking liberals had not considered possible.

A Questioning of Belief

The triumph of Afrikaner nationalism in 1948 led to Brookes once more abandoning the political terrain, especially after his failure to be reappointed by the government to the Native Affairs Commission in 1950. African politics in Natal began to become radicalized by the late 1940s as the Congress Youth League, led by figures such as Jordan Ngubane, attacked the old-style boss politics of Champion in Durban. As early as 1948 the issue of boycotting elections to advisory boards exposed rifts between groups Ngubane termed "liberals" and "democrats". Brookes's political base began to look increasingly fragile.[84] He hinted at a possibly more aggressive political style in 1949 when he wrote to Rheinallt Jones: "We may be in for many years of reactionary rule with no obvious escape except revolution or appeal to the outside world, neither of which I want to see. It has seemed to me that now or never is the time for militancy."[85]

It was not really clear how this "militancy" was to be directed. In a Hoernle memorial lecture to the Institute of Race Relations in 1950, Brookes saw the warnings of Arthur Keppel Jones in his book *When Smuts Goes* (1947) as uncannily accurate in their nightmare vision of a "semi-totalitarian" government emerging in South Africa. Brookes felt that the "spirit of the age" was against this trend in South African politics, which represented "a very unexpected sequel to our participation in our war against nazism".[86]

Brookes did strongly oppose the ANC's support for passive resistance in its 1949 *Programme of Action*. Patrick Duncan tried to convert him to such a view in the early 1950s, but Brookes resisted the appeal of Gandhian-style *satyagraha* which he felt would get nowhere. Still at heart a conservative, he felt that time would act as the great healer of racial tensions.[87] He had been initially impressed by the young Duncan, whom he had considered a potential Principal of Fort Hare, and had suggested to Smuts in 1949 that Duncan be adopted as a United Party MP. By 1952, the outlook of Brookes and

Duncan began radically to diverge as the latter became drawn into supporting the ANC Defiance Campaign of that year.[88] Brookes, on the other hand, was forced out of politics by a coronary which confined him to hospital before the 1952 election to the Senate. He was succeeded as senator for Natal by the conservative Durban advocate Douglas Hemming who had for a number of years had the support of Allison Champion.

After the 1953 election, Brookes decided to return to university life following an invitation from E. G. Malherbe, the Principal of the University of Natal, to teach at the newly created university. University life enabled him to make a reassessment of his political ideas. Liberalism was increasingly on the defensive in South African politics as apartheid became entrenched. On the international plane, too, liberal ideas became subordinated to a realist political outlook seeking the defence of the West in the era of the cold war. During a rather bleak period of mounting domestic conflict, Brookes tried to see South African politics in a more international context.

Unlike many South African liberals, Brookes had a first-hand acquaintance with the changing international opinion on race. In 1947 he had attended a UNESCO conference in Mexico City where he met the Catholic thinker Jacques Maritain whom he considered "the greatest political philosopher of our time".[89] Maritain's philosophy reinforced Brookes's increasing disillusionment with nationalism. In *Man and the State* in 1951 Maritain castigated the "plague of nationalism" and looked to the idea of the "body politic" embracing a vision of duty to Christian ideals. It was possible, Maritain pointed out, for this idea of the body politic to arise "in the bosom of a national community". This "national community" could only be a "propitious soil and an occasion for the blossoming" since "the idea of the body politic belongs to another, superior order. As soon as the body politic exists, it is something other than the national community."[90]

Maritain's notion of a Christian body politic kept open the idea of human free will to transform the political realm in accordance with transnational ideas of duty. It enabled liberals to break free from the more static conception of the "liberal spirit" that Hoernle had impressed on the thinking of many South African liberals, though Brookes remained, in public at least, a strong admirer of Hoernle's "acumen and outstanding ability".[91] The approach, though, could also reinforce a flight from political struggle into the inner realm of the human spirit as a form of compensation for political defeat.

The latter course began to emerge in Brookes's 1953 study, *South Africa in a Changing World*, where he declared that "ultimately salvation lies not in changing political organisations, but in the inner resources of the human spirit. The movements of history are not in our own hands: our reactions to them are."[92] Brookes recognized that with sovereign nation states as the core units of international politics, there appeared to be little that the international community could effectively do against the illiberal creed of apartheid. This was an era when any suggestion of employing sanctions against the South African government commanded very slender political support in most political circles opposed to South African government policy.[93] There appeared to be no world-policeman to enforce the liberal creed on the South African government in the same way that the United States federal government could impose its core values. The Swedish social analyst Gunnar Myrdal, in his important study *An American Dilemma* (1944), had termed these values "the American creed" and he had seen them as based on the Enlightenment ideas of reason and justice and the perfectibility of man. They were likely sooner or later to supersede the minority creed of Southern segregationism which stood in opposition to the values of the rest of the United States.[94]

Brookes recognized that the slender roots of the South African liberal tradition left it in a far weaker position than the dominant "American creed" to define the core values of South African society. He pointed out:

> To the extent to which segregation and separation are made ideals in South Africa, and linked up with the noblest and holiest in Afrikaner tradition, this particular type of inner conflict is partly avoided, or directed into a defensive aggressiveness against a misunderstanding outer world. It is never wholly silenced, for the voice of conscience still speaks: but the dilemma of America is not reproduced in its acute form.[95]

Brookes felt a growing sense of despair during the 1950s as growing state authoritarianism undermined what was left of parliamentary government. In 1956, at the time of the removal of the Cape Coloured franchise, he wrote that the "English genius for compromise" was not "appreciated" by the Nationalist government. It became necessary to examine what the "unconscious first principles are on which our experience is based", for a battle was to be fought for the "inner citadel of truth".[96]

Such considerations led him to turn to the fundamentals of Christian political belief. Political action had ultimately to be founded on a Christian ethic, though the same year he warned Z. K. Matthews not to expect too much from this, for "God has never promised freedom from injustice, but freedom in it. Our circumstances we cannot control, but we may turn to Him in them, and whatever persecution we have to face our spirits can remain free and the creativeness of love and faith can still work in our lives".[97] Unlike later advocates of liberation theology, he did not see Christianity as a message of political liberation.

Brookes became attracted by the ideas of the fifth-century North African bishop St Augustine. In 1959, as the government prepared legislation to extend segregation to the universities, he gained temporary respite through a sabbatical year at Oxford, where at the High Anglican Pusey House he wrote what he came to regard as his most important book, *The City of God and the Politics of Crisis*. The book was deeply distrustful of all state power, even when it was held by a nominally "liberal state". Though it was true that liberalism stood for values that the church could not but approve, "yet she loses her soul when she agrees that these are the final and absolute truths."[98] There was an element of resignation in the book. It refused to accept that Christians had any major political struggle on their hands in their moral opposition to apartheid. The "startling thing to discover," wrote Brookes, was that "we need not consume ourselves in the effort to retain ... civilised values, that it is really true, literally true, that if we seek first the Kingdom of God and his righteousness all these things will be added unto us."[99]

The return to the Augustinian notion of a City of God was symptomatic of a growing doubt held by a number of Western liberals in the unqualified pursuit of Enlightenment reason. Since the publication in 1932 of Carl Becker's seminal series of essays, *The Heavenly City of the Eighteenth Century Philosophers*, a "climate of opinion" (a term employed by Becker) had been created among many liberals internationally that the achievements of the eighteenth-century *philosophes* were somewhat limited; that the medieval cosmic order had been rebuilt anew on secular terms and the heavenly city of Augustine brought down to earth.[100] These doubts on the metropolitan plain had not really penetrated the thinking of South African liberals before the Second World War, partly because of the continued political optimism of international missionary opinion and partly because of the detached position of the South African academic community at that time.

However, by the late 1950s Brookes was able to articulate the growing theological doubts of a number of liberal Christians in South Africa. He did not go anything like as far as Trevor Huddleston, whose controversial book *Naught For Your Comfort* in 1956, internationalized the South African issue by challenging the whole idea that whites had any moral leadership left in South Africa as they stood guilty of the sin of "racial pride" that was similar in kind to Nazi Germany.[101] But Brookes did hope that his writings would stir an internal re-examination of the liberal Christian conscience in South Africa.

Brookes supported the Progressive Party when it was established in 1959 but became a member of the Liberal Party in 1962. He was voted chairman two years later following the banning of Peter Brown. By 1963 he moved towards support for a universal franchise, though still hoped in the book *Power, Law, Right and Love* that nationalism could be banished from political thinking, for it was only an "inevitable step between the attainment of equal human solidarity and 'colonialism' which has its day of usefulness, but which can easily become an evil barrier on the path of progress".[102]

He continued to stress the importance of a change of heart on the part of the ruling regime and emphasized the Christian notion of *love*, drawing on the writings of the German theologian Paul Tillich. While it was necessary for liberals to recognize the reality of state power and the tempering of it through the rule of law and the recognition of rights outside those of the state, love nevertheless had the last word. It stood indeed above any "prudential" arguments to the "Afrikaner people", whose emotions were "too deeply engaged". There was still the hope of "winning them by the call of love which is implicit in any Christian faith, however twisted and distorted".[103]

Brookes began rather belatedly to understand before the end of his life the challenges facing blacks as well as whites in South Africa. In 1965 he recognized the force of James Baldwin's case in *The Fire Next Time* that whites who came only to "give" to blacks were merely being patronizing.[104] These doubts towards the traditional liberal attitude of wanting to "help" blacks were further strengthened by a visit to the United States in 1968. Like his first visit half a century previously, the US proved to be a therapeutic jolt to Brookes' ideas on race. Lecturing at a number of university campuses he became acquainted with the strength of the Black Power movement amongst black American students during a period of mounting protest against the continuing US involvement in the Vietnam War. He recognized that all great changes in human societies were originally initiated by small minorities. Black Power was important for helping to initiate a new sort of world, and he cautioned against the US adoption of an economic and political imperialism in international politics.[105]

At one level these were radical sentiments on a foreign issue which Brookes had not been prepared to mount closer to home. He did talk the same year of a need for "intellectual liberation, deep religious conviction, passionate rebellion against the trammels of the past" in order to shift whites in South Africa from their "instinctive faith" in apartheid.[106] This was talking a language of liberation which was to have such a marked influence on South African politics in the following decade. To this extent, Brookes developed as an important representative of the classical liberal tradition in South African politics during a period when it came under mounting political attack from an authoritarian state.

Brookes had during a large part of his career directed liberals towards the ruling political bloc that dominated the South African state. Until the 1960s he had only a tardy recognition of the growing significance of African nationalism. Some black writers have viewed Brookes for this reason with great suspicion, though the Zulu writer H. I. E. Dhlomo wrote of the conflict between Brookes the politician and public man and Brookes the Christian and private individual. The paradox Dhlomo explained in terms of the fact that "we are victims of circumstance, condition and fortune, and must at times be content to teach in philosophy and precept, in verse and art, what we cannot fully live and do".[107]

Brookes's liberalism now appears politically weak in its refusal to condemn the exploitation of the poor by the South African state. Alan Boesak has attacked the Christian church for failing to confront the "painful truths" behind a "facade of myths and real or imagined anxieties". Boesak accepted the basic message of Christian love, though he argued that its significance lay in its ability to challenge separation and alienation, for otherwise love in the world of apartheid has a "stifling, destructive character that cannot but deny the true essence of Christian love".[108] Brookes was not totally opposed to such an interpretation and by the early 1970s, as the next chapter shows, he took a strong stand against efforts in liberal quarters such as SPRO-CAS to seek a devolution of power on a group as well as an individual basis. He was thus important for updating the classical tradition of liberalism in South Africa from its roots in the Cape and trying to make it relevant to a world that had been so drastically transformed by the impact of apartheid.

4
LIBERALS, RADICALS AND THE POLITICS OF BLACK CONSCIOUSNESS

Brookes's search for a moral anchorage for liberal values in the Augustinian conception of a City of God indicated that a crisis had developed within English-speaking South African liberalism in the years after 1948. It became increasingly apparent that the English Whig inheritance of relying on progressive political reform through parliamentary structures was being increasingly nullified by state repression. At the same time, Hoernle's efforts to stimulate a debate on the nature of liberal values in South Africa failed to come to fruition in the years after 1945 as the white English-speaking population increasingly opted out of politics. Though there were periodic upsurges of political protest by English-speakers against the course of Nationalist policy, these failed to coalesce into a strong opposition movement. The Springbok Legion and the Torch Commando, for instance, were mobilized by ex-servicemen horrified at the apparently Nazi complexion of some the state's policy, but they lacked any clear political direction and failed to confront directly the issue of racial segregation in their own ranks.[1]

Many of the bodies that had been founded in the inter-war years, such as the SAIRR and the Joint Councils, continued to shape the central direction of English-speaking opposition politics in the years after 1948. They were joined after 1953 by the Liberal Party which was formed by a number of English-speaking professionals after the United Party's second election defeat, though not without the considerable misgivings of some older liberals such as Margaret Ballinger.[2] For a period, the Liberal Party managed to hold together a fairly disparate group of activists ranging from conservatively inclined figures such as Margaret Ballinger and Bernard Friedman to radicals such as Randolph Vigne and Patrick Duncan, who after 1958 edited the party's magazine *Contact*.

The Emergence of Common Society Liberalism

The period of the 1950s proved to be a fertile one for liberal debate in South Africa. Though the Liberal Party had refused to participate in the 1955 Congress of the People which led to the Freedom Charter, there were moves towards trying to update liberal ideology for a more democratically inclined age. To many liberals during the period of the cold war it seemed essential to try to meet the challenge of an increasingly revolutionary situation in South African politics as the ANC and allied organizations began to drift towards mass action. "The choice is between revolutionary evolution," wrote Alan Paton in 1957,

> or just plain revolution. It is the role of liberal forces to hasten evolution so as to avoid revolution. Revolution in South Africa will not be what revolution was in North America, when it led to the creation of the world's great democracy. Revolution in South Africa would lead to a totalitarian state, but also it would lead to a poorer spiritual and material life for all.[3]

The main impulse behind South African liberalism was cut adrift in the cold-war years from the revolutionary traditions of late eighteenth- and nineteenth-century liberalism. South Africa was not seen as a society ready for mass popular revolt to attain democratic goals in the manner of Europe in 1848. This was partly due to the deep distrust of the South African Communist Party, which tended to exhibit strongly Stalinist leanings and close links with Moscow. Though the party was banned under the Suppression of Communism Act in 1950, many Communists remained active in underground South African politics and the left-leaning Congress of Democrats (COD) was widely believed to be acting as a Communist front organization. Nevertheless, many African nationalists in the ANC, such as Nelson Mandela, Walter Sisulu and Oliver Tambo, began moving towards a close political alliance with the SACP despite their earlier suspicions as members of the Congress Youth League (CYL) of Communist influence in African politics.[4]

A number of leading liberals considered it essential to try to spell out the sort of goals they envisaged for a future South Africa. In the course of the 1950s, debate intensified on the nature of the "common" or "multi-racial" society which liberals hoped to build once apartheid was removed. One of the figures who had a considerable influence on this was the African anthropologist and political leader Z. K. Matthews. Though Matthews never formally belonged to the Liberal Party, he did influence liberal ideas through a number of articles and addresses. Matthews emerged as a figure of national prominence in the wake of the suspension of the Natives Representative Council in 1946 when he had been able to articulate the sentiments of the councillors against what was widely perceived to be a powerless "toy telephone". He tended though to be treated with suspicion by many of the members of the Congress Youth League, for he remained sceptical of tactics of immediate and outright boycott of bodies such as the NRC and the Native Advisory Boards given the poor level of organization within the ANC. Matthews tried to act as a mediator between the African National Congress, of which he was Cape president, and liberal bodies such as the SAIRR in the hope that this could expand the level of African political contacts and enhance its pressure on the government in Pretoria.

Matthews stressed the role of "co-operation" between whites and blacks in furtherance of the multi-racial goal. This ideal had an advantage, he wrote in 1949, over the older inter-war liberal ideal of "assimilation" which conjured up the notion of "inter-mixture and dull conformity". Equally it was a more active notion than the other fashionable ideal of racial "integration" which implied "a kind of passive becoming in which things happen to the individual instead of the individual consciously shaping or participating his [sic] own destiny".[5] "Co-operation" had a moral appeal for many liberals since it denoted some idea of action against a government whose ideology of apartheid represented the very denial of this in the form of non-cooperation between races.

Matthews's political ideas were partly derived from an earlier era before World War Two when many African leaders sought incorporation into a single South African society without stressing the element of nationalism. In the course of the 1940s he was forced to respond to the emergence of a newer nationalism fired by the Congress Youth League, whilst also facing an increasingly remote central government following the defeat of Smuts's United Party government in 1948.

As the ANC committed itself to a Programme of Action in 1949 leading to the Defiance Campaign in 1952, it appeared to Matthews that older liberal strategies based on Hoernle's notion of group-based accommodation looked increasingly anachronistic.[6] Returning from a lecture tour in the United States for the year 1952-3, Matthews called on the ANC leadership to consider calling a Congress of the People to pass a Freedom Charter. He shifted towards a more populist political position, though still kept open the option of a dialogue with the central government. This became increasingly difficult when Matthews was charged with treason along with 155 other defendants in the Treason Trial that began in 1956.

Despite major harassments from the government, Matthews continued over the next few years to press for the ideal of a common society. One major venue was a "Multi-Racial Conference" held at the University of the Witwatersrand in November 1957, which called for "inter-racial talks" in order to draw up a constitution guaranteeing civil rights as well as equal rights of citizenship and universal suffrage on a common electoral roll. The conference had been originally called by the Interdenominational African Ministers Federation (IDAMF) and had only weak links with the Congress movement, though a number of prominent figures from the ANC, including Z. K. Matthews and Govan Mbeki, contributed papers. The conference tried to define the nature of economic, social and political duties in a "common society" and was hailed by some observers as being one of the most representative gatherings ever held in South Africa, though the National Party, The United Party and the DRC all refused to be represented officially. The Anglican Bishop of Johannesburg, Ambrose Reeves, considered that the conference gathering "demonstrated the possibilities inherent in the method of consultation".[7]

Matthews's paper to the conference noted that South Africa appeared to be "as good a laboratory as can be found anywhere for the testing out of arrangements in a real multi-racial society".[8] What later became disapprovingly termed "common society liberalism" was of relatively recent origin in South African political discourse and experimental in nature. It was impelled by a growing sense of crisis generated by the entrenchment of apartheid and the need to try and steer African political leadership from more radical political goals. A number of the contributors at the conference were from within the mainstream of African nationalist politics and a dialogue occurred between liberals and Charterists before the government clamp-down in 1960.

Matthews in particular warned the conference against the path of ethnic group accommodation. "Even if we succeed," he wrote,

> in getting beyond thinking of people in terms of race, we may fall into the similar error of looking at them in terms of groups such as white and non-white, the Afrikaans-speaking and the English-speaking, the Indian or the Coloured, and think of their political rights in terms of the groups to which they belong.[9]

It was recognized by some at the conference, such as Govan Mbeki, that Africans did have group interests, but these were considered largely defensive since they were forged in reaction to segregationist policy stretching back to the 1913 Natives Land Act. "Unless these groups assert their right to live," Mbeki argued, "they will be exterminated": an interesting application of "survival politics" that has now been adopted by Afrikaner nationalists.[10]

The "common society liberalism" that was developed in the 1950s was by no means hostile to all groups in politics. The Freedom Charter itself recognized the rights of social, cultural and religious groups, as it proclaimed that "there shall be equal status in the bodies of state, in the courts, and in the schools for all national groups and races".[11] But these were ultimately subordinated to a social model organized around a single and equal citizenship.

Radical critics have seen this model as static and failing to recognize class divisions, though it did mark a significant ideological development on the inter-war liberal segregationism that dominated so much of the discourse of the English-speaking liberals of the time. This earlier liberalism had often been content to compromise on the issue of egalitarianism for, as Jan H. Hofmeyr had written to James Rose Innes in 1930, "The advocacy of egalitarianism can only strengthen the forces of reaction and ... we can do better service to the cause of the native by seeking to find another way".[12] The theme of democratic rights has not always been an inherent feature of the liberal tradition in South Africa. It was mainly in the period after 1945, under the pressures of a populist African nationalism, that mainstream liberalism was impelled towards a democratic commitment.[13]

Even after 1948, there were countervailing forces within South African liberalism, pushing it back towards a more conservatively inclined paternalism. In part this was aided by the naive search for political adventure of some of the younger radical liberals who emerged in the early 1960s through NUSAS and became involved in the (rather inappropriately named) African Resistance Movement (ARM). The crushing of this movement in 1964 and the decision of one of its main organizers, Adrian Leftwich, to turn state's evidence did considerable damage to the mainstream Liberal Party. Edgar Brookes was appointed President the same year following the banning of Peter Brown in an effort to restore some sort of credibility to the organization.

The ARM episode brought into sharper focus political divisions within the English-speaking intellectual community – divisions between a faction of conservatively inclined liberals concerned to try and achieve what short-term gains they could through the existing structure of power and authority and a small fraction of radicals anxious for a more thoroughgoing alternative political agenda to that of apartheid. The conservative paternalists proved to be more resilient than many of the radicals imagined. They were partly assisted by the vacuum in politics created by the banning of the ANC and PAC in 1960, the decision of the revolutionary wing of the *Umkhonto we Sizwe* to resort to armed struggle in 1961 and the flight of many of the younger white radicals at the time of the ARM debacle.

The Paternalists and the SAIRR

The conservative strand of South African welfare liberalism reached a high-point in the Second World War when it appeared that the logic of industrialization was finally beginning to break through the barriers of racial segregation. The resurgence of Afrikaner nationalism after 1948 appeared to many of these liberals to be an atavistic throwback to a pre-industrial era governed by an anti-capitalist racial ideology derived from the frontier.[14] The tradition continued to enjoy an extended lease of life, due in part to the international reputation enjoyed by the SAIRR, though it failed to generate significant degrees of financial support from organized business. By the 1960s the Institute's membership settled down at the modest figure of some 4088 members in 1961, and by 1973–4 it was still only 4300.

In the early 1960s, the Institute continued to reaffirm its "historical and accustomed role, serving as a clearing house of ideas and a channel of communication between groups".[15] The period was notable for the emergence of a more militant black radicalism in exile Congress politics that sought a severing of the ties with liberal and reformist bodies. But many of those active in the SAIRR saw the organization as having a vital role in disseminating information on conditions in South Africa even if its role as political mediator looked less and less credible.

The disappearance of the Liberal Party in 1968 forced a re-evaluation by a number of bodies within the South African "liberal establishment" of their position, now that a central political buffer had been removed. Many activists in the English-speaking churches as well as the South African Institute of Race Relations had been able to take a somewhat detached view of the political process so long as the Liberal Party had been in existence. The Party's conferences and publications had provided a forum for open political debate that enabled the SAIRR to avoid too high a political profile in order to focus upon welfare work and empirical research. Some of those involved in the Institute were well-known liberals and one past president, Leo Marquard, went so far as to proclaim in 1963 that the Institute was "a liberal body" whose "only fear need be that it will cease to be liberal".[16] But most of the leadership of the SAIRR avoided too close a political identification during a period of mounting apartheid legislation, which threatened to put its future in jeopardy.

Broadly speaking, the Institute's 1954 statement of its overall goals *Go Forward in Faith* reflected the thinking of a considerable section of post-war South African liberals in its emphasis upon economic growth eventually leading to some form of "racial integration" into a common multi-racial society.[17] The problem was how to advance these ideas on the political plain and impress them on to an apparently intractable body politic. Since the early 1950s, many of the Institute liberals had emphasized the need for a more indirect strategy of trying to influence progressive-minded sections of the

Dutch Reformed churches and the younger Afrikaner intelligentsia.[18] Signs of an early form of *verligtheid* had been apparent at the time of the debate in the DRCs on the Cottesloe Consultation called by the World Council of Churches in 1960. This had stimulated hopes that a more independent minded group of dominees would emerge within the DRCs who would be less compliant to government dictats.[19]

This attempt to establish a political dialogue with Afrikaner moderates did not go without some criticism. For some of the more radical clerics in the Church of the Province such a Fabian effort at influencing government policy appeared doomed to failure. Bishop Reeves of Johannesburg was particularly critical in 1958 of attempts by the Director of the Institute of Race Relations, Quintin Whyte, to intervene in church affairs and seek to promote a dialogue between the Dutch Reformed churches and the Church of the Province. Accusing Whyte of acting as an "errand boy" for the DRCs, Reeves pointed out that two-thirds of the members of the Church of the Province were black and would exert a "strong reaction" to the Anglican communion meeting with the DRC leaders at an all-white conference.[20] Reeves, however, was deported in 1960 and more moderate forces came into play over the following decade.

The Institute's Assistant Director, Fred van Wyk, helped organize the Cottesloe Consultation, held between 7 and 14 December 1960 between the South African member churches of the World Council of Churches and a WCC delegation. The Consultation encouraged a number of English-speaking churchmen to try to persuade the South African government to move towards a more amenable platform with regard to the moderate black political leadership.

The Institute still acted as an important platform for traditional liberal criticisms of government apartheid policy. In 1963, Judge O. D. Schreiner, in the Institute's annual presidential address, attacked the emphasis upon group as opposed to individual rights in South African liberal thought and argued for an evolutionary view of political change that would progressively widen the franchise and lead to the growth of political parties that would not seek a power base simply in ethnic ties.[21]

Such sentiments fell increasingly out of favour in the early 1960s as disillusion set in with progressive Whig models of political decolonization. A number of figures in the Institute began to look towards group-based political models in order to try to reform and humanize government policy from within. Quintin Whyte, for example, became anxious over the absence of direction among many of the political liberals. After replacing J. D. Rheinallt Jones as Director of the Institute in 1946, Whyte steered it away from indirect political involvement in natives' representation and looked towards American liberal ideas on race relations, which emphasized the pursuit of an "educational" as opposed to a "moralistic" or "exhortatory" approaches to "inter-racial justice".[22]

By 1963 Whyte began to doubt the "strategy and manoeuvring" of the Progressive Party which, he thought, was in danger of reacting to government initiatives in an *ad hoc* manner. White considered it likely that the South African economy and polity would ride the storm of international criticism, and it appeared increasingly essential to start thinking out a longer strategy of accommodation with the Bantustan policy. "Why cry to high heaven that the plans of the Government in the Transkei are eyewash," he privately noted, "and say that the Xhosa people are having something imposed on them when the fact of the matter is that all the vast majority of the Xhosa people want independence?"[23] He suggested in an Institute memorandum that liberals should seek to work within the framework of the Homelands policy and put pressure on the government to develop them further economically short of outright independence. Such a strategy was, he felt, in accordance with R. F. A. Hoernle's argument in his 1939 Phelps-Stokes lecture that total segregation was not incompatible with the liberal spirit. The important point was to shift from being concerned simply with the means of government policy towards the ends involved.[24] At the end of 1963, Whyte suggested in a memorandum to Harry Oppenheimer of the Anglo-American Corporation that a high-level international team be formed on the basis of funds from the Ford Foundation to come and report on South African conditions and make recommendations. It was important "to plan changes which will take into consideration external opinion and internal realities".[25]

The attempt to engage international experts was a reflection of the rather desperate mood that overtook a number of South African liberals in the early 1960s as the government clamp-down drove a number of activists either into exile or silence.[26] The earlier hopes, stretching back to the 1940s, in economic growth dissolving the structures of racial segregation appeared to be increasingly chimerical. The South African liberal historian C. W. de Kiewiet wrote in the American journal *Foreign Affairs* in 1964 that while liberal forces remained "the single most vital element of light in darkness and hope in despair" there remained the problem that "the cloud of resentment produced by South Africa's racial policies hides the liberal elements in its murk. They feel abandoned, and some have become bitter and angry".[27]

Quintin Whyte in some degree reflected this outlook of growing isolation. Following a visit to Britain and the United States in 1966, he began to recognize that South African liberals had to go it alone. "The foreign experts have not been to South Africa and have no 'feel' for anything," he wrote, "– only a disembodied empathy with the oppressed. U.N. has had 18 years scarification [sic] of South Africa result – Nil".[28] He looked to the Ford Foundation for funds to help develop the Institute's programmes, partly as a result of the contacts that had been built up over the years by E. G. Malherbe, the Institute's president in 1968. Once it was clear that the 1968 Prohibition of Political Interference Act did not threaten the Institute's status, Ford agreed to fund the Institute over the next five years with the generous sum of $500,000.[29]

The Institute leadership came out of the 1960s somewhat battered after attempts were made to smear it. In 1965, a bogus organization, "The League for Liberal Action", distributed a pamphlet stating that the Institute was "assisting liberalism" in the Dutch Reformed Church. Quintin Whyte was forced to deny that the Institute was attempting to "sow the seeds of discord in the Afrikaans churches".[30] Similarly the SABC depicted the Institute in 1967 as standing completely outside the mainstream dialogue in South African politics and gloatingly concluded that "if the Institute wishes to take part in it, and to make a meaningful contribution, then it will have to draw nearer the main, though turbulent stream, of South African thought".[31] In 1969, Whyte confessed to de Kiewiet that growing Afrikaner political self-confidence and the apparently new agenda initiated through Prime Minister John Vorster's "Outward Looking" policy indicated that "liberals will have to re-think themselves in light of all this and adopt new strategies to be directed towards the same general ends. But don't ask me what these should be!".[32]

By the end of the 1960s, a political impasse had been reached, especially as the demise of the Liberal Party enhanced the general sense of political isolation in the Institute. This became further evident as the Institute's position began to come under renewed attack from more radical forces both within its own ranks as well as externally from a militant younger generation of black and white intellectuals.

Black Consciousness and the Upsurge of Democratic Radicalism

The loss of political direction in the SAIRR occurred at the same time as a renewal of democratic radicalism in South African politics. There were a number of sources of this, including the upsurge of student radicalism in Europe in the late 1960s which encouraged the spread of militant ideas both in NUSAS as well as the black South African Students Organization (SASO) after its secession from NUSAS in 1969.[33] The advance of decolonization in Africa during the 1960s encouraged the spread amongst black radical intellectuals of Fanonist ideas of anti-colonial struggle. These in turn came to grip the imagination of some black consciousness advocates in South Africa in the early 1970s. One of the most potent sources came from the United States where the spread of Black Power ideas in the late 1960s encouraged a distrust of white liberals, who were accused of trying to stifle independent black political assertion.[34]

The spread of black consciousness had a strongly radicalizing effect on a number of white radicals who had become disaffected from the cautious line of the Institute in the course of the 1960s. In 1963 the Christian Institute had been established under the directorship of Dr Beyers Naude as part of a drive for ecumenical unity in South African churches following the Cottesloe Statement of 1960. The general tone of the CI in its periodical *Pro Veritate* in the 1960s was one of a Reformed theology derived from the struggle for a Confessional Church in Nazi Germany. By the 1970s, it was being increasingly influenced by liberation theology and Black Power ideas.[35] Despite a small membership of some 2000, the CI did establish contacts with African churches, especially those that were organized by the Inter-denominational African Ministers Association of Southern Africa (IDAMASA). Grants of R1000 from the World Council of Churches and R2000 from the Bantu Welfare Trust (organized under the SAIRR) provided IDAMASA with a secretary and office assistant in 1964, and a number of young black churchmen began to be sent to the Federal Theological Seminary at Alice in the Eastern Cape on bursaries provided by the Theological Education Fund in New York.[36]

IDAMASA approached the Christian Institute for assistance in establishing a theological school, theological correspondence courses in African vernaculars as well as theological "refresher" courses. The CI saw this as an opportunity for developing "Black initiated agencies under Black leadership",[37] though in the case of Nyanga in Cape Town in 1966 it was still the case that little had been done to get white members to "come together" with the black membership.[38] The CI assisted in the establishment of a Council of African Independent Churches (AICA) which had a membership of 261 by March 1969, as well as a theological school at Alice and a Womens Association of African Independent Churches. Fred van Wyk and Beyers Naude also acted as "advisers" to IDAMASA, before van Wyk left to take over the directorship of the SAIRR from Quintin Whyte in January 1970.

The work with the independent churches was disappointing since inadequate funding prevented the establishment of any substantial organization to reorganize the churches. The churches were prone to sectarian splits, especially after the establishment of a rival to IDAMASA in the form of the Reformed Independent Churches Association (RICA) under a white minister of the NG Kerk, Rev. N. J. van Loggenberg. Beyers Naude encouraged AICA to become more independent financially and he tried to steer the CI away from any involvement with AICA's own internal splits or "a false image of AICA being created through its close association with the Christian Institute". No further financial assistance was given after 1973 and the link with the independent churches declined before the CI's banning in 1977.[39]

The CI became more closely drawn to black student politics through the University Christian Movement and later through SASO after its establishment in 1969. Many of those involved in establishing the CI saw black consciousness as challenging some of the central tenets of traditional white "welfare work". By 1970 the CI noted that "more and more Black students and intellectually awakened youth will move into a position of Black power, rejecting all offers of assistance on the part of Whites to aid them in their struggle towards freedom".[40] It was stimulated into trying to rethink new modes of political, economic and social change in South Africa. It began to raise the question of how far there had emerged in South Africa a "serving middle class" among Africans, such as teachers, nurses, journalists, clergymen who could be the "pattern setters" for the rest of black society.⁴¹ Considerations such as these prompted the establishment, conjointly with the South African Council of Churches, of the Study Project on Christianity in Apartheid Society (SPRO-CAS), which consisted of six study commissions embracing 150 academics and researchers in the fields of economics, education, law, the church, and the social and political sciences. The project was directed by a former Assistant Director of the SAIR, Peter Randall, who had become disillusioned by the late 1960s with the Institute's general lack of political direction. The South African Council of Churches supported the initiative following the 1970 Statement by the World Council of Churches consultation on racism. For many in the SACC the statement reflected the fact that the South African churches had failed, in the words of one executive member Calvin Cook, to "convince their brethren overseas of their bona fides, even where these may exist".⁴² A new course of action clearly had to be thought through.

The work on SPRO-CAS appeared to many of the conservative paternalists as potential ground for assessing the potential worth of group-based models of liberalism. South Africa's "political ills", Quintin Whyte wrote to Randall, were "largely due to a completely false and outmoded idea of the nature of the nation or a group in society and its function". It was necessary "somewhere to argue the true nature of groups in society which are based on interests commonly held between members".⁴³ This outlook helped shape the work of the various commissions, especially the one on political change.

Many black-consciousness (BC) activists saw this attempt by the churches to act as a forum for political dialogue as irrelevant. One SASO document reprinted as a SPRO-CAS background paper declared the whole notion of racial "integration" to be pivoted on liberal "arrogance" and a product of "conscious manoeuvre" rather than the "climate of the inner soul". "The myth of integration as propounded under the banner of liberal ideology must be tracked and killed," it continued, "because it makes people believe that something is being done when in actual fact the artificially integrated circles are a soporific on the blacks and provide a vague satisfaction for the futility stricken whites".⁴⁴

This distrust of the work of SPRO-CAS One by many BC radicals encouraged it to become a highly academic forum for debating various models of political, economic and constitutional change. Most of those involved were white male academics, though this was in part due to the reluctance of some long-standing liberal activists like Alan Paton to become involved and the inability to find any significant black intellectual support for the project.[45] The work of the Political Commission encouraged debate on the political and ethical basis of South African liberalism. Peter Randall as director of the project was considerably impressed by the work of the political scientist Andre Du Toit at the University of Stellenbosch, who stressed the need for a group-based approach to liberal rights and duties. Du Toit considered that a "parting of the ways" was at hand between the "doctrinaire liberals" and "those willing to look to new approaches and alternatives".[46] Some more classically minded liberals such as Alan Paton, however, warned that there could be no simple blueprint for a federal system in South Africa that incorporated group identities, even if this might be expected from the Project.[47]

The SPRO-CAS Political Commission contained the radical figure of Rick Turner from the University of Natal, though a banning order prevented him from fully engaging in the latter stages of its report, *South Africa's Political Alternatives*, in 1973. Turner's presence helped to shift some of the initial discussions away from the traditional liberal theme of how to change racial attitudes towards a more sociologically penetrating debate on the nature of the South African "plural society". Turner was generally perceived as a radical political figure, who was concerned with formulating a notion of "white consciousness" to meet the ideological challenge presented by the emergence of black-consciousness doctrines. He stressed that white liberals should not be perceived by radicals as a significant political force capable of overthrowing apartheid and that the term "white liberalism" as it had come to be employed by many BC radicals was "uselessly broad". It was necessary to categorize whites into groups of racists, liberals and radicals, and these terms could equally be applied in black politics as well. Once these shared political perspectives were recognized, it should then be acknowledged that the notion upheld by many BC advocates that only blacks could talk to blacks was based upon an inadequate theory of communication. In essence there were differences of degree rather than kind between blacks and whites in South African and white radicals could still make a useful contribution to the overthrow of the apartheid system.[48]

Turner developed this critique of orthodox liberalism in his work for the SPRO-CAS Political Commission. In a draft section on economics he stressed the importance of sociological models of pluralism derived from the work of the anthropologist J. S. Furnivall in Indonesia. In the original conception of pluralism the emphasis had been centred on the role of economic forces and the market place in determining social relationships. Turner elaborated on this by drawing on the theoretical work of the former South African sociologist John Rex, who explained the economic base of the South African "plural society" in terms of a neo-Marxist model of colonial capitalism and the need for a ready supply of labour. Turner saw this as reinforcing the argument that "group conflict" in South African society was really underpinned by a conflict of economic interest, while the roots of racial prejudice lay in "the objective relations of domination set up by the conquest and the institutionalisation of conquest, and they are not likely to be extirpated until this is pointed out, nor are they likely to stop rerooting themselves while the system of economic inequality persists".[49]

Turner had tried to shift the Political Commission's attention away from the issue of group as well as individual rights. The final report, he suggested in some notes, should be concerned with the distribution of both political and economic power and should contain an ideal model "in terms of which the situation should be judged". Such a model should contain both ethical concepts as well as the form of their expression, meaning the "common society approach". The key to this notion was democratic control over social resources and whether it should be capitalist or socialist. It was at this point that the Commission should be concerned with "the problem of what to do about the situation", for it was possible analytically to distinguish between change in the direction proposed by "voting Christians" (that is, whites) or changes by "non-voters" developing the power to force it.[50]

The approach raised questions concerning the structural nature of South African society and its resulting capacity to cope with change towards a non-racial and democratic political system. These issues the Commission tried to minimize in order to secure some form of common consensus amongst its members. It became clear in the course of 1972 that Turner's radicalism added to an already complicated situation in which there was a considerable divergence between different parties to the Commission. On one side, Edgar

Brookes as a more classically orientated liberal emphasized individual rights and looked at the emphasis upon groups as a new form of adaptation to segregation, a failing he felt he had been guilty of, as we saw in chapter 3, in the 1920s.[51]

On the other side, Dennis Worrall argued for a more conservative emphasis upon groups and attacked what he termed the "common society" approach within liberalism, arguing instead for "multi-nationalism" and some form of confederal political solution.[52] Worrall's attack was dressed up in academic terminology, though later in 1973 he applied to join the National Party and urged his fellow-English-speakers not to "under-estimate Afrikaner idealism".[53]

Given these growing differences of view among the Political Commission's members, Peter Randall supported Du Toit's effort at a "middle course" emphasizing both group and individual rights. This went some way towards preserving the idea of a "common society", but more radical notions of a structural shift in the locus of economic power tended to be discarded.

South Africa's Political Alternatives did show some signs of Turner's influence, especially in its discussion of plural society theory. The Report marked a significant break with the strand of post-war liberalism which had relied on economic growth as eventually inducing political change. It recognized that in its existing condition South Africa was a "divided plural society", though it contrasted this with the ideal of an American-style "open pluralistic society": the question it then posed was how far a transition from the first to the second was possible. Turner's emphasis upon the structural underpinnings behind the cleavages in the plural society model and the demand for labour was downplayed in favour of a more authentically liberal discussion on the "complex interplay" of the processes of "integration" and "acculturation".[54] The Report viewed black consciousness as possibly presenting a "countervailing separatism" to that of the "imposed separatism" of government policy.[55] It raised the option Hoernle had originally suggested of "true separation" in contrast to the existing segregation that favoured white supremacy.[56]

The Commission Report rested on firm liberal concepts of the rule of law, personal freedom and civil liberties and equality of opportunity. It opposed the egalitarian ideal of equality of wealth. It also expressed severe reservations on the applicability of a Westminster-style system of parliamentary government in South

African conditions. The Christian concepts of "love and brotherhood", it considered, could not, like the negative claims of freedom and equality, be translated easily into political arrangements. It tried to avoid any wide-ranging utopian social values in its ideals for a future South African society. It was far more concerned with developing a feasible model of a devolution of political power away from that of the administrative echelons of the central state in order to facilitate access by the unenfranchised majority to political power. Such an incremental approach led to a two-stage model of consociational bargaining between groups, leading to the eventual attainment of an open pluralistic society on lines similar to a Western political system.[57]

Short of advocating violent or revolutionary change, the Commission Report was presented as one possible way out of the political impasse that liberals found themselves in by the early 1970s, drawing upon rational models of bargaining from the social sciences. To some critics, there still appeared to be an element of utopian idealism involved in the Report which, *The Argus* declared, presented "yet another manifesto of radical, redemptive politics; yet another all-including socio-political system – a political idealism within which a new South Africa would arise purged from its inhumanities".[58] In Progressive Party (PP) circles, however, the Report had some impact. One of the PP's senior figures, Colin Eglin, admitted to Quintin Whyte that the Party's policy of a federal solution for South Africa had led it to "play down the fact that it is committed to the redrawing of the Constitution and has ignored almost entirely any steps in transition from the present situation to the one it sets as its goal".[59] More conservatively inclined liberals went even further. Dennis Worrall saw the report as an counter-attack against the "common society liberalism" that he saw as a phenomenon that had gripped the imagination of English-speaking intellectuals in South African universities in the 1950s and 1960s and which had as a consequence widened the gap between the intelligentsia and politicians in power. The Report, in Worrall's eyes, went some way towards restoring the more pragmatic liberalism of Hoernle that had been abandoned in the post-war years.[60]

For radicals, the top-down nature of the Report's consociationalism divested it of any major significance for long-run political and economic change. Rick Turner had been critical of it in its draft stage, arguing that its employment of a consociational democracy approach appeared to ignore the problems of economic conflict almost entirely.[61] Turner refused to identify himself with the Report in its final form and proceeded to publish through SPRO-CAS a strikingly alternative utopian political vision for a future South Africa in the form of the essay, *The Eye of the Needle*, in 1973. The book managed to have a fairly powerful impact on political debate, selling 2000 copies before being banned by the government. It emerged at a time when the ideals of the Freedom Charter had faded to a rather distant memory and there seemed to be few clear conceptions of what kind of society a post-apartheid South Africa would be. Turner's essay reflected an ethical socialism in a tradition that stretched back to such Victorian figures as John Ruskin and William Morris. Its concern, too, for shifting power away from the central state to local bodies was in keeping with the student radicalism of the late 1960s in Europe as well as a longer tradition that in Britain went back to the guild socialist movement during and after the First World War.

Turner stressed the importance of utopian thinking in the development of more theoretical thinking on South African politics. One critic, W. A. de Klerk, retorted that this had been precisely the problem with apartheid which had itself been based on utopian political thought.[62] Utopianism for Turner was part of a wider project to engage more directly with the present as history, which could no longer be seen as something abstracted from contemporary processes. His thinking was on similar lines to that of some other radical figures at this time in South Africa – figures such as Nadine Gordimer, for example. As the next chapter points out, novels such as *The Late Bourgeois World* (1966) and *The Conservationist* (1974) moved beyond a "liberal humanist" framework towards situating characters within a more immediate historical process that could look beyond the immediate parameters of white rule.[63]

Turner looked towards a "participatory democracy" emerging in a future socialist South Africa, partly modelled on experiments such as Ujamaa villages in Tanzania as well as workers' co-operatives in Yugoslavia. The remnants of the "communal and person-orientated" values of tribal society he saw as a possible "counter-culture" to the effects of conservative socialization, even if there were flaws in the concept of African socialism and its mythical view of a classless and timeless African past.[64] Turner also recognized the importance of black consciousness, though he stressed its essentially middle-class quality. Being black was not really a political programme and the black-consciousness advocates had not as yet spelled out what new values were entailed by the doctrine.[65] Despite its strongly socialist tone, the book was not hostile to the work of white liberals, whom Turner saw as important for possibly being able to steer the society away from a "final bloody show-down" whilst at the same time helping to "inject a greater element of rationality into white thinking".[66] This assessment was doubtless one of the reasons why the book in its American edition earned warm praise from Alan Paton who considered it an essay on the South African condition "as searching as any that has ever been written".[67]

The Eye of the Needle's utopianism led it to a commitment to what Turner termed a "transcendent morality" concerned with the ultimate purposes of human life as opposed to the more immediate "internal morality" of paying debts and not cheating or stealing. It saw capitalism as essentially an alienating and unChristian form of social system and looked to a society that treated people not as means but as ends in themselves. This certainly put it at odds with the main thrust of *South Africa's Political Alternatives*. A number of the liberals involved in that project received the work somewhat coolly, though Peter Randall defended its utopianism on the grounds that it was essential to have an ideal yardstick by which to formulate "conscious goals for the improvement of our society". The work was, he claimed, "a serious attempt to relate the values of Christianity to the structures of our society".[68]

At a seminar in Stellenbosch, from 29 September to 1 October 1973, on strategies for political change, Frederick Van Zyl Slabbert argued that *The Eye of the Needle*'s utopianism led it away from the path of feasible political action. Politics was "not the abstract universal search for a common good," he declared, for it was the "process of synthesizing a variety of interests within a common policy, and only those interests which appear in the political process get included in the final policy".[69] It was not clear either where the increased awareness for the kind of society that Turner envisaged was going to come from. Some participants, such as Geoff Budlender, suggested that radical whites could accept the basic tenets of the black-consciousness model and play an essentially supplementary role in helping black solidarity, on the one hand, and fragmenting the white power bloc on the other.[70]

Andre Du Toit at the seminar contrasted the book's macro-political approach to change with the more micro-political approach of the SPRO-CAS Political Commission, which he claimed was aiming less at "participatory democracy" than "effective participation in government". Du Toit considered that it was important not to resort to a "moral emigration" away from current social and political problems but to turn to political action to try to remedy them, action that should also be governed as far as possible by criteria of political effectiveness. For students to seek involvement on these lines the chief aim should be *exemplary action*, whose value could be quite high.[71]

The broad thrust of the discussion indicated that there was some basis for organized action by white radicals extending beyond merely symbolic politics of the kind that had often been associated with student radicalism in Western Europe in the late 1960s. Pressure for such action made itself especially felt in the discussions on the SPRO-CAS Two Programme in early 1972 where there was strong pressure for staff-initiated projects that were not centrally controlled by the executive. Neville Curtis and Rick Turner urged a Youth Programme that would be directed at high-school and university students, "young workers" and "opt outs". A Black Community Programme (BCP) was also launched after 1971 involving a survey of black organizations and a programme of consultation focusing on training in administration, committee operation and secretarial skills. The BCP was under the direction of a former worker in the YMCA, Bennie Khoapa, who helped gather together a group of black-consciousness radicals around the Programme, including Steve Biko and the trade unionist and journalist Bokwe James Mafuna.[72]

The academically inclined work of the Study Commissions led to pressure for more co-ordinated action that would involve both the Christian Institute as well as possibly the SAIRR in a broadly based programme of radical change. SPRO-CAS staff met Fred Van Wyk, Clive Nettleton and Dudley Horner of the SAIRR to discuss co-ordination of their work.[73]

Along with these moves there was strong pressure within the BCP for politically autonomous control over its functioning. Khoapa made it clear to Peter Randall that the black staff on the project would find unacceptable any proposal for a joint steering committee to oversee the work of both the black- and white-led programmes.[74] This position emerged in response to a much harder stand being made by some of the radicals within the BCP. There were growing suspicions in the organization over the nature and direction of the

SPRO-CAS project, and one black activist, Rev. Clive MacBride, accused both SPRO-CAS and the SAIRR of being "liberal organisations" that "get money on our ticket [blacks] and very little of the money really filters through to the grass roots". Others such as Steve Biko saw the issue as raising broader questions over the relationship of whites and blacks in the SPRO-CAS programme and on the sources of the money that was financing it. Khoapa urged an acceptance of the fact that the programme had been sponsored and encouraged work from that starting point. In the event, some broad agreement was secured around the idea that the BCP would create as few "structures" as possible and that the Programme would act as the "midwife" to "real community organisations which may or may not be created by the people themselves when the programme draws to a close". It was hoped that the black panels would be able to develop their own national panel which could act as a "guiding body in terms of broad policy principles and other recommendations that it deems fit".[75]

By the end of 1972, black-consciousness ideology was beginning to exert a major impact on the work of white-run liberal organizations in South Africa. The SPRO-CAS Programme had led to strong demands by its black members for their own autonomous area of space for the formulation of specifically black political demands. This was significantly occurring at a time when there was a major political vacuum in black politics, though one that Gatsha Buthelezi in Kwa Zulu was hoping to try to fill. For many of the more conservative figures in the Institute of Race Relations the challenge by both the white radicals and black-consciousness activists was one that should as far as possible be contained. The black-consciousness radicals consciously adopted a policy of refusing to debate with whites the "pros and cons" of the doctrine, and this in a sense reinforced the hand of the conservative critics who argued against a strategy of major concessions.[76] The Institute's "old guard" clearly felt much was at stake in keeping open what thin lines of communication they already had with the government in Pretoria. Over the following year a strong line of resistance ensued which undermined the hopes of political unity in the liberal camp.

The Response from the Institute of Race Relations

The conservative paternalists proved quite adept at organizing an effective resistance within the South African Institute of Race Relations against proposals for closer links with SPRO-CAS and the

CI. In the wake of the demise of the Liberal Party, the SAIRR was feeling itself in quite an exposed position, even though it was considered by one observer, Heribert Adam, in the early 1970s to have emerged as "the most significant and almost sole representative of traditional liberalism in South Africa".[77] Its response to the new pace of political events in the early 1970s was somewhat protracted and still shaped by the view that apartheid was a historical product of a pre-industrial frontier that had governed its thinking since the 1930s.[78] There was considerable opposition to allowing the younger Institute members to forge links with radical organizations, a proposal which Leo Marquard likened to a form of "moral blackmail" of the older members. "The Institute might be compared to a good cart horse," he wrote to Fred Van Wyk, "bred for that purpose and doing a good job. The young people want it to be a race horse. If it tries to be one it will lose its character and will end by being neither a good carthorse nor a racehorse." He strongly urged the maintenance of a fairly hierarchical organization in which no staff members should attend meetings of the executive as of right and "should not take part in debate unless asked for an opinion, and should certainly not have a vote".[79]

Nevertheless some of the Institute's leadership recognized that the traditional strategy of trying to act as a bridge of communication between different racial "groups" was no longer working and that some reforms were necessary. Quintin Whyte urged shortly before his retirement in 1969 a "shaking up" of the Institute, for "the effectiveness of liberalism, as it were, has declined here as in America. We are entering a new period when old ideas on all sides will have to be shaken up."[80]

The Institute's new Director, Fred Van Wyk, was sympathetic to such arguments while continuing to emphasize the traditional white liberal areas of support, such as voters for the Progressive Party. It was important, he maintained, for the Institute to continue seeking an "informed public", while at the same time maintaining a degree of "caution and care" in persuading the "older generation" in the Institute of the views of a younger generation that was emerging within it.[81] Over the following three years, this cautious strategy continued to dictate Institute policy, which was confirmed in 1972 as being committed to a peaceful and non-cataclysmic mode of political change.[82] The Institute's leadership was generally reluctant to be seen to bend before the challenge of black consciousness which Van

Wyk saw as containing the same sort of racial separationism which the Institute had been fighting in the form of apartheid.[83] This view was reinforced by the appointment in 1972 of Duchesne Grice to succeed William Nkomo as President of the SAIRR. Grice was a Durban lawyer with connections with commerce and industry and was widely viewed as a "middle-of-the-road" figure who was anxious not to chart any new course or the Institute in the 1970s.[84]

Political support for Van Wyk's position also came from Ellen Hellman, who had developed a strong influence on Institute policymaking since the early 1960s and was notable for standing on a number of the Institute's committees including the one concerned with research. As an anthropologist trained in the "culture contact" school of Malinowski, Ellen Hellman had been concerned with emphasizing, since at least the late 1930s, the power of acculturation in South African society. "All evidence," she had written in 1948 "points to the willingness of the Bantu to accept the admittedly superior western culture."[85] An admirer of Hoernle's thought, she campaigned throughout the 1950s for the idea of a "shared society" and common citizenship, though she was on occasions prepared to try and reconcile this with the idea of territorial partition. "When a country is partitioned," she wrote in 1956,

> individuals have the right to choose to remain in the new state, even if they do not belong to the majority group of that state, and are then entitled to enjoy the full rights of citizenship. The Arabs who did not flee but remained in what was Palestine are today citizens of Israel.[86]

Ellen Hellman was one of the Institute's leaders most resolutely opposed to its radical critics on the issue that emerged early in 1973 of whether or not to give evidence to the government's Schlebusch (later Le Grange) Commission, appointed to examine the workings of universities, NUSAS and other liberal organizations. Both Hellman and Grice agreed to appear before the Commission since they thought that to do otherwise could be used as an excuse for further government attacks.[87] Ellen Hellman viewed the announcement by the Christian Institute of support for staff in SPRO-CAS who would refuse to appear before the Commission as mere "fun and games". "As far as the IRR is concerned," she wrote to Quintin Whyte, "I believe that the loss of 'activist' or radical young people and the disaffiliation of NUSAS as well is pretty well inevitable and not a tragedy at all."[88]

The Institute's decision nevertheless caused an embarrassing split within the white liberal establishment at a time when it could ill afford to be seen to be divided. Though some English-language newspapers like *The Star* supported the decision, to a number of observers it appeared an indefensible cringing to government authority. Helen Suzman fell out with Ellen Hellman's stand on the issue after initially assuming that the Institute would side with the CI.[89] Some of the Institute's younger members, such as Michael Savage, Horst Kleinschmidt and Jonathan Paton, announced that they would not give evidence to the Commission, and the Reverend Clive McBride called for mass resignations from the Institute.[90] Jonathan Paton called for a new body to replace the Institute and Peter Randall bitterly attacked it for being after forty years a "white-led, white dominated, bourgeois organisation. It stifles black initiative. It is an obstacle to change and a hindrance to progress."[91] Patrick Lawrence in *The Star* detected a general attack from "radical liberals" on the Institute's standpoint.[92]

Within the Institute, an effort was made by the group of younger radicals to give their criticisms of the leadership some focus. Clive Nettleton, the organizer since 1970 of the Youth Programme and a former NUSAS activist, urged a number of changes in Institute policy in a memorandum in May 1973. He considered it essential to get away from "white, middle class academic values" and to develop publications with a stronger political commitment and wider audience appeal. It was also necessary to recruit more black staff and move away from the negative image which most blacks had of the Institute.[93]

The radical whites had a generally shaky political base to mount an attack on the Institute conservatives. The issue in some ways recalled the previously unsuccessful effort to goad the Institute leadership into a more political standpoint by Douglas Buchanan and Alfred Xuma in 1942–3.[94] Outside the Institute the work of SPRO-CAS One was already complete while the community-based work of SPRO-CAS Two had forged an uneasy alliance with the black radicals led by Biko and Khoapa. Some of the most committed of the radicals, such as Horst Kleinschmidt, had already resigned while it became clear towards the end of the year that the Institute conservatives led by

Ellen Hellman were determined to resist the demands for major change.

Ellen Hellman considered that the white radicals were only interpreting what they thought were "Black Power demands or stances", while the Institute itself had received no direct calls from blacks, with the exception of Clive MacBride. She disputed Clive Nettleton's urging of a more populist publications' policy, pointing out that previous efforts in this direction had been unsuccessful and the material pulped.[95] Support for this view came from academic bodies such as the Centre for Inter-Group Studies at the University of Cape Town and the Institute for Social Research at the University of Natal.[96] Cautiously sympathetic activists at the local level, such as F. O. Joseph, the Regional Secretary in the Cape, felt impelled to point out:

> A factor that always has to be borne in mind is that the existence of the Institute, as it is presently organised, depends on the goodwill and generosity of benefactors – mainly large industrial and business enterprises and mining houses. We must, unfortunately perhaps, take this into consideration in contemplating any change.[97]

By the time of the Institute's Council meeting in January 1974, the radicals had been effectively marginalized. A programme of cautious reform was agreed to involving attempts to increase both Afrikaner and black membership, though it was accepted that there should be "no need for any drastic changes in the Institute's approach and work".[98] The Institute's Youth Programme continued for another year under the control of Clive Nettleton, but in a reduced form, and at the end of 1975 Nettleton left the Institute. Links with business, especially the mining industry, tended to become closer. In June 1974, Alex Boraine, a labour practices consultant for Anglo-American and a member of the Institute's executive, was elected as a Progressive Party MP for Pinelands in the Cape. The 1975–9 fund-raising campaign got off to a good start in its endeavour to raise R1 million by gaining the sponsorship of Harry Oppenheimer. This ensured an income of R150,000 a year and helped to make up some of the gap in income as the aid from the Ford Foundation fell from some R75,000 in 1974 to R26,000.[99]

From the mid 1970s, the Institute executive began to take a

growing interest in consociational methods of political reform on lines similar to *South Africa's Political Alternatives*. The period 1974–5 was one of growing talk of "detente" in the wake of the April 1974 coup in Lisbon. The Prime Minister, John Vorster, told the Senate in October that the country was "at a crossroads" and the cost of confrontation would be "too high for southern Africa to pay".[100] The Institute's Council discussed in early 1975 a number of papers outlining models of political change. At this meeting Andre Du Toit introduced some of the basic ideas behind the SPRO-CAS Report *South Africa's Political Alternatives* in a paper outlining the idea of a "common area" in South Africa. Du Toit argued that such an idea gave political substance to the long-held Institute ideal of a "common society" except that this was now the *terminus ad quem* of a strategy of "pluralistic devolution" of powers away from the centre towards bodies like the Coloured Persons Representative Council and the Urban Bantu Councils.[101] The paper reflected that in a society such as South Africa ideas discussed originally on the peripheries of politics in the early 1970s started to move quite rapidly towards mainstream political discourse.

The Institute of Race Relations in effect had begun to adopt a policy of seeking to influence the direction of policy in Pretoria rather than meeting the challenge of black consciousness head on. Its continued search, however, for some form of "dialogue" with the white state, which had kept its hopes alive even in the bleakest years of the 1960s, further underlined the isolation of the black radicals in SASO and the BPC. Such a separation from the ideological influences of white liberalism created a political space which gave many black-consciousness activists a growing sense of hope in ultimate victory.[102]

Black Consciousness and the 1976 Soweto Revolt

The development of black-consciousness doctrines occurred at an uneven rate in the early 1970s. The appeals of "*Being* Black, *acting* Black and *thinking* Black" gained most support amongst the growing secondary-school and university intelligentsia, though an effort was made at a more nationwide process of political conscientization after the establishment of the Black Peoples Convention (BPC) in 1972.[103] Many BC radicals such as Steve Biko saw the importance of the doctrine in its challenge to "common society liberalism". It also reinforced a notion of black self-reliance without the intervention of paternalistic white do-gooders.

The period of the early 1970s was relatively fluid as a new political generation sought to cut for itself its own distinct path. "We blacks must sit down to examine the various power groups in our midst," declared Njabulo Ndebele in 1972 at a SASO symposium, "with a view to finding out which of these groups can be most effective and relevant towards our necessary, and hence natural, struggle for a meaningful participation in the shaping of our country's destiny."[104] Unlike many BC rhetoricians, Ndebele stressed the political potential of the peasantry in addition to black urban workers, whilst also pointing out the economic basic to apartheid. "Apartheid is no longer a pseudo-ideology," he argued.

> It has become an economic principle. This is an important development for the black person. It means that the black man must be careful of concentrating on the racial struggle, to the detriment of the economic struggle, because the latter may have become more important than the former.[105]

Black-consciousness thinking was still rather ragged, though it was free of the rigidities of "scientific socialism" that became a later characteristic of radicals in movements such as AZAPO and the National Forum in the early 1980s.[106] There was no clear political programme before the upsurge of protest in the schools in 1976, and in a number of ways the black intelligentsia who had started off by disseminating the BC doctrine allowed it to run out of control. In part this can be ascribed to the continuing difficulties of political organization in the early 1970s, with continued bannings and a massive diversion of energy into the trial of BC activists tried under the Terrorism Act in 1976.[107]

There was also a strong faith in various forms of black economic self-reliance, whether in co-operatives, shops, farms or "buy black" campaigns. Some of the concepts of rural black self-reliance espoused by some pre-war white missionaries, such as Father Bernard Huss in Natal and Transkei, began to resurface in a somewhat different guise.[108] Marxism and methods of class analysis had been effectively peripheralized in the course of state repression in the 1960s and would only start to make a renewed impact in the late 1970s in the course of the development of the black trade union movement and more militant methods of struggle in both the factories and the townships. The BC intellectuals were forced to turn inwards towards more romantic concepts of anti-capitalism, similar to the agrarian nationalism of Anton Lembede and the Congress Youth League of the middle 1940s.[109]

In essence, the BC intellectuals sought a strategy of racial reassertion in an era when Pan Africanism had declined in its political appeal. They did not seek a heroic golden age, but simply the ideal of black national unity which C. M. C. Ndamse called "the new day". "No member of the white community in any part of South Africa," Ndamse continued, "can harm the weakest or meanest member of the black race without the proudest and the bluest blood of the nation being degraded."[110] Whites were inextricably part of the common national society, though one no longer governed by colonial trusteeship as the older liberal doctrine had presumed.

The impact of black theology, especially from the writings of James Cone in the United States, was important at this time for stressing the need for black collective pride in liberation and in the notion of a black Christ. This led to a rejection of the idea that blacks could only be liberated when whites came to "love" them. It was still difficult, though, for black theologians to break completely from the mainstream Christian message of loving one's enemy as oneself and Cone admitted that "the presence of Black people in America ... is the symbolic presence of God and his righteousness for *all* the oppressed of the land".[111] At the Black Renaissance Convention in December 1974, many of the tensions between different factions of BC radicals began to surface as there were worries that the doctrine could end up being treated either as an intellectual curiosity or as the basis of a cultural rather than political revival.[112]

By this stage a pattern of organization had already been established at the school level through the South African Students Movement (SASM), which had its first general congress at Roodepoort in March 1972. In contrast to the rather rambling pattern of organization through the Black Community Programmes or the Black Peoples Convention, a network of school branches was linked to regional executives, aided in 1976 by a R4000 overseas grant for a full-time organizer.[113] SASM was by no means the simple creation of SASO, despite the importance of BC ideas in galvanizing it into political action. It was the SASM Action Committee, elected on 13 June 1976, which formed the basis for the Soweto Students

Representative Council. The movement within the schools ran considerably ahead of the BC intellectuals in SASO and the BPC, which were only banned a full year after the 16 June revolt in Soweto. The first phase of BC radicalism had by then come to an end, as the moral and intellectual impact of BC thinking had been demonstrated, especially in breaking former links with white liberals.

The first phase of BC was crushed in the government clampdowns in 1977, leading to the banning of the BCP, the CI and the murder of Steve Biko. Many of the ideas generated fed into a new debate that began to emerge in the late 1970s and early 1980s surrounding the upsurge of unrest among black labour. By this time, some of the ideas for top-down consociational political reform, held by a number of white liberals in the early 1970s, had begun to permeate the thinking of the state itself, leading to the introduction in 1983 of a new constitution based on a tricameral parliament.

To this extent, the ideological debates of the early 1970s had played a crucial role in the emergence of more mass-based political struggles in the following decade, as well as acting as a catalyst for rethinking ideas in South African politics. It also indicated that the rapidly escalating pace of events were leaving a number of the English-speaking liberals behind. It was significant that one of the most prominent radical figures to emerge from this period was Beyers Naude, a former Broederbond member with impeccable credentials for membership of the Afrikaner *volk*. The early 1970s can in this regard be seen as a watershed period in which the ethnic cohesion of the English-speaking intellectual community, fostered as it had been throughout the post-war period by organizations like the SAIRR and the Liberal Party, began to fall apart. New avenues for political and intellectual engagement began to emerge over the following years as the domestic political crisis continued to mount.

5
LIBERAL REALISM IN SOUTH AFRICAN FICTION

The years between the Second World War and the 1960s were crucial for English-language writing in South Africa. Given the cultural diversity of South African society and the colonial legacy of its literature, there has traditionally been a crisis of identity for many English-speaking South African writers. Their output as a consequence has been subject to fits and starts. World War Two acted as a dampener on the work of the pre-war years, as South African military involvement threw the country back on to the cultural links with Britain and Europe. This had the effect of inhibiting, for a period at least, the development of an indigenous literary tradition.[1]

The effort at asserting an English South African literary identity also became linked to growing ethnic and class cleavages in national politics. The small groups of English-speaking writers, both white and black, lacked a clear enough sense of cultural direction to override these cleavages, although many politically shared a liberal distaste for racial discrimination. This in part derived from the wider lack of political direction in English-speaking liberalism in the years after 1945. It meant, though, that South African English literature in the decades after 1945 faced a strong up-hill struggle in the objective of widening the genre of English-language writing to encompass the full breadth of the society's historical and cultural experiences.

As this chapter seeks to show, the period from Alan Paton's *Cry the Beloved Country* (1948) to Nadine Gordimer's important prophetic novel *The Late Bourgeois World* (1966) was a cultural watershed for English-language literature in South Africa. In the field of fiction the tenets of literary realism, which most major writers saw as the basis of the English South African literary enterprise, were found to be increasingly irreconcilable with a generally liberal world-view. The crisis of English cultural identity thus produced an internal crisis of literary form as the assumptions of individual characterization began to come under strain.

By the early 1960s, English-speaking writers in South Africa were confronted with an ideological dilemma. To some it appeared to be essential to try to move out of the dominant tradition of liberal realism which had been experimented with over the previous decades – the genre indeed stretched back to Olive Schreiner's *The Story of an African Farm* in 1883 and had slowly emerged out of the romance formulae of the English writers of imperial fiction in South Africa – Rider Haggard and John Buchan, for example.[2] Some experiments were made with "socialist realism" by writers such as Peter Abrahams who in his novel *Mine Boy* in 1946 envisaged colour differentiation being superseded in industrial conflict by a shared set of class interests of black and white workers. Abrahams had been important for his Pan Africanist sympathies, and in 1945 he helped organize the Fifth Pan Africanist Congress in Manchester. By the early 1950s, though, Abrahams became estranged from South Africa and eventually settled in Jamaica.[3]

The efforts at a "socialist realism" were thus rather fitful in post-war South African English literature, though as will be seen in the case of Phyllis Altman's *The Law of Vultures* (1952) they did periodically surface. On the whole, though, the left-wing radicalism which had momentarily seeped into English-speaking political discourse during the war years became progressively marginalized in the years after 1948.[4] The main impulse towards literary realism was liberally inclined in intent until the crisis of self-confidence in the late 1960s and 1970s, leading to such postmodernist experiments as J. M. Coetzee's two novels *Dusklands* and *In the Heart of the Country*. It is this progressive loss of literary self-confidence, reflecting a wider political crisis at the heart of post-war South African liberalism, that is the theme of this chapter.

The English Realist Tradition

The employment by English-speaking liberal writers of the realist mode occurred at the very time when it was itself undergoing a crisis within metropolitan culture. As Nadine Gordimer has pointed out, the South African novelist began to create a literature at a time in world history when the community which had originally been such an important part in its creation was on the decline and a "technological collectivity" was taking its place.[5] The "community" for English literature since the eighteenth century had been a class-bound society with its own recognizable codes of character and social conduct. In the novels of Jane Austen and Charles Dickens, for example, there is a direct correlation between social and economic position and a character's state. In its classic form the English novel was in effect what Daiches has termed a "public instrument" closely inter-relating the internal and external dimensions of character on an agreed standard of moral conduct.[6]

The "realism" employed in this novelistic tradition also reflected a bourgeois philosophical tradition. The rise of the novel closely coincided with the growth of a middle-class reading public whose attitudes and values were structured around the holding of property, the division of labour and a tolerance of free speech that facilitated the rise of parliamentary government. It was broadly allied to a liberalism that was centred upon the particularity of the individual and his or her social development over time. As Ian Watt has pointed out, the "history" of such characters as Tom Jones or Barry Lyndon is to be contrasted with the timeless quality of ancient, medieval or Renaissance literature.[7]

This historical consciousness was the product of an outlook conducive to a mechanistic sense of duration born of the scientific discoveries of Isaac Newton. The discourse that helped shape the English novel in the eighteenth and nineteenth centuries was derived from the transformation in European thought which led to a divorce between thought and nature, symbolized by the Cartesian division between thinking and being – *cogito ergo sum* – and the violent manipulation of external reality.[8] It emphasized the autonomy of competing individuals in a social system strongly analogous to that of the model of the free market.

The realist depiction of the individual derived from a tradition of European thought that celebrated man's domination of the natural world by a superior technology. The ideal of the individual was in essence that of an "imperial self" which was symbolized by the lone individual, Robinson Crusoe. Defoe's novel portrayed a model lone entrepreneur able to bend nature to his will in the interests of survival as well as mixing his labour with nature in order to embody a model *homo economicus*. The ideal of Crusoe underpinned many later English novels during the period of imperial self-confidence and expansion in the late eighteenth and nineteenth centuries. It also extended into the imperial adventurer genre. As the next chapter shows in the case of the writer Laurens van der Post, this enabled it to survive much longer than in mainstream metropolitan literary tradition.

However, from the 1870s onwards the mainstream tradition of liberally inclined literary realism began to enter a period of crisis which became increasingly evident by the years after World War One. The self-confident individualism at the heart of the tradition began to be cast into doubt while Victorian imperialism went on to the defensive, especially in the years after the Anglo-Boer War of 1899–1902. The entrenchment of realism had been based upon a conservative resistance to the penetration of romanticism into the novel form and a defence of traditional notions of hierarchy and status by means of a bourgeois concept of gentility.[9] There was, though, a contradiction at the heart of this project. By the 1870s and 1880s an urban literary intelligentsia had emerged within the environs of the capital, which was cut adrift from the traditional "intellectual aristocracy" that had defined Victorian notions of progress and moral conduct. This intelligentsia gravitated towards a literary modernism that had developed in France and Germany and championed the untrammelled and indulgent pursuit of art and aesthetics. It lived rather uneasily with the dominant orthodoxy of imperialism. The modernist outlook was thus often depicted as standing in opposition to the ethic of imperial conquest, as in Rudyard Kipling's novel *The Light That Failed* (1890) where the conflict is resolved by his central blind character abandoning a career as an artist for the dream of empire in the Sudan.

The onset of modernism at the heart of the British imperial metropolis had far-reaching literary and cultural consequences. It led a number of writers such as Thomas Hardy, E. M. Forster and D. H. Lawrence to turn inwards and pay closer attention to landscape in a wave of literary naturalism. The "counter-culture" of pastoralism, epitomized by Hardy's *Tess of the Durbervilles* (1891) began to break down some of the assumptions of a cohesive English culture that had underlain the realist tradition up till then. It was also reflected in Forster's *Howards End* which set up the English country house as the embodiment of English culture and counterposed it to the extraneous forces of Empire.[10]

For many writers in England modernism reflected a crisis of belief in the imperial vision. Joseph Conrad's *Heart of Darkness* (1902) undermined the notion of an absolute set of moral values behind the imperial enterprise and hinted that "civilization" was itself relative. The novel embraced a modernist notion of the *Angst*-ridden individual in the character of Kurtz, who is cut adrift from his own society and social order. This leads to a portrayal of complete solitude and isolation as Kurtz is left in the "invisible wilderness", crying the words, "the horror! the horror!"

This vision of the isolated individual pushed "beyond culture" into the abyss of nothingness is prophetic of a more recent postmodernist nihilism in the era after 1945. However, many modernist writers preferred to preoccupy themselves with a less grandiose literary agenda based on the pursuit of new codes of moral and social conduct in the relative freedom of European urban culture. They were hesitant to confront head on the full weight of European imperial values.

This was also the case with the small group of writers in South Africa centred around the magazine *Voorslag* in the mid 1920s – writers such as William Plomer, Laurens van der Post and Roy Campbell, for whom modernism amounted to little more than a plea for art in a rather philistine society and for a re-evaluation of the controversial subject of "miscegenation". It led to no major intellectual challenge to the premises of white rule and both Campbell and van der Post were later to become ardent champions of order against the metropolitan liberal critics of Empire.

William Plomer's *Turbott Wolfe* (1925) is nevertheless a good example of an experiment by a young writer with the modernist novel form in South Africa. The novel came a year after Sarah Gertrude Millin's *God's Stepchildren* which dealt with the theme of "miscegenation" by presenting its effects through four generations following the decision of the Reverend Andrew Flood to marry a Hottentot woman. Marrying a woman of another race is linked to social decline and degeneration in the novel, which continued to be cited in pro-apartheid propaganda years later. By contrast, *Turbott Wolfe* produced an uproar in South Africa due to its uninhibited portrayal of sexual relationships across the colour line. The novel was important for extending the boundaries of South African literature from those of a rational reformist belief in social progress into a direct confrontation with the racial cleavages of South African society.[11] It failed to generate a new novelistic tradition in South Africa, for its engagement with sex and race is really only a device to explore the possibilities open for the free individual at a particular time and place.

The plot of *Turbott Wolfe*, such as it is, centres upon the political activities of a young missionary, Rupert Friston, and his Society of Young Africa, the main focus of the novel being really the affair of a black member of the Society, Zacchary Msomi, with a young white woman, Mabel van der Horst. Friston dabbles for a time with communism and marries Msomi and van der Horst before leaving for "Swedish East Africa" never to return. His "papers" include some notes added as an appendix to the novel, on the "politico aesthete" – notes which reflect Plomer's own uncertainty of the relationship of the aesthetics of modernism to political engagement. The "politico-aesthete" is a man "hemmed in by wireless telegraphy", who "staggers, poor man, under the weight of the past; and he struggles, poor man, under the load of the future.... He would like to focus his attention on the point where the rational in the character coincides with the concupiscle; but it is really his character, he wonders – ?".[12]

As a young man's first novel, *Turbott Wolfe* reveals a strongly self-indulgent tone. It failed to make a major impact in South Africa, though van der Post's *In a Province* was preoccupied with similar themes. By the 1930s all three of the *Voorslag* literary coterie had left South Africa. Literary modernism was too metropolitan and urban in orientation to have a major influence on South African writing in the pre-war years. Traces of it can be discerned again, however, in the new upsurge of English South African writing after 1945. By this time, two major traditions of writing began to emerge which were to define the course of novel-writing over the next two decades.

Two Traditions

South African English writers by the post-Second World War period confronted, in some respects, a literary situation similar to that of England in the latter part of the nineteenth century. As has been pointed out, in the English context there had been a progressive split between a path of modernism and a search for the autonomous self in an urban setting and a naturalistic retreat back to the rural landscape. A similar situation presented itself in the South African setting.

For the South African writers two main streams of writing developed. One was an updated naturalist conception of the rural terrain as the locus of the South African identity, and the other was an urban modernist concern with new codes of social conduct that could be capable of transcending the fixed racial barriers of segregation. Both streams reflected an interest in what Rabkin has termed "social problems", for both related to a deeper tradition of writing stretching back to Olive Schreiner. These traditions will be examined in turn.

The search back to the rural landscape

The pastoralists in South Africa, like the English romantics, were uneasy with the values of an urbanizing industrial culture. For this tradition, the publication of Alan Paton's *Cry the Beloved Country* in 1948 was a major event since the novel marked a re-establishment of English South African writing after the war. The author was a second-generation Natalian of Anglo-Scottish descent who was deeply influenced by the poetry of the nineteenth-century romantics, especially that of Robert Louis Stevenson. The descriptions of the Valley of the Ixopo serve as a crucial point of moral anchorage in the novel and are tinged with a nostalgia which becomes clearer when it is realized that the novel was written during a period of major economic and social change in rural Natal as agricultural commercialization had a major impact on the landscape. "The sad fact is," Paton later wrote in his autobiography,

> much of the beauty of the Ixopo countryside has gone, because the grass and bracken and the rolling hills and farms have in large part given way to the endless plantations of gum and wattle and pine, and the titihoys do not cry there anymore. Many of the farmers have gone, and their farmsteads are now the homes and offices of timber managers, and the lowing of the cattle has given way to the whining of saw mills.[13]

The realism of *Cry the Beloved Country* is qualified by a deeper romantic nostalgia for "one of the fairest valleys of Africa", placing the novel more strictly in the tradition of South African romances stretching back to Rider Haggard and John Buchan.[14] The novel deals with "social problems" rather than adventure as in the imperial adventurer mode, and really conforms to a romance formula. The novel is shot through with a Christian eschatology of heaven and hell which underpin two separate and contrasting worlds. These worlds can, after Northrop Frye, be termed the "idyllic world" and the "demonic world" and they in turn counterpose the placid and idyllic rural terrain of Natal with the demonic world of the morally corrupt Witwatersrand.[15]

The result is that the novel ends up bypassing the emergent black African urban culture of the townships and slums of the Witwatersrand. These are only depicted through the deadening lens of a paternalistic moralism which had been fortified by Paton's own experiences as warden of the Diepkloof Reformatory for African boys outside Johannesburg. Here Paton had experimented with the then fashionable theories of the eugenicist Cyril Burt by trying to manipulate the environment of the reformatory in order to engineer a new and morally sounder individual. While he upheld the Christian belief in free will, Paton's fiction is shot through with an environmental imagery that powerfully shapes the choices that individuals can make. There is a fatalistic inevitability, for instance, in the career of the character Ha'penny in the story *Ha'penny* who, despite efforts to escape the gangland culture of the townships, knows that it will catch up with him in the end and exact its revenge.[16] Similarly in *Cry the Beloved Country* there is an environmental distinction drawn between the characters who drift to the towns and those who stay behind. The first are exemplified by Absolom and John Kumalo, the son and brother of the Reverend Steven Kumalo. The first has been sucked up by the urban culture of the townships to become a murderer while the second ends up as a corrupt politician. On the other hand, Letsitsi, the agricultural demonstrator, embodies a hope for a rejuvenated peasant culture back on the land in contrast to the moral disintegration of life in the townships.

The crucial link figure in the story is the Reverend Kumalo who travels between the two worlds in the course of the novel in an endeavour to track down his lost son Absolom. Once cast into the demonic world of the city the Reverend is lost. As soon as he reaches Johannesburg train station he is cheated of a pound by a young African boy. It is only with considerable difficulty that he manages to trace Absolom, via his daughter Gertrude, who has become a prostitute. The novel presents an image of a pathological African family structure in the urban areas which was not born out by some of the research evidence of the period. At the time of the novel's publication there were already some psychological tests conducted by Wulf Sachs suggesting that the influences of early childhood were the same for Africans as for whites.[17] Paton, however, chose to perpetuate an image of African otherness rooted in a rural and "tribal" past that did much to inhibit the literary recognition of an urban black cultural identity.

Paton's depiction of moral disintegration in urban black African culture was by no means new. It continued a vein begun by William Plomer in *Ula Masondo* (1927) and W. C. Scully in *Daniel Venanda* (1923). *Cry the Beloved Country* was distinctive for linking the theme with a more assertive liberalism which had been fortified by the experience of South African involvement in the Second World War. Paton was an admirer of R. F. A. Hoernle in the early 1940s and he is mentioned by name in the novel. Arthur Jarvis, a white social worker who is murdered in the novel, embodies Paton's own hopes for liberalism in the South African context. His death represents a sacrifice for a wider ideal of South African "civilization", and a manuscript he is writing at the time of his murder reflects on the basic dilemma that confronts liberals. "The truth is", it stated,

> that our Christian civilisation is riddled through and through with a dilemma. We believe in the brotherhood of man, but we do not want it in South Africa ... even our God becomes a confused and inconsistent creature, giving gifts and denying them employment. Is it strange then that our civilisation is riddled through and through with dilemma? The truth is that our civilisation is not Christian; it is a tragic compound of great ideal and fearful practice, of high assurance and desperate anxiety, of loving charity and fearful clutching of possessions. Allow me a minute ...[18]

At this point the manuscript breaks off and Jarvis goes off to his death like an early Christian martyr. The fact that it is left unfinished personifies the unfinished nature of South African liberalism. The "tragic compound" of "great ideal and fearful practice" is one that Paton sees as being ultimately resolved. The novel is significant for mapping a terrain of Christian hopes like *The Pilgrim's Progress*, though how these were to be realized remained unclear.

The year of *Cry the Beloved Country*'s publication saw the election victory of the Nationalists under D. F. Malan over Smuts's United Party government. The triumph of Afrikaner nationalism put many English-speaking liberal writers on to the defensive in the course of the 1950s, though there were efforts to break out of the straightjacket of literary naturalism. Patons's response was to shift the focus of his next novel, *Too Late the Phalarope* (1955), from the theme of "inter-racial contact" to exploring the psychological landscape of the Afrikaner mind. The form of the novel marked a technical advance on *Cry the Beloved Country*, especially through its penetration of the hopes and fears of the white mind in South Africa. Paton had long been interested in trying to explore the inner consciousness of the white mind in South Africa, especially in the authoritarian and patriarchal society of Afrikaner communities in the rural *plattelana*. He was especially disappointed by the failure of Olive Schreiner to realize her full literary potential, while later in his biography of Jan H. Hofmeyr he was fascinated by the failure of one of South Africa's foremost white liberals to realize his full political potential. Both appeared in effect to represent a "darkness of the soul" and a loss of faith.[19] Paton was by the early 1950s in his tentative explorations in white interiority exposing some of the limitations of conventional liberal realism.

Too Late the Phalarope is also important, though, for its tackling of the theme of inter-racial "miscegenation". The novel is mostly a monologue by the aunt of Pieter van Vlaanderen, an Afrikaner policeman and rugby champion in a Transvaal town. Van Vlaanderen is a man deprived of paternal love: his father, Jakob, does not smoke the pipe his son chose for a birthday present and refuses to allow him to continue collecting stamps after he fails to come top in class at school. Burdened by an unhappy marriage, van Vlaanderen seeks comfort in a "forbidden" liaison with an African girl and is eventually discovered and convicted under the 1927 Immorality Act.

The novel manages, in V. A. February's words, to unravel a "picture of human and personal tragedy, during the course of which the insularity of the Afrikaner microcosms is laid bare with a razor's edge".[20] It ends up ascribing the roots of white South African racism to the anxieties and fears of Afrikaners dominated by a frontier past. The black characters tend to be mere playthings in this internal white psychological drama and have no independent moral authority of their own.

Too Late the Phalarope does little to move beyond the conventional stereotype of an unchanging Afrikaner mind burdened by ceaseless tribal fears and guilts. Its explanation for van Vlaanderen's liaison is in terms of one of the traditional formulas of the colonial novel: Pieter van Vlaanderen is really an aberration from the dominant norms of his society. He is portrayed as having unusually "feminine" characteristics of gentleness and a keenness to read books. He was in fact "always two men":

> The one was the soldier of war, with all the English ribbons that his father hated; the lieutenant in the police, second only to the captain; the great rugby hero of thousands of boys and men. The other was the dark and silent man, hiding from all men his secret knowledge of himself, with that hardness and coldness that made men afraid of him, afraid even to speak to him.[21]

The reader is left guessing at the end of the novel the real explanation for the actions of the "dark and silent man" who wrote his feelings in a secret book, which the all-knowing authorial voice refuses to divulge at the end of the story. There is a hint here of infantile regression of a mother-fixation reminiscent of the "rosebud" theme in Orson Welles's film *Citizen Kane*. The novel can be read as a bitter extension of Paton's own conflicts with the Malan and Strydom governments in the 1950s as it depicts Afrikaner culture through a gendered model of dominant *tannies* (an Afrikaans word for domineering aunt-like women) and infantilized men that is impervious to reasoned ideas. Even the book, *The Birds of South Africa*, that Pieter gives to his father gets destroyed once the truth of his betrayal of his tribal race purity becomes known. The voice of Pieter's aunt, however, embodies a hope at the end of the novel that the triumphant Afrikaner nation will not abuse its power once it has:

> ... left the trodden and the known for the vast and secret continent, and made there songs of heimwee and longing, and the iron laws. And now the lord has turned our captivity. I pray we shall not walk arrogant, remembering Herod whom an Angel of the Lord struck down, for that he made himself a god.[22]

Paton's interest in the psychological dimension of the Afrikaner mind led away from the novel form over the next few years as he got involved in the biographical study of Hofmeyr, though this could only be published after the death of the politician's mother.[23]

Paton did not play an especially prominent part in the South African literary scene after the mid 1950s. His absence clearly harmed the development of the English-language literary tradition, though new figures continued to emerge. One rather more radical experiment was published in 1952 by Phyllis Altman in her novel *The Law of the Vultures*.[24] This lacked the psychological penetration of *Too Late the Phalarope* and still embraced the major theme of the rural African migrating to the city and falling foul of the law and becoming embittered as a consequence. The main character, Thabo Thaele, comes from a mountain community in Lesotho and struggles against almost impossible odds to improve his education while working in an office as a clerk. After being mistakenly accused of stealing money, Thaele is sent to gaol and emerges deeply embittered against whites. He sets up an Africanist "People of Africa Society", though this has no political programme and is milked of funds by its parasite of a secretary, Jobula. Thaele tries to win over the other main African character in the story, Nkosi, who is also embittered by failing to receive compensation for the loss of his livestock while fighting in the South African army in North Africa during World War Two. A rival for Nkosi's support emerges in the form of the trade union organizer, Dhlamini, who points out that the only really hopeful strategy for Africans is organization of the work-force.

The Law of the Vultures is hardly an urban novel, though it does show some understanding of the limited choices available to the urban African working class and departs from the high-minded moralism of Paton. It signally fails to explain why Thaele lurches into such an anti-white stance after his vaguely liberal employer, Dent, betrays him in favour of his white staff. Altman's novel suggests in a Marxist formulation that, as opposed to the working class (which will turn to trade unionism), those blacks with leanings towards individual advancement will be more likely to turn to a racial Africanism. Both Thaele and Jobula are shown to have no interest in trade unionism, and while Jobula is a professional parasite on African political movements, Thaele is portrayed as a naive dreamer.

Critics have pointed out that Altman's novel contains an evolutionism at the heart of her socialist radicalism. African political organizations need to follow the "true" course of action on Western-style trade union lines and must not be diverted by individual self-seekers, who may still be casualties of a racially discriminatory society.[25] The novel failed to find any significant successors and remained rather isolated in the 1950s in its efforts to understand the urban African condition. It bore many of the traits of the English investigative novel and would eventually be followed by writing such as Richard Rive's *Emergency* (1960) which examined the state of a whole urban community — in this case, District Six under growing state pressure.

The major English writer to emerge in South Africa in the mid 1950s was another person from Natal, Jack Cope. His work has been copious, though in many ways it follows in logical succession to *Cry the Beloved Country* — the novel which Cope has seen as marking the foundation of a specific style in English South African fiction. He was particularly moved by what he saw as the novel's assertion of "a true fellow feeling between the white and black man as we have never had before",[26] and his own novels have also tried to advance this ideal.

One of the features of Cope's work has been the imaginative use of pastoral imagery as a backdrop to the ideal of a cohesive South African culture. In his novels of the 1950s he invested characters with a humanity derived in part from the surrounding landscape. *The Fair House* (1955), for example, dwelt on the theme of inter-racial relationships at the time of the 1906 Bambata rebellion. Tom Erskine, a white soldier, has a boyhood friendship with an African, Kolombe Pela, who joins the side of Bambata. Tom falls in love with Linda, an Afrikaner girl, who fervently supports the white settlers against Bambata. Tom is sickened by the violence employed against the black rebels and leaves the army, though in the end he does not marry Linda. Instead he chooses the more intellectual Margaret O'Neill. Kolombe is saved from being killed by the white troops and lives to fight another day.

The novel counterposes an image of nature against war and human struggle and is significant for challenging the Social Darwinism of the imperial adventurer genre of Haggard in which human struggle is seen to be derived from a violent nature. The pastoral is employed to invest his characters with a humanity, such as when Linda, sitting by Tom on a horse-drawn cart seemed

> to unfold like a flower once the tension of life has burst upon

the calyx and it can smooth out its cramped petals until they are startlingly large and flawless and iridescent, breathing perfume and colour from their whole surface. Her eyes seemed darker; the whole veld singing for the morning after the down-pour and a richer and deeper colour and the air was more dense with the scent of tree gums and wild herbs.[27]

To Tom, too, while struggling through the forest undergrowth in search of the rebels, the "wildness and glory and secretiveness of the forest were never meant for war.... Nature followed its blind, pitiless cycles here, yet nothing in its countless ages was more savage than the manhunt he was engaged in".[28]

Cope's novel is underpinned by an evolutionism, even if not of the Social Dawinist sort. The Africans are depicted as divorced from the landscape and as victims of a shattered culture resulting from their defeat by the colonial forces. For Kolombe and his men the landscape is merely backdrop without any of the symbolic associations that it has for the whites:

> Kolombe collected his rifle and cartridge belt from Umtakati and went up into a sheltered ravine to see the fighting leaders Macala and Mganu. The two men, armed with rifles, revolvers and crossed bandoliers, held council together in the open sunlight. A great rock-capped spur jutted from the side of the ravine which fell almost vertically to the mountain torrent below. Among the smooth cold rocks, aloes were flowering and brilliant blue, green and scarlet sunbirds flitted around them sucking honey with slender curved beaks. Kolombe made his report of the situation at the Drifts and the country beyond.[29]

The landscape here provides an element of continuity in a situation of violent cultural and political conflict. Cope's pastoral description of it bears some similarity to that of H. E. Bates's pastoral novels, especially those concerning colonial situations, such as *The Jacaranda Tree* (1949), *The Scarlet Sword* (1950) and *The Purple Plain* (1952).

The Fair House portrays racial discrimination as a product of childhood fears, rather as *Too Late the Phalarope* does. One of the liberal characters in the story, Margaret O'Neill, sees that there is "room enough in this country for all of us but that's not good enough for some people. If we were children, white and black and brown children fighting over every inch of a garden, it would be sickening, but we are adults and it's criminal".[30] But it is significantly no longer simply the Afrikaner nation that is guilty of infantile regression but all the ethnic groups in the South African conflict. The society itself is seen as immature and needing collectively to grow up in multi-racial harmony, though Cope, unlike Altman in *The Law of the Vultures*, does not indicate that this would necessarily occur through industrial organization. Its historical nature indicates that Cope shares some of the assumptions of frontier historiography: it is the colonial encounter which has shaped current racial conflict in South Africa.

Cope is a good example of the optimism contained in some of the liberal thinking of the 1950s. His novels embrace the hope that through education and learning black South Africans can eventually participate in a common society and politics, though the achievement of this may still entail some violence. It is Kolombe rather than Bambata who realizes the full implications of the rebellion as he urges his followers to recognize that

> your day of war is still to come. Hate the White House, but learn from them. Learn from the mistakes we, your elders, make. Listen while I teach you something. This is the last war with assegais; this is the last war with chiefs and doctors; it is the last war where our battle cries give us away like children playing in the dongas.[31]

Kolombe is like Buchan's character, Laputa, in *Prester John*, since he too has used his foreign education to try to organize a black revolt against white rule. But Kolombe is unlike Laputa in that he knows that education has to be the main way rather than armed insurrection. He is in fact aware of the forces of historical change:

> He had in his heart the dream of a new kind of black army, an army of such boys grown to manhood with all the bravery and endurance instilled into them from the ancient ways, but also with new ideas and commanders and weapons.[32]

Cope does not explore this possibility in terms of urban change, seeing the African future mainly in rural and pastoral terms, but his novel is a significant work in imagining a process of acculturation of African society towards "Western" values. Other writers, though, lacked the same sort of historical perspective, preferring to counterpose the "civilized" values of the metropolis to those of the backward rural areas of South Africa.

An example of this can be seen in the Jewish writer Dan Jacobson's novel *A Dance in the Sun* (1956). Here a contrast is drawn between the arid landscape of the Karoo which is incapable of any real growth and the desperate clinging to "civilization" by the white man Fletcher in the face of the moral evil of his brother-in-law, Louw. The moral conscience of the story lies in the student narrator who, along with his colleague Frank, is hitchhiking from Lyndhurst (Kimberley) to Cape Town. The cultural bleakness of the terrain hearkens back to *The Story of an African Farm*, though Jacobson's story questions the rectitude of liberal ethics in so far as they represent the intrusion into this rural wilderness of the city values of Lyndhurst.

This clash can be seen when the African servant Joseph asks one of the students, Frank, for help in his struggle against his employer, Fletcher, and actually offers some money as payment. Some liberal assumptions become jolted:

> ... Then I thought I saw a way out.
> "We have more money than you."
> "You don't know how much money I've got," Joseph gently reminded me.
> "No," I said. There was no way out: he had exposed the tenacity and duplicity of my own feelings of white baaskap – my own 'liberal' intolerances, my own assertion of where his place should be, and where mine. And to my surprise I saw that for the first time in all my dealings with him, Joseph's stiff and deliberate manner had relaxed, as he bowed his head and smiled doubtfully bowing almost as if he were waiting for a reproof.[33]

Joseph's strength in being able to manipulate a situation to his advantage rests on the moral weakness of Fletcher, in the face of the power and violence of Louw, who has both an incestuous relationship with Fletcher's wife and gets Joseph's sister pregnant. Louw breaks up the house of the Fletchers' and goes off after refusing to take Mrs Fletcher with him. Fletcher's own life is revealed to be a hollow sham and he is left at the end of the story under the influence of Joseph, who can no longer be sacked from the farm. He is indeed in a state of pathetic helplessness:

> We turned to look at Fletcher. Fletcher was dancing. Along in the veld, in the middle of his dusty piece of ground, Fletcher was dancing with humiliation and rage and despair. He stamped his feet into the dust, and gnawed his knuckles, and twisted his ears, and pulled his chain, and brandished his fists. He was still lifting his knees, he was still raising the dust from his ankles when we turned our backs on him.[34]

This is a powerful image of white impotence and what one critic has termed "an eloquent symbol of the culturally isolated in an adopted land".[35] Even so, the story rests upon an apolitical view of African cultural identity. It is illiteracy that forces Joseph to turn to the white students in order to understand the letter he has stolen from Louw to Fletcher announcing his arrival at the farm. Joseph's situation is a narrow and cramped one, suggesting a dependency of Africans upon the technology of "white" South Africa. His story emerges second-hand through the white narrator of the tale and emphasizes the difficulties of mobility as Joseph searches for his sister who has disappeared after becoming pregnant. Like the Reverend Kumalo, Joseph is involved in a desperate search for relatives lost through the harshness of South Africa's segregated society.

Joseph's story reveals a different and alternative morality to that of "white" South Africa. It is "my sister" whom Joseph is looking for and the narrator is compelled to reflect that:

> The profundity of this family feeling of his did not arise, it seemed to me, out of pride, or dynastic ambitions, or a desire to protect a self-regard extended in an unwarranted manner to the members of his family. Nor was it merely an obedience to an imperative from an almost forgotten tribal past, whose commands were to be grudgingly heard and grudgingly carried out. It was not even a matter of love – the protean emotion that excuses as many evasions as it encourages selflessness. The precepts that he was obeying were those of his own morality – a morality that acted on its own level, almost wordlessly, without

fuss. In its closeness and unquestioned necessity it presented itself simply as part of life: what he was doing was the act of living.³⁶

This morality remains generally impenetrable in the story. The character of Joseph has an "otherness" which sets it off from the moral code of the white characters, such as that is. There is, therefore, a continuing colonial formula at the heart of this device that is comparable to the "noble savage" characterization employed by Laurens van der Post in his depiction of bushmen. The simple and pre-literate culture and morality of the colonized in both contexts is used by sympathetic white liberal writers to explore the moral failings within white colonial society rather than to explore the culture of the colonized on its own terms.

Joseph is nevertheless rather more than the passive stereotype of Stephen Kumalo, and the story indicates that a development was occurring in the white liberal literary imagination in South Africa at this time towards a fuller realization of African character. The terrain for this lay in the city rather than the remoter landscape of the Karoo.

Urban modernism

In the years before World War Two English-speaking writers had considerable difficulty in portraying an urban African identity. Africans seemed alien to the urban metropolis. Until at least the 1930s many liberal writers felt a benevolent and liberal segregationism was a means of freeing African society from the horrors of a Victorian-style urbanization. Novels such as W. C. Scully's *Daniel Venanda* (1923) and Ethelreda Lewis's *Wild Deer* (1929) portrayed African characters as essentially lost in the urban metropolis and only finding true peace back in the countryside. It was not indeed until the 1950s in the era of *Drum* magazine that a reassessment began to take place by many English writers and intellectuals of urban African identity, often as a result of a first-hand acquaintance with writers such as Casey Motsitsi, Can Themba or Bloke Modisane.³⁷

One key novel to reflect this changing outlook among liberal whites is Nadine Gordimer's *A World of Strangers* (1958). In this novel Gordimer was concerned to explore the increasing potential opened up by the city for social manipulation of relationships. In the world of Johannesburg in the mid 1950s a number of new avenues had opened up for social interaction between black and white liberals and radicals who went to one another's parties and slept in one another's beds. The novel depicts the world of emerging multi-racial political activity in the wake of the 1955 Freedom Charter, when magazines such as *Drum* and *Golden City Post* reflected a new urban consciousness amongst an urban black working class.

The central character in *A World of Strangers* is an outsider to South African society, Toby Hood, an English journalist with an upper-class but politically radical background (his father fought in the Spanish Civil War). Toby is able to negotiate the different world on the Witwatersrand with relative ease, moving from the upper-class world of his first mistress, Cecil Rowe, to the more radical milieu of his next lover, Anna Louw, and the black townships through a black acquaintance Stephen Sithole. All this occurs within a landscape that is quintessentially artificial in nature:

> ... as if people had been presented with an upland plateau and left to finish it, to create a background of natural features instead of to fit in with one – and at the same time curiously empty, as if truly abandoned to man. Between the factories that thinned out from the perimeter of one town, almost meeting the last industrial outpost of the next, there was a horizon of strange hills. Some of them were made of soft white sand, like the sand of the desert, piled up on colossal castles ...
>
> There were no valleys between these hills for they were simply set down on the flat veld. Patches of tough green grass and short waving grasses showed, but mostly the growth was weird, wet and thin; a few cows would stand in the reeds of an indefinite swampy patch where the ooze shone mother-of-pearl, like oil: a rectangular lake out of which pipes humped had sheets of violet and pink, like a crude water colour. In some places there was no earth but a bare, grey scum that had dried and cracked open. And there was black earth, round a disused coal mine, where someone had thrown a peach away, and it had grown into a tree, making out of the coal dirt some hard hairy green peaches.[38]

This image of a dead artificial landscape is one that was probably designed to shock the overseas reader in Britain, so used to images of a "natural" rural landscape. At the same time it taps a traditional literary revolt against urban industrialism. Life, though, can grow on this terrain, but it has to do so under harsh conditions. The novel ends on an uncertain note with the death of Stephen Sithole in a car crash, the arrest of Anna Louw and Cecil's marriage into the white upper class. As Toby leaves for a month in Cape Town, it emerges that he has been ultimately unable to bring these different worlds of "strangers" together in any meaningful way, indicating the continuing fragmentation of South African culture under apartheid. The composer Sam, a friend of Steven, sees Toby off at Johannesburg station with a note of continuing anxiety as to the possible future of inter-racial relationships in such a society as South Africa. "Who knows with you people, Toby, man," he says. "Maybe you won't come back at all. Something will keep you away. Something will prevent you, and we won't –" and here he gets lost as the two go down separate stairs, watched by the symbol of white state power, "a young policeman with an innocent face, on which suspicion was like the serious frown wrinkling the brow of a puppy".[39] The novel can be seen as driven by a search for "wholeness", reminiscent of the search by Victorians such as Matthew Arnold for a cohesive "culture" in the face of the advancing "anarchy" of industrial capitalism. As Robert Green has pointed out, though, the novel never really brings into any balance its essentially liberal commitment to private life and the "harsh stolidity" of the social forces arrayed against it.[40] Even at his stage, there is an emerging doubt in Gordimer's mind over the credibility of individual characters in such a society where massive social engineering has intervened so drastically into private lives.

If *A World of Strangers* was burdened by an uncertain vision of human relationships across the racial divide in South Africa under apartheid, this doubt was only to increase in the following years. By the early 1960s, in the wake of Sharpeville and the banning of the ANC and PAC, Gordimer's writing reflected an increasing sense of alienation in the English-speaking South African liberal imagination. Many of the earlier relationships that had been forged in the heady era of the mid 1950s became shattered by bannings and the flight into exile by a number of political activists. Furthermore, the confidence of the English liberal tradition became progressively undermined by the advance of Afrikaner nationalism. In 1961 South Africa became a republic and the literary journal *Contrast* caught some of the changing mood amongst many English-speaking liberals in pointing out that the English-language group "cannot live on delusions of controlling its own destiny". It was impossible for English-speaking writers to dissociate themselves from apartheid, though at the same time guilt about its effects emerged from "intense and probably unrealised anxieties" for "we wronged the Boer-Afrikaner and therefore we deserve to be punished. At the same time we affront his language and denigrate his cultural status and so justify our own loss of guilt as part of the nerveless minority."[41] The journal pointed out that the only way for writers to try and free themselves from this cycle of guilt was by going to the root of the problem by seeking to free themselves from the burdens of race. "Until the artist can touch all humanity with compassion," it concluded, "he has not advanced beyond the blundering steps of the primitive".[42]

This plea for renewal of faith in a colour-blind liberal humanism was, though, undermined by the growing isolation of the white artist in the growing repression and bannings of the early 1960s. A humanism of sorts was being forged in the world of the 1950s, even though there was a rather naive optimism that this was going quickly to shape a new society. But as the contacts were severed after the 1960s a new set of challenges emerged.

It is the state of alienation of the white liberal artist which is the main theme of Gordimer's novel, *The Late Bourgeois World* (1966). In 1959 Gordimer wrote that whites were going to feel increasingly rebuffed by the advancing black nationalism in Africa. This was going to be damaging to the ego of many liberal whites but something they were going to have to learn to live with, for it was produced by a "nationalism of the heart that has been brought about by suffering. There is no share in it we can hope to have. I for one can read this already in the faces, voices and eloquently regretful but firm handclasps of my own African friends".[43]

This sense of cultural alienation was further compounded by the failure of white radicals in the early 1960s to organize any significant resistance to increasingly authoritarian state power. *The Late Bourgeois World* was written to penetrate the atmosphere of advancing social and political isolation in South Africa in the early 1960s. It was designed, Gordimer later said, "to look into the specific character of the social climate that produced the wave of young white saboteurs in 1963–64". The novel is divested of many of the liberal humanist assumptions that marked *A World Of Strangers*. By the time it was written the rule of law in South Africa had been seriously undermined by the security legislation of the early 1960s such as the

1963 General Law Amendment Act that allowed the state to incarcerate a prisoner for eighty days without charge. At the same time a number of younger members of the Liberal Party had become frustrated by the failure to secure change by non-violent means and formed themselves into a terrorist group called The African Resistance Movement (though most of its members were white). The group was soon rounded up, though one member, John Harris, was hung in 1965 for planting a bomb in Johannesburg railway station that killed a passer-by. Later the same year Bram Fischer was arrested after being on the run for a number of months, and effective white opposition to the regime had come to an end. Most of the leading activists in the ANC, too, had been silenced after the 1964 Rivonia trial that sentenced Nelson Mandela to life imprisonment.

It was in this context of growing political repression that *The Late Bourgeois World* was written. The novel can be seen as a landmark in post-war South African literature especially in its mature modernist form, though it was fully anchored in the culture of Western technology and the moral possibilities that this offers.

The novel is set one day in the life of Elizabeth van den Sandt, the former wife of a radical white political activist, Max, who has committed suicide by driving his car into Cape Town harbour (Max was one of the false names used by Bram Fischer while on the run from the police). Max's family are wealthy upper-class representatives of the English-speaking bourgeoisie and his father was a United Party Member of Parliament. But his career was one of revolt against the values of his parents. As a student he joined the South African Communist Party and, after the party's banning in 1950, the left-leaning Congress of Democrats, followed later by the Liberal Party. Max is politically and emotionally volatile. After taking part in the 1952 Defiance Campaign, he began to turn towards more underground activities. He is arrested for sabotage, causing his father to resign his parliamentary seat. His wealthy parents are able to save him through their social connections and Max remained a somewhat flawed character, unable to break out of his parent's world, despite his ranting at his wedding reception against the world's "moral sclerosis".

The character of Max is one drawn in some degree from the romantic adventurism of characters involved in the white opposition in South African politics – characters such as the younger Patrick Duncan, who tried to steer the Liberal Party in the 1950s towards a more radical political position based upon Gandhian passive resistance.[44] Gordimer also portrays the limitations of upper-class radicals in such a highly charged political milieu as South Africa, whilst also showing the important inter-relationship between the inner emotional landscape and the wider political culture. Max's white, male and radical emotional state remains blocked as was the wider political opposition against apartheid during the 1950s and 1960s. It ends up being eclipsed by the emotional development occurring within the central female character in the novel, that of Elizabeth. In the course of the day, Elizabeth visits her son Bobo at his school outside Johannesburg to inform him of his father's death, goes to see her senile grandmother and has dinner with a black radical activist, Luke. In the morning and the afternoon she is with her lover, Graham, who also acts as the conduit for the central piece of information occurring outside the main story, that of the first American space walk, a powerful symbol of Western technological prowess.

The novel can be interpreted on three separate levels: that of an examination of the political resistance by both white and black radicals in South Africa during the 1950s and early 1960s to growing state power; the nature of this power in relation to the wider theme of modern Western technology symbolized by the American space walk; and the relation of the artist, and indeed the novel form itself, to these other two themes.

It is probably the third of these levels which engages Gordimer, as novelist, the most directly. The character of Elizabeth van den Sandt is the medium through which Gordimer, as a white female artist, can herself relate to the wider events depicted within the novel, and can approach the question of her own role within a rapidly changing social and political situation within South African society. The title of the novel, *The Late Bourgeois World*, gives a clue to the dilemma as Gordimer then perceived it. Elizabeth asks Graham, "What *on earth* do you think they'll call it in history?" and Graham replies that it will be "the late bourgeois world" after a book he had just read by an East German for "... it exists in relation to the early Communist world – shall we call it. Defining one, you assume the existence of the other. So both are part of a total historical phenomenon."[45]

The book in question is Ernst Fischer's *The Necessity of Art* first published in Dresden in 1959 and in English in 1963. It is a Marxist work that states an alternative teleology to the Western idea of progress. The Western bourgeois world is thus "late" because it is in its final stages before the emergence of a socialist culture which can restore art to the community. The point about contemporary Western bourgeois art, Fischer argued, was that it was essentially commercialized whereas "socialist art" is able effectively to take over the Western notion of progress and transform it into a genuine vision of the future:

> ... in the long-term view socialist art has the advantage over late bourgeois art. The latter, although it has much to offer, lacks one thing: a large vision of the future, a hopeful historical perspective. Despite disappointments, this vision still belongs to the socialist world. It is far more than a question of the bread and space rockets, prosperity and technical perfection: it is a matter of the 'meaning of life', a meaning that is not metaphysical but humanist.[46]

The idea of the bankruptcy of modern Western culture has been a strong one in Gordimer's novels, though the notion that the West lacks a vision of the future now looks strikingly dated in the context of the demise of the Cold War and the failure of the socialist project in former Eastern bloc states such as the German Democratic Republic. But Western art has appeared to Gordimer as an extraneous intrusion into South Africa: she has satirized the collections of European art found in the homes of upper-class whites in the northern suburbs of Johannesburg, such as Marion Alexander's rather dingy Courbet "find" in *A World of Strangers* or the absurd pornographic plastic nude of Brandt Vermeulen in *Burger's Daughter*. Such art is perceived as divorced from the interests and needs of the majority of black Africans in South Africa and from their popular culture. Her attack on it marks an effort by Gordimer to be not just the entertainer of the white bourgeois world but to try and break through as far as possible to this community of popular readers, even though this may itself be breaking down as a result of the impact of modern technology.

At the time of *The Late Bourgeois World*'s publication this technology did appear triumphant, especially as all effective opposition to the South African state had been effectively smashed in the years 1960–65. Not only was it triumphant in space but it was rearranging the South African landscape with an impetus nothing short of demonic. As Elizabeth drives out of Johannesburg to see Bobo she notes:

> Caterpillar tractors were grouped as statuary in the landscaped gardens of the factory that made them. For more than a mile I was stuck behind a huge truck carrying bags of coal and the usual gang of delivery men, made blacker by gleaming coal dust, braced against the speed of the truck round a blazing brazier. They always look like some cheerful scene out of hell . . .

It is the African workers who make this system work, and whites are cut off from being able to forge any humanistic ties with them as a result of a system of entrenched racial segregation. Elizabeth sees the workings of a vibrant African popular culture as an outsider:

> They didn't care a dam either. There was a young man with a golfer's cap pulled down over his eyes who held on by one hand while he used the other to poke obscene gestures at the black girls. They laughed back or ignored him; no one seemed outraged. But when he caught my smile he looked right through me as though I wasn't there at all.[47]

While Toby Hood can mix socially quite freely in the lively world of the mid 1950s, Elizabeth meets Luke alone and secretly in the privacy of her flat. Here she is confronted with a moral dilemma that Toby did not have to face, whether to allow her grandmother's bank account to be used as a means for channelling foreign funds to the underground Pan Africanist Congress. She initially refuses, but she suspects that in the long run she will concede to this request for she finds her relationship with Luke far more honest, based as it is upon mutual self-interest, than the pretence of her relationship with Max:

> Luke knows what he wants, and he knows who it is he must get it from. A sympathetic white woman hasn't got anything to offer him – except the footing she keeps in the good old white reserve of banks and privilege. And in return he comes with the smell of the smoke of braziers in his clothes. Oh yes, and it's quite possible he'll make love to me, next time or some time.

That's part of the bargain. It's honest, too, like his vanity, his lies, the loans he doesn't pay back: it's all he's got to offer me.[48]

The novel leaves Elizabeth, like Molly Bloom in James Joyce's *Ulysses*, in a state of suspended consciousness in bed. The story makes a bid to escape from the mechanical notion of linear time. Like the American spacemen flying high up overhead, Elizabeth moves into a state of moral suspension, freed from the fixed moral norms of goodness and evil which had locked Max into a futile fight against the system of his parents. She can choose to help or not help Luke in his more engaged struggle against the system of racial oppression in South Africa; he is significantly a member of a more distinctly Africanist and anti-white movement than the more multiracial ANC. Her own autonomous heartbeat comes to symbolize a revolt against the fixed notion of Western linear progress:

There is no clock in the room since the red travelling clock that Bobo gave me went out of order, but the slow, even beats of my heart repeat to me, like a clock, afraid, alive, afraid, alive, afraid, alive ...[49]

Elizabeth comes to symbolize the individual's ability to transcend constricting social values and embody a search for moral autonomy and freedom from the burdens of history. She reflects the dilemmas facing many white liberal intellectuals in the face of advancing black nationalism. Gordimer herself toyed with the idea of leaving South Africa but resolved to stay, recognizing that whites would have to try and fit into the newly emerging African societies as immigrants to a new country. This would mean abandoning the "old impulses to leadership, and the temptation to give advice backed by the experience and culture of Western civilization – Africa is going through a stage when it passionately prefers its own mistakes to successes (or mistakes that are not its own)".[50]

It was a matter of having to adapt to a loss of power and the emergence of a new society not governed by the same rhythms and rationality as that of the West. This theme was to be taken up by a number of South African writers over the following years. It had, though, already been understood by another writer who had developed in a considerably different manner from Gordimer. As the next chapter shows, Laurens van der Post moved from a relatively liberal literary ideal in the 1930s to an attempt to remoralize British imperial power in post-war Africa through an understanding of the African "tribal" mentality and the figure of the "Bushman", the new "noble savage" on the continent.

6

LAURENS VAN DER POST
The Noble Savage and the Romantic Image of Africa

Laurens van der Post has been considerably neglected in the re-evaluation of South African literature in the post-war years. This can perhaps be seen as a result of van der Post's own rather ambivalent relationship to the mainstream English-speaking South African literary tradition. His family background was located in the Afrikaans-speaking rural community of the Orange Free State, where he was born in 1906, and in 1909 he was taken as a young child by his father to the Convention that established South African Union. He grew up in a period before the entrenchment of Afrikaner nationalism when there were efforts in the nascent white liberal intelligentsia to forge a bi-lingual culture rooted in English and Afrikaans.

In 1925 he helped found the short-lived literary journal *Voorslag* with William Plomer and Roy Campbell, which was devoted to the ideal of trying to establish a South African literary identity. Within a year, though, he became disillusioned with this project and visited Japan in the ship *Canada Maru*. He returned to South Africa and wrote for the *Cape Times* before moving to London to publish with the Hogarth Press his first novel, *In a Province*, in 1934.

At one level van der Post's early career showed all the makings of a bi-lingual white South African novelist. His subsequent writings never broke from the basic precepts of the inter-war colonial novel and, if he had chosen to stay inside South Africa, he might well have fitted into the tradition of liberal realism developed in the years after 1945 by writers such as Jack Cope and Alan Paton.[1]

Van der Post is interesting, however, for his early rejection of the general course of South African segregationist policies. In the wake of the publication of *In a Province* he spent the rest of the 1930s in Britain where he acted as a diplomatic correspondent for *The Times*, before signing up to fight in the British army in the Second World War. Combat in Ethiopia, North Africa and the Far East, where he was taken prisoner by the Japanese, did much to reinforce van der Post's generally cosmopolitan outlook. His story *The Seed and the Sower* (1963)[2] reveals a remarkable absence of bitterness over his brutal treatment as a prisoner of war and a strong determination to try to transcend cultural barriers and understand the outlook of his captors.

The experience of the Second World War and his service under Lord Mountbatten in Java after his release as a prisoner of war enabled van der Post to build close ties with sections of the British military and political establishment. He became rather estranged from South Africa, especially after strongly condemning Nationalist policies of apartheid after 1948. Van der Post favoured a system that provided some scope for African political advancement in a single political system, though he was sceptical that British policies of "partnership" in the Central African Federation in the 1950s were going fast enough. In *The Dark Eye in Africa* (1955) he supported Colonel David Stirling's Capricorn Africa Society which campaigned for a federation of British colonial territories in East and Central Africa under an enlightened system of British rule.

This involvement in British colonial politics in Africa in the twilight years of Empire rather alienated him from the hard-pressed South African liberal establishment, though friendships were kept up with such figures as Uys Krige, Roy Campbell and Alan Paton. But he wrote at a distance about South Africa and this is probably why he has not received more critical attention in South Africa itself. To some liberals his writings appeared to manifest a lack of sensitivity to the specific problems and dilemmas that South African writers faced in the years in which apartheid was being entrenched.

Van der Post championed the ideals of the British Commonwealth in the post-war years, though like a number of writers of this period, such as Nevil Shute, he began to realize increasingly that British imperial power and influence were on the decline.[3] In his travel writings, such as the Nyasaland journey narrated in *Venture to the Interior* (1952), he attempted to recreate the idea of an untapped African wilderness waiting to be explored by the intrepid traveller and adventurer. This was an increasingly unconvincing project in an era of rapidly expanding tourism and mass communications. The Africa of van der Post's childhood was rapidly disappearing by the 1950s and 1960s and this occasioned no small regret. He tried to move beyond being a writer of colonial nostalgia and has linked his ideal of an uncivilized African wilderness with a concern to recover values within metropolitan Western culture that appear to have been submerged by urbanization and industrialism.

This enterprise was partly made possible by his acquaintanceship with the psychologist Carl Gustav Jung through Ingaret Giffard, whom he married in 1949. His account of Jung's ideas *Jung and the Story of Our Time* (1976) marked a new phase of his writing career in which he began actively to champion the surviving communities of "Bushmen" (San) in the Kalahari in Botswana, seeing them as embodying many of the simple values of love and a collective sharing of goods which have been eroded in modern industrial societies. The heroic figure of the "Bushman" became the subject of two adventure novels, *A Story Like the Wind* (1972) and *A Far Off Place* (1974). The religious symbol of the Mantis in the extinct culture of the Southern Bushmen, narrated in the stories collected by W. H. I. Bleek in the nineteenth century, formed the basis for a link with the Christian ideal of love in *A Mantis Carol* (1975).

By the late 1970s van der Post had acquired a considerable reputation in Britain, both for his literary works and television documentaries on the San, and he received a knighthood in 1981. He is godfather to Prince William and a strong supporter of Mrs Thatcher, whose policies he championed in *A Walk with a White Bushman* (1986) as a means of morally regenerating British society through strong government.[4]

His writings on the San are also important for reviving the theme of the noble savage as a means of exploring more fully some of the basic values of Western society. David Maughan Brown has suggested that this recreation of the noble savage myth was also linked to a literature of counter-insurgency as the bush war in Southern Africa began to spread by the late 1960s and 1970s.[5] Van der Post, therefore, does have a relevance to contemporary issues of race and politics in South Africa.

The Noble Savage Ideal

The idea of the noble savage had an appeal for van der Post, for it had romantic and apparently anti-rational roots. The noble savage was a term coined by the poet Dryden in 1672. It developed in the late eighteenth and early nineteenth centuries as part of a romantic naturalism that championed childhood, scenery and peasant life. The noble-savage idea provided an ethical yardstick by which to evaluate European societies. It represented what Hoxie Neale Fairchild has termed "any free and wild being who draws directly from nature virtues which raise doubts as to the value of civilisation".[6] Just as the idea of a Golden Age enabled critical observers to imagine a state of primeval innocence, so the idea of a noble savage in distant places outside European society acted as a device to expose the corruption of civilized society. Some critics have pointed out that the noble-savage notion facilitated an advance of knowledge about non-Western societies, even if this did remain highly biased.[7] The idea had at its heart what Hayden White has termed a fetishization of man in that it ascribed to him super-human powers. This paradox derived from an ambiguity in the "noble-savage" concept since the very idea of nobility or aristocracy stands in opposition to the presumed wildness or savagery of other social orders. The noble savage represents not so much the elevation of the savage but the demolition of the nobility.[8]

The noble-savage myth served as part of a critique of European society as it was undergoing a transition to capitalism. This could take a variety of different forms. It offered in the eighteenth century what Peter J. Weston has termed a "potential radicalism" in some works of prose fiction that imagined native Indian societies in North America to be utopias free of economic exploitation. It also had tendencies towards a sentimental nostalgia that failed to challenge the dominant values of metropolitan society and ended up celebrating little more than a displaced rural idyll.[9] The radicalism contained in the noble savage concept was rather ambiguous since it was based on a primitivism hostile to luxury, corruption and the misuse of wealth. This could lead on occasions to a more sophisticated radicalism (such as that developed in Europe in the wake of the French revolution) or to a more reactionary sentimentalization of poverty as in the case of the later Wordsworth.[10]

In South Africa the myth of the noble savage initially emerged in the romantic nature poetry of William Burchell and Thomas Pringle in the first quarter of the nineteenth century. It was a notion that lived rather uneasily with the perceptions of African landscape by Boer and British colonizers.[11] There were slender possibilities for developing the noble-savage concept in Southern Africa on lines similar to North America. The Boer settlers trekked into the interior without the same kind of optimistic outlook of the North American pioneers. Theirs was a culture with only tenuous links to the eighteenth-century Enlightenment, and the African communities they encountered appeared too menacing to embody notions of autonomous reason. As J. M. Coetzee has pointed out, the Boer communities in Southern Africa could not conceive of the San and Hottentot societies they encountered as being in a state of innocence before the Fall, and so they did not think of them as being in any manner the originals of civilized man.[12]

The noble-savage figure that did emerge in South Africa was really the creation of what Northrop Frye has termed "manufactured romance" in the popular adventure fiction and romances of such imperialist writers as Rider Haggard and John Buchan. The finest example of the noble savage in this writing is probably Haggard's character, Umslopogaas, who combines a homespun wisdom with a sense of proud tradition and history. But he is eclipsed by more menacing figures embodying actual rather than noble savagery: Haggard's female witch, Gagool, in *King Solomon's Mines* and Buchan's sly black character, Laputa, in *Prester John*. These savage characters reflected the emergence of a racist Social Darwinism by the latter quarter of the nineteenth century, which located black figures on a lower rung of the great chain of being. This led to the widespread assumption that those aspects of reason that had been acquired, such as Laputa's American education, were only a thin veneer over a savage interior which would soon emerge once the character was set back in his native environment.[13]

The rise of segregationist ideology in South Africa by the early twentieth century also had little time for the idea of the noble savage. Some segregationist ideologues such as Dudley Kidd were willing to embrace the notion of an African rural idyll, since they saw African culture as reflecting a timeless form of primitive socialism. But Kidd had no time for any rebellion against the European idea of rationalism and progress and saw African societies moving gradually in the direction of European ones.[14] Segregationists, as chapter 1 pointed out, were mostly concerned to maintain social control over African societies through tribal forms of authority and were scarcely anxious to romanticize African rural life.[15] They did not see Africans as embodying Western concepts of reason, for they were viewed as easily led by political agitators and highly prone to waves of irrational emotion: Laputa, for example, leads an unsuccessful black revolt at the end of *Prester John*, while George Heaton Nicholls's novel *Bayete* (1923) also ends with a black revolt stirred up by a foreign-educated African leader, Nelson.[16]

A major problem confronting novelists trying to develop the imperial tradition in fiction represented by Haggard and Buchan was the degree to which it was possible to depict black characters moving from an apparently pre-rational, rural and tribal society towards a modern, civilized, rational and European one. The issue was particularly exemplified by the contentious issue of marriage and "miscegenation" between white and black in the years before and after Union at a time of periodic "black peril" scares.[17]

In some cases, such as in the novel *Margaret Harding* (1911) by Perceval Gibbon, an attempted solution to this dilemma is to portray the black lover, Kamis, as having a white European character based on an education he had received in England, despite his black skin.[18] This was a rather isolated case, and by the end of the First World War English-speaking South African writers usually perceived the issue in terms of a threat to the moral fabric of white colonial society. In the novels of Sarah Gertrude Millin, such as *Dark Water* (1921) and *God's Stepchildren* (1926), "miscegenation" was depicted as a process that would lead to a degenerate "half caste" progeny lacking cultural roots and undermining white rule.[19]

The Development of van der Post's Writing

William Plomer's novel *Turbott Wolfe* represented a brief rejection of this trend, and became the subject of mounting hostility from the white press following its publication in 1926. The novel exemplified the intrusion into South African literature in the 1920s of an outlook that was partly shaped by the somewhat misnamed jazz age and its interest in promoting black African culture. The literary milieu in which both Plomer and van der Post wrote was at this time one influenced by the modernism of T. S. Eliot and the Bloomsbury Group.[20] This modernism contained an apocalyptic vision of decay and decline from within that David Trotter has linked to a wider imperialist vision of white racial collapse. At various points in Eliot's

The Waste Land there is a linkage between decay in the urban metropolis and a vision of "hooded hordes swarming/Over endless plains" (the threat from Communist Russia). The post-war modernist movement in poetry did exhibit anxieties concerning possible imperial collapse, even though many of the writers concerned were anxious to distance themselves from mainstream imperialist writers such as Kipling who were by then seen as increasingly out of tune with the temper of the time.[21]

Similar themes intrude into van der Post's first novel, *In a Province*, in 1934. The novel concerns the relationship between a young Afrikaner, Johan van Brederpoel, and an African, Kenon Badiakgotla, in the city of Port Benjamin (Cape Town). Their encounter initially takes place in the urban setting of Port Benjamin. The novel at first envisages a cultural harmony occurring between the metropolis and surrounding mountain wilderness of nature where "van Brederpoel saw yellow squares of cultivated land, houses flanked by long avenues of oaks, stable and graceful witnesses of a fruitful co-operation of nature and man".[22] But this vision becomes undermined in the course of the novel.

Both the main characters look back nostalgically to their rural roots. In van Brederpoel's case this involves a memory of an African nurse and a teacher, Meneer Broecksma, at his father's farm of Vergelegen. Broecksma suggests to Johan's surprise that he consider sleeping with a black girl on the farm, Johanna, on the grounds that "every time I look at her, I feel that we lose a hell of a lot by being civilized. Look at her yourself and be inspired".[23] This is a suggestion that Johan does not take up.

It is Kenon's sexuality that is explored in the novel rather than Johan's who remains mostly uncommitted in the general action of the story. Kenon's career in the city follows the conventional "Jim comes to Jo'burg" genre of white South African literature, as he becomes crushed by the pressures of urban life and falls for the temptations of coloured prostitutes. The description of Kenon's departure for the city from the kraal of his father, Mlangene Badiakgotla, is a forerunner of *Cry the Beloved Country*. Van der Post avoided at this stage a romantic description of the African landscape in the idiom of tourist-agency literature. He asks his white middle-class readers if they know "that there are far too many people for so seemingly rich a soil, that often it does not rain, that the taxes are heavy, and that on the other side of the hill there is a Kenon setting out from his father's hut, envying you the speed of your car?".[24]

In a Province reveals at times an understanding of the economic forces that impel black migration, though van der Post hesitated to accept the idea of a fully urbanized black working-class movement. There is a tentative recognition of the black cultural renaissance of the post-war years, and in the boarding house that Johan stays one of the guests plays Paul Robeson singing "Old Man River". But van der Post does not get as far as exploring the idea of the "new African" that was at the basis of cultural debate amongst some black and white intellectuals in South Africa at this time.[25]

The novel, though, reflects some of the political activity in Cape Town in the early 1930s, following the splits in the International and Commercial Workers Union and the emergence of the Garveyite followers of "Professor" James Thaele in the Western Cape.[26] Van Brederpoel attends a meeting of the African Workers Union where a pretentious speech is made by an African leader, "the Doctor", who attacks white society for failing to be really Christian. The action is set within a wintry landscape described in terms reminiscent of a Munch painting:

> On the black and sodden bark of the trees appeared small explosions of green. Soon the avenues were covered in shade. The sky hardened and stretched taut over the town until life seemed imprisoned in a sphere of steel. An atmosphere, vivid but insubstantial like that of a dream, gathered over the houses. Wood and stone and steel lost their look of solidity and appeared only violent vibrations of colour on planes of smoke and vapours of heat.[27]

There is a mood of crisis and hollowness within the urban civilization itself, which the political challenge from the African Workers Union meeting only throws into sharper relief. Van Brederpoel is unable to shrug off the meeting like the other whites present and is driven to reflect on the forces that create both revolutions and churches. He realizes that he has lost faith in both and remembers a painting back in Vergelegen by the Dutch painter De Groot showing a street in Leyden on the banks of the Schildersgracht where a mother in eighteenth-century clothes hands her daughter a porcelain flask. The painting represented a secure and contented society by a painter whose own life was the opposite. The painter had nevertheless been able to give expression "to the salient characteristics of the life of his time – a life of which the calm and security were so strong that they annihilated, or placed in a tradition of order, his own sense of disorder".[28]

Van Brederpoel fails to resolve this dilemma before the dramatic ending of the novel. He rejects the overtures for a Marxist commitment from the white revolutionary figure he encounters, Burgess, who bears some similarity to contemporary revolutionaries in South Africa such as S. P. Bunting, Eddie Roux and the Trotskyite chemist, Max Gordon, who were active either organizing African trade unions or seeking a following in rural areas like the Transkei.[29]

The novel's hostility to the communists is almost equalled by its opposition to the activities of the white liberals on the Joint Councils. The "Bantu-European Approach Association" appears to represent racial discrimination in reverse and to consist of unattractive and anti-social types. The novel has the facets of a quest for meaning and purpose in a society that appears hollow.

At the end of the story van Brederpoel re-encounters Kenon in the town of Paulstad on the edge of Bambuland where Burgess seeks to organize the local African population. Van Brederpoel toys with the idea of buying a farm to avoid returning to Port Benjamin. He also sympathizes with the jaded figure of the local magistrate, Mags, who is out of tune with the conservative atmosphere of the local white citizenry. This aimlessness is finally resolved when Kenon and van Brederpoel die in a violent confrontation between the Africans organized in the African Workers Union and local police and white vigilantes. This vaguely existentialist act confirms Johan's humanism in opposition to the Marxism of revolutionaries such as Burgess who "sow out of their love of the oppressed the seeds of hate".[30]

Van der Post's first novelistic effort was in keeping with the inter-war white interest in "the native question" in South Africa and the question that a number of liberals asked, namely, how far was it possible for "traditional" Africans to adapt and survive in the modern city? The intrusion of an apocalyptic modernism in the novel was rather unusual for South African literature of this period, especially as South Africa was itself seen as part of the colonial "frontier" to which European modernist writers turned for the moral regeneration of metropolitan society.

Van der Post did develop this aspect of this writing, mainly because when he came to Britain with the manuscript of *In a Province* in the early 1930s he experienced rapid disillusion with one of the fountainheads of modernism in the form of the Bloomsbury Group. Few of the group, he later recollected, "seemed to me to be interesting in the sense of being on course with life and their own natures". He found himself revolting against the apparently contrived world of London literary intellectuals in the 1930s where aesthetics had become a religion.[31]

The years up to the outbreak of World War Two were rather empty ones for van der Post. His character Jacques Cellier probably spoke for his outlook at this time in the story *The Seed and the Sower* when the essential hollowness of his existence came to an end with the war itself which would "soon put an end to this shadow boxing that I had endured for so many years. Yes, I even felt a kind of grim satisfaction at the thought."[32] The experience of armed conflict provided the possibility for moral repurification after the dead years of the 1930s. Van der Post did not see the conflict as hastening the collapse of European imperialism and felt, at the end of the war, that white colonizers had a civilizing mission to perform. He was sent by the British government to advise the Dutch government at the end of the war to abandon any hopes of returning as straightforward colonizers to the Dutch East Indies (Indonesia). But he appears to have believed in a continuing white colonizing mission in at least part of these far-flung islands. He later confessed to his friend, Leif Egeland, then South African High Commissioner in London, to feeling "v. sad" over Java, "because I fear a 'white race' has flung away quite shamelessly a magnificent opportunity there. I do not think much can be done except by God + time to put the situation right."[33]

Van der Post was deeply struck by the moral cohesion of Japanese culture while being a prisoner of war in Java. He had originally become acquainted with Japanese society as a result of the visit in *Canada Maru* in 1926 and this proved an invaluable aid when it came to understanding the harsh conditions as a captive. He saw Japan as a society which had acquired modern Western technology before it had gained the psychology to handle it, though the surviving strength of its warrior and samurai traditions he found deeply impressive in their ability to provide meaning and order in life. Japanese culture, as Ruth Benedict wrote in her seminal work *The Chrysanthemum and the Sword* after the war, appeared to have attained a balance of martial and aesthetic virtues in striking contrast to the West.[34] Van der Post was especially moved by the "heroic" idea of love, in contrast to the "sloppy debased" view of it in the West. The autobiographical figure of John Lawrence in *The Seed and the Sower* considered that the Japanese had "romanticized death and self destruction as no other people. The romantic fulfillment of the national ideal, of the heroic thug of tradition, was often a noble and stylised self destruction in a selfless cause".[35]

Van der Post avoided any worshipping of military heroism. The strength and tenacity of the Japanese warrior tradition was really another yardstick to evaluate a declining British imperial power. With this outlook in the late 1940s and 1950s, a new phase in van der Post's writing career commenced as he joined battle against the radical critics of empire in Britain.

The Cold War, Decolonization and New Literary Departures

The ending of van der Post's military career in 1948 occurred at the same time as the onset of the Cold War in Europe. Demobilization allowed him to return to studying the role of myth in European history which had initially attracted his attention before 1939 when he had begun a book on the role of mythology in Hitler's rise to power, a process he termed "the mythological dominant in history".[36] This interest in myth became broadened in 1949 by the start of an acquaintanceship with the psychologist Carl Gustav Jung through his wife Ingaret Giffard, who was finishing her training at the time at the C. G. Jung Institute in Zurich.

Jung's ideas fascinated van der Post by their preoccupation with European penetration of a supposedly savage African continent and the potential for savagery in civilized man once the boundaries of a rational society cease to exist. Gloria Young has pointed out the strong parallels between Jung's *Memoirs, Dreams and Reflections*, recalling a journey to Africa in 1925, and that of Joseph Conrad's *Heart of Darkness*, based on a visit to the Congo in 1890. Both works are obsessed by the primitive and the notion that the civilized traveller or adventurer faces the risk of lapsing back to a savage atavism unless strong control is maintained over civilized behaviour.[37]

Jung used the idea of a primitive mentality as the basis for a theory of the "collective unconsciousness". This drew upon Freud's idea that there were "archaic remnants" in the unconscious mind, which surfaced in dreams. The components of the collective unconsciousness could have both positive and negative aspects, and Jung impressed van der Post by his assertion that many of the troubles of "modern man" arose from the divorce between his instinctive and primitive self, which he had come to despise and repress.[38] This idea contained a number of assumptions about black African culture which was seen as essentially prehistoric. The consciousness of black African adults became equated with that of white children, while the black consciousness was likened to the white unconscious. Jung had a deep fear of the supposed irrationality of black people, while the process of dreaming became a kind of psychological laboratory in which the "modern" and "civilized" man discovers his primitive past, one which could be equated with the actual state of contemporary black African society.[39]

Van der Post shared many of Jung's assumptions concerning racial differences, especially the idea – born of the work of the French ethnologist Levy-Bruhl – that African society was based on a "primitive mentality".[40] Van der Post was, nevertheless, emphatically opposed by the early 1950s to the policy of apartheid and he began to champion policies that would end racial discrimination.

Van der Post's ideas became reinforced at this time by debate over the nature of the Mau Mau movement in Kenya in the early 1950s. Opinion in Britain became divided between a conservative group of writers who broadly shared the white-settler image of the movement as an expression of an atavistic tribal savagery and a liberal group of writers who supported a more sympathetic view of the issue, seeing it as a result of discriminatory policies which had dispossessed the Kikuyu of their land. Both groups tended to see the movement as less of a peasnt insurrection against colonial rule than as a relapse to a more primitive form of behaviour. This view was reinforced by the publication by the government in Kenya in 1954 of a pamphlet by Dr L. C. Carothers entitled *The Psychology of Mau Mau*. Carothers saw the movement emerging as the result of a collapse of the supportive influences of traditional Kikuyu tribal authority and the survival of traditional "magic".[41]

Van der Post interpreted Mau Mau in a similar manner in a book, *The Dark Eye of Africa*, in 1955, based upon a talk given to The Psychological Club in Zurich the previous year. He saw the movement as exemplifying a wider crisis in which Africans had been cut adrift from their cultural roots. Mau Mau was, he declared, a result of the African way of life becoming discredited under colonial rule with no "honourable alternative" being put in its place. The movement was "a desperate attempt on the part of the Kikuyu to prevent ... a loss of national soul".[42] The "European" in Africa was "blindly and ignorantly provoking all these events in Africa because, in his deepest nature, he is provoking them in himself" since "European man" had been effectively at war with himself since the Reformation".[43]

Racism was interpreted by van der Post as a product of psychological repression within European culture rather than of the structures of African colonial rule. He acknowledged that this racism had intensified since the first arrival of Dutch settlers in South Africa in the seventeenth century, but was in essence a reflection of inner fears which threatened the stability of the continent unless directly confronted. Racism was more of a "black man's burden" than a "white man's burden" since it was black Africans who were having to bear the "terrible unconscious projection" of "modern European man".[44] He was concerned to confront the irrational aspects of modern culture and berated the critics of colonial rule on the left in British politics for failing to acknowledge this. He complained bitterly to Leonard Woolf, his publisher at the Hogarth Press, of the lack of thoroughness of the Labour Party's colonial experts. "They do not seem to me to worry very much about facts, these boys," he wrote, "and the sort of people whom they send abroad go not to find African eggs to bring back to their political incubation but merely take along an egg of their own to hatch en route."[45]

By the mid 1950s van der Post found himself becoming increasingly out of tune with liberal opinion in Britain on colonial issues. He refused to acknowledge that there was an African nationalist challenge to European colonial rule and saw the issues confronting the African continent eclipsed by a wider set of cosmic and global forces. Some liberal critics such as Thomas Hodgkin in the *Spectator* were impressed by the comparison van der Post drew between the white subjugation of blacks in Africa and the Japanese subjugation of European prisoners of war in World War Two.[46] But it was by no means clear what van der Post's criticisms implied for future colonial policy.

In the novel *Flamingo Feather* (1955) van der Post tried to awaken British public opinion to the dangers of a lethargic colonial policy in the Cold War. The novel marked a lurch towards more traditional kinds of imperial adventure fiction in the vein of Rider Haggard and John Buchan. The story concerns the unravelling in 1948 by a gentleman adventurer Pierre de Beauvilliers of a Russian-inspired plot to foment a black revolution in Africa through a fictional people known as the Takwena – a broad amalgam of Zulu- and Xhosa-speakers in South Africa. The murder of a member of the Takwena royal family, Kawabuzayo, outside Beauvilliers's home in Cape Town leads to a scheme to draw back the superstitious Takwena to their ancestral homeland through the symbol of a pink flamingo's feather, which indicates a powerful traditional dream of reuniting the divided people. Beauvilliers's adventures take him to Durban where he uncovers a Russian plan to land arms on the East coast of Africa to aid the black uprising, as well as the use of members of the Takwena royal elite by the Russian conspirators Harkov and Colonel John Sandysse who was captured by the Russians in Manchuria during World War Two and who proves to be a double agent.

Beauvilliers is an authority on the customs and culture of the Takwena and is engaged in a study *The Mind and Myth of the Amangtakwena*. He sees the failure by colonial policy-makers to understand the degree to which the Takwena have been excluded from colonial society as the explanation for their resort to oathing ceremonies. Van der Post curiously refuses to acknowledge at any point in the novel that South Africa is an independent state and it appears as just another British colonial possession complete with governor and district commissioners! The British mission Beauvilliers arrives at, to warn of the impending insurrection, seems oblivious of the apparent dangers and is snowed under by bureaucratic inertia. It is the heroic lone figure of Beauvilliers who stops the insurrection when he reaches the royal kraal of the Takwena and who convinces the king that the dream which the Russians are trying to impose on the Takwena through their embittered follower, Ghinza, and the *Umbombulino* (medicine man) is false. The dream that had been dreamed by the royal ancestor 'Nkulixowe was not one in which he was black, as the *Umbombulino* argues, for he was yellow and neither white nor black. Ghinza and his followers commit suicide once the truth is revealed and the attempted insurrection collapses.

Flamingo Feather has many facets of a *Boys Own* adventure, but can be read at another level as exploring many of the anxieties of the British upper-class imperial establishment. It appeals to a Tory imagination with its strong sense of social hierarchy and natural fitness to rule. Beauvilliers is a hero who knows the African terrain thoroughly and has loyal servants such as Ticky and the Somali Said. He is skilled in bushcraft and shoots rhinoceros, hippopotamus and leopard. Van der Post appears to hope that this social order can be put on a newer and sounder footing in order to prevent the prospect of a race war engulfing the subcontinent in which fifteen million armed Africans would confront two million whites. The plan to overthrow white rule even includes a plot to spread amongst the black servants millions of poison-filled cigarette lighters in order to kill their white employers! Beauvilliers has despaired of appealing to the sentiments of the whites south of the Limpopo and looks more to a change of heart in British political circles, though the Colonial Service appeared to be "rapidly becoming a kind of museum, artificially preserving dead values and stuffed attitudes".[47]

The novel strongly hinted at the survival of an African "primitive mentality". It began with a quotation from Levy-Bruhl, "Le rêve est le vraie dieu des primitifs", and saw African superstition as an inevitable facet of their living closer to the natural world than whites. Africans were also prone to manipulation by well-organized Russian communists who had schooled some of their leaders in a special university in Tashkent for ideological subversion in the West. The communists themselves, though, were without any real belief of their own, since this had "been cut so short at its instinctive roots by their coldly materialistic and intellectually willed Marxist dogma: a belief only in the dubiousness of all belief".[48] Even the communists were not credited with the original idea of the plot since they were tribal Mongols and Tartars; it came from an embittered German refugee, Lindelbaum, who had twice had his businesses burned down in anti-German riots in South Africa.

The novel urges its readers to restore their faith in Western values in the context of the ideological struggle of the Cold War. It is deeply suspicious of liberal appeals to reason, considering this to overlook the irrational and instinctive elements in the human make-up. The central character, Beauvilliers, is left at the end pondering whether the Great Trek of his Boer ancestors cannot be continued in the modern era in another dimension, so as to extend it from "world without" to "world within".[49]

Van der Post's novel was written at a time of re-evaluation in British imperial policy, though before the rush to decolonize in the years after Harold Macmillan's "Winds of Change" speech in Cape Town in 1960. It was written during a period of rising African nationalism and Africans scarcely emerge as "noble savages". The novel marks a regression from *In a Province*, since it has no interest in Africans in the urban setting. Neither does it see rural African society as a yardstick by which to judge the failings and limitations of the European metropolis. The Africans are either menacing or gullible in the story and their culture is prone to flaws, since both the keeper of the people's memory and the *Umbombulino* interpret the dream of 'Nkulixowe wrongly. Their culture may only be potentially of importance if the Takwena can be reunited under the leadership of the moderate and "responsible" figure of the existing king, and the bad (racial) dream replaced by a non-racial yellow one.

Flamingo Feather was not taken especially seriously even by critics on the right. James Stern in *Encounter* considered it an excellent school-boy story and praised the description of the landscape and wildlife. He felt that he might have admired Beauvilliers as a character in his teens but now felt him somewhat of a prig and know-all with a patronizing attitude to those less fortunate than himself.[50]

Van der Post's depiction of static African societies in Southern Africa began to be eclipsed by the late 1950s by a more informed and mature public opinion in the metropolitan societies of Europe. This was now more familiar with the anthropological research that had been conducted amongst various African communities over the previous four decades, though anthropologists themselves were divided over whether religion and mythology were examples of "pre-logical" modes of thought compared to scientific rationality.[51]

Van der Post looked nostalgically back to African societies as the modern exemplification of pre-rational modes of thinking. This became the base for his critique of scientific modes of reasoning especially when applied to human affairs. He rejected the very notion of a social science and the "phony new disciplines" that had been created in new universities.[52] He linked these with collectivist political ideology and became fascinated by the figure of the Bushman (San) as a means of asserting a more individualistic ethic in the apparently conformist societies of the West.

In Search of the San

For van der Post, the Bushman contained a vital simplicity and closeness to nature, whilst at the same time he was not such a threat to the white colonial presence in Southern Africa as black African societies. In *The Lost World of the Kalahari* (1958; the subject of a documentary film) and *The Heart of the Hunter* (1961) he began to campaign for the preservation of the San culture in Botswana and to oppose schemes for the economic development of the region which he had himself supported a decade earlier.[53] The Bushman needed to be kept as far as possible isolated from contamination by the West, for "he was essentially so innocent and natural a person that he had only to come near us for a radio-active fall-out from our unnatural world to produce a fatal leukaemia of the spirit."[54] Preserving San culture was part of a general interest in conservation of flora and fauna, for the Bushmen were "part of the natural fullness of the life of our continent".[55] Van der Post was grateful that recruitment of the San by the South African Chamber of Mines was terminated.

The anthropological study of San culture and history at the time van der Post began his explorations was extremely limited. Most research work over the previous three decades had focused on African societies such as the Bemba, Pondo and Lovedu, and few writers had bothered to concern themselves with San culture. The Bushmen societies in the Kalahari appeared to be a sad remnant of much wider settlement that had been driven back in the face of both black and white settlement. The most important work had been done on the San language by the scholar W. H. I. Bleek in the nineteenth century together with a collection of folklore gathered from a group of San prisoners in Cape Town. These had been published posthumously in 1911 as *Specimens of Bushman Folklore* by his sister-in-law Lucy Lloyd.[56] The volume appeared at a time of a renewal of interest in the San, following the posthumous publication in 1905 of George William Stow's *The Native Races of South Africa*. This work was based on Stow's extensive work in ethnology that was begun soon after his arrival in South Africa in 1843 and was strongly influenced by Victorian evolutionary ideas. The volume took a generally catastrophic view of the Bushmen in South Africa who were seen as irreparably doomed to die out in the face of the advance of stronger races.[57] Bleek's volume appeared to confirm the same tendency. In the introduction the historian George McCall Theal considered the collected stories to reveal "a people in the condition of early childhood", though he acknowledged that "in the great chain of human life on this earth the pygmy savages represented a link much closer to the modern European end than to that of the first beings worthy of the name of men."[58]

The stories from Bleek's collection, together with an additional volume *The Mantis and his Friends* (1923), made a powerful impression on van der Post during his boyhood and early teens. Some were read to him by a San nurse on his mother's and grandfather's farms in the Orange Free State. It was a period when few writers bothered to take any notice of the San, the one notable exception being W. C. Scully, who reported Bleek's work sympathetically.[59]

The figure of the "Bushman", however, got lost in van der Post's early fictional work due to his enthusiasm for black African culture in the 1920s while working for *Voorslag*. *In a Province* reflected the poor image that the "Bushman" had at this time as Kenon insults a Coloured girl calling her a "Bushman girl".[60] *Flamingo Feather* exhibited no concern for San culture either and it was not until his later fiction starting with the two novels *A Story Like the Wind* and *A Far Off Place* together with the exploration of the life of Hans Taaibosch in the United States in *A Mantis Carol* (1975) that the real interest in the San begins.

Van der Post's view of San culture was heavily shaped by the work of Bleek, though this led to a number of distortions. The "Bushmen" were credited with having a religious divinity based on the insect known as the praying mantis, though this has been more recently shown to have been the case only amongst the now extinct Southern Bushman whom Bleek interviewed in the nineteenth century and not to the communities in the Kalahari. Furthermore, the "Bushmen" emerge from Bleek's story collections as rather puritanical figures with little or no interest in sex. This may simply have been due to Bleek's own Victorian prudery leading him to fail to record bawdy stories that more recent folklorists have noted in San story-telling.[61]

The mantis became a central symbol of San religious thought for van der Post, as it appeared to embody the spirit of creation. In the Bleek collection, Mantis is married to the dassie Kauru and has three children by her together with an adopted daughter, the porcupine.[62] In another story the Mantis appears sitting between the horns of a hartebees, a creature whom the Bushman likened to the mantis due to the shape of its long neck and head. The intermarriage and union of such different creatures appeared to van der Post to represent "the image of the great togetherness of life and time, of the whole which our existence on earth experiences only in part".[63] To this extent, the Bushman myth appeared to embody the Jungian notion of the collective unconscious, and van der Post significantly dedicated *The Heart of the Hunter* to Jung.

This interpretation of San mythology shaped van der Post's two adventure novels, *A Story Like the Wind* (1972) and *A Far Off Place* (1974). These recount the experiences of a young *Boys Own*-type of hero, the thirteen-year-old François Joubert, somewhere in the "remote interior" of Central Africa. François is forced to rely much upon his own devices in the face of great adversity in the form of some Chinese-trained guerrillas who seek to overthrow white rule in Southern Africa. He befriends the Bushman Xhabbo whom he rescues from a trap and it is Xhabbo who warns François of the impending guerrilla attack. François is left with only his faithful dog, Hintza, and the daughter of an English baronet, Nonnie, and has to flee across the Kalahari to Namibia in order to warn of the impending incursion. The story is like *Flamingo Feather* in its failure to understand African nationalism: the guerrillas are an amorphous group with no social roots and led by two marginalized and embittered European revolutionaries, one a Buchan-type Scotsman from Glasgow and the other a Frenchman who had formerly fought in Indo-China (training usually associated with mercenaries in Africa). The Africans van der Post feels most at ease in depicting are the faithful servants on the farm of Hunters Drift, such as the Matabele Bamuthi, who dies in the massacre committed by the guerrillas.

The Africans are also depicted as deeply superstitious and subject to manipulation through a myth that records that thousands of miles to the west of Hunters Drift there is an ancient tree that is reputedly the tree of life. The tree was reputedly in the keeping of a "white female presence" as had been depicted in the Bushman painting in Namibia, popularly known as the "white lady of the Brandberg".[64] François hears from the white hunter Mopani Theron that the tree is the nearest that the African peoples had to a common religious temple and from which they can receive their commandments.

It is this legend which the guerrillas try to use to foment a black revolution by forcing a Portuguese woman, who was kidnapped in Angola, to sing near it as if the songs come from the tree itself. François encounters the tree in his flight west from Hunters Drift and the prophecy is ended as the woman gets mistakenly killed by the guerrillas. Through careful bushcraft and survival in the desert with the help of Xhabbo François manages to reach the Namibia coast and alert a British naval contingent.

Van der Post managed to intertwine in the two novels a conventional imperial adventure story with a rather more innovative formula based on the noble-savage figure of the Bushman Xhabbo, whose name derives from Bleek's *Specimens of Bushman Folklore*. Xhabbo embodies the ideal of living in harmony with the forces of nature. François is able to speak Bushman and uses the language to communicate with his dog, Hintza. François is reassured by an old Bushman, Koba, that "all the animals, birds, reptiles and insects of Africa, and also all the plants, understood the onomatopoeic Bushman tongue".[65] François also sympathizes with and understands Bushman customs and folklore, quite unlike the African workers on the farm. The novels project an alternative pattern of human relationships which transcend the appeals of nationalism and political ideology, which are seen as narrowly prejudiced and discriminatory. These relationships are pivoted around a rigid set of gender distinctions. Van der Post emphasizes universal tendencies towards domesticity and maternalism. Luciana and Nuin-Tara, the woman of Xhabbo (named after a story in Bleek of Ko-G!Nuin-Tara, who was "wife of the dawn's heart star") both perform domestic roles for the men, even in the desert while fleeing from the pursuing guerrillas.

The novels reveal a certain uncertainty with the traditional forms of political leadership. The story is no longer focused on the archetypal gentleman adventurer, as in *Flamingo Feather*, for it is only the young boy François who appears to recognize the full extent of the danger at hand. The traditional figures of authority fail to be of any assistance: François's paternalistic father gets sick and dies in Cape Town; the game-hunter Mopani Theron disappears and only re-emerges to congratulate François on his achievements at the end of the story; Luciana's father, the eccentric English aristocrat Sir James Archibald Sinclair Monckton, is caught asleep by the guerrillas and murdered. Compared to *Flamingo Feather* the novels indicate a growing anxiety with the state of the governing mind and its apparent inability to recognize the dangers from African revolution or communist penetration of Africa. Van der Post hints at the need for a new learning process, exemplified by François and Luciana being left together at the end of the story, realizing the need to stay on the farm in Africa and go to university to get proper training.

The novels were rather an anachronistic hangover from the Second World War since their depiction of guerrilla activity has a decidedly dated quality. These are not guerrilla units equipped to fight on a hit-and-run bush war, but a large mass complete with lorries and aircraft ready for a full-scale conventional assault on white power in Southern Africa. This appears to derive from fears in some political quarters (both left and right) in the West in the 1960s that the continuing entrenchment of apartheid would lead to a full-scale race war.[66] Van der Post's novels lack any form of sophisticated insight into differing class and ethnic patterns in Southern African societies and reproduce a rather crude set of stereotypes concerning African tribalism and superstition.

Van der Post's employment of the noble-savage theme continued in the 1970s with the short story *A Mantis Carol* in which he explored the career of the Bushman Hans Taaibosch in the United States. The story refuses to see Taaibosch as becoming significantly urbanized in any form in the United States but depicts him as a "child of the desert" complete with "pointed Pan-like ears". From the photographs that were taken of Taaibosch while he was alive in the US in the 1920s and 1930s van der Post considers that he was "one of the truest of true Bushman".[67] Unlike Xhabbo, Taaibosch is depicted as embodying the theme of love in its more Christian form, for as a child of nature he embodied the exhortation "to become children again if we were ever to find the way to the united Kingdom called Heaven".[68] The apparent survival of this "natural man" in the urban wilderness of the New York metropolis appeared to van der Post to be a demonstration that humanity was not simply a product of its environment. Van der Post also saw him as an example of human individuality in contrast to the collective pressures of modern life. Taaibosch embodied the natural self which is imperilled in modern man and his existence in the US a confirmation that,

> this love, this improbable calling for wholeness in life, had to be experienced first in loneliness and isolation by a single heart and lived out in the small round of one unique life, however powerless and absurd it may appear to itself, before the great impersonal and arrogant collective spirit of our time would be moved to imitate it.[69]

A Literature of Exile

Van der Post's work can be read as in part a literature of exile. His autobiography entitled *And Yet Being Someone Other* indicates a conscious attempt to construct an alternative identity to that of his white South African birth.[70] The memory of the bushman stories of his childhood became the base for the construction of a myth of man of nature, though these were themselves stories of exile told by prisoners such as Xhabbo in the Cape Town jail.

The construction of the noble-savage myth marked, though, a sentimentalization of the African terrain and the San people. The "potential radicalism" of *In a Province*, with its concern for black African identity in the urban environment of South Africa, became transformed into the imperial-adventure formulae of the post-war novels. Van der Post's writing serves as a recent example of the adventure-fiction tradition which Martin Green has posited as the popular alternative to the Leavisite great tradition in modern English literature.[71] Earlier writing, such as *In a Province*, tried to emulate the literary modernism of T. S. Eliot and Bloomsbury. However, by the late 1930s van der Post became more preoccupied with the role of myth in contemporary Western life. The post-war fascination with Jungian psychology became combined with a concern for a revitalization of Western values in the period of the Cold War. In the 1950s, he became interested in the idea of the noble savage as part of a more wide-ranging attack on both collectivist values in metropolitan society and a concern for a revival of the lone individual adventurer.

This has been, therefore, an archaic romanticism that has sought to adapt the genre of imperial-adventure fiction to the late twentieth century. Van der Post sees Western culture as containing within it the salvation of the rest of the world precisely because "Western man has the experience – through the experience of empire".[72] The association of this genre with white racial superiority has been down-played, though characters such as Beauvilliers and François reflect themes of traditional imperial-adventure fiction such as courage, heroism and innate, as opposed to intellectual, intelligence. These themes, however, have survived rather uneasily in a late twentieth-century urban culture that is pivoted so strongly around the mass media. His literary work may prove to be enduring for other reasons. Van der Post writings serve as an important early example of a concern for the retrieval of the "natural" from the wilderness of the urban jungle. His novels are probably read more for their descriptions of the African landscape and wildlife than for their contrived plots and anachronistic heroism.

The lone character of Hans Taaibosch is also rather too remote a noble savage to stimulate an interest similar to earlier noble-savage figures based upon black African societies in the eighteenth and nineteenth centuries. Van der Post's championing of the San may be comparable to similar work to preserve South American Indian cultures such as Peter Matthiessen's *At Play in the Fields of the Lord* or the film *The Emerald Forest*. He has more recently admitted his failure to take sufficient account of anthropological study of San culture.[73] Rapid changes in the last few years, in which many "Bushmen" in Angola and Namibia have been employed by the South African Defence Force have contributed to a demythologizing of San society and culture.

Van der Post's depiction of both African and San people is thus deeply flawed by an imperialism that fails to see them as anything other than an "other" to the white European colonial adventurers. His work falls into a colonial tradition that began to be challenged by white liberal writers in the early 1960s. The black writing that has emerged in South Africa in the last thirty years also marks a reaction to the proprietorial view of nature contained in the genre of imperial adventurer fiction. To this extent van der Post's work is as anachronistic as the Western in the United States of recent years – a genre similarly based on the conquest of landscape.[74] Its depiction of African nationalism as a superstitious force manipulable by international communism looks increasingly irrelevant to the contemporary politics of South Africa following the end of the Cold War, though it bore some relationship to the South African Defence Force's notion of a "total onslaught" by communist-backed guerrillas against white power in the late 1970s and early 1980s. Van der Post's ostensibly non-racial ideals will still be difficult to relate to the cultural climate of a post-apartheid South Africa, for they will be perceived as the product of a former British imperial imagination that became marginalized from South African politics and society in the years after 1948.

7
THE DECLINE OF THE IDEA OF CIVILIZATION

Origins of the Idea

White political ideology in South Africa during the first half of the twentieth century was frequently characterized by a concern to protect "civilization" within the society from the threat of "savagery" or "barbarism" without. The opposition of these two notions in political thought provided a form of intellectual direction over the question of "native policy" and the degree to which Africans should be incorporated into a common South African society.

The idea that South Africa was a "civilization" enabled politicians and intellectuals to relate their goals and ideals to a wider set of cultural traditions, that of "Western civilization", of which South Africa was seen as an offshoot. The notion of "civilization" was well implanted in Western political thought. As its meaning changed so too did the opposing form to it, "barbarism", which had been initially associated with unabashed primitivism. The "barbarian" was usually seen as a savage warrior who intruded on the peace of agricultural communities, most classically in Central Asia.[1] By the nineteenth century, though, it acquired a new meaning in terms of being a state outside the cultural space created by European imperial expansion.

In Europe and America many intellectuals shared the view that "Western civilization" was part of a broad historical process that was the culmination of earlier civilizations stretching back through the

Middle Ages to Greece and Rome and to the earliest patterns of human settlement in Egypt and the Middle East.[2] From the 1920s and 1930s a different view began to emerge based on the work of such theorists as Oswald Spengler and Arnold Toynbee. Civilization was now seen not as a continuous development but the product of distinct societies, each with their own separate identity. This newer view began to undermine the idea that Europe was the "microcosm" of an expanding world economy destined to transform all other civilizations into its own image.[3] This revisionist notion began to find its way into some English-speaking South African thought.

By the early twentieth century the Victorian imperial idea that there was a simple hierarchy of cultures began to be challenged by a cultural relativism which stressed the equal worth of separate cultural traditions. This owed much to the emergence of anthropology and the considerable impact of such travel writers and observers as Mary Kingsley and Flora Shaw.[4] In South Africa, a debate emerged – particularly amongst English-speaking writers – which reflected this shift in thought in Europe. From the latter part of the nineteenth century, a number of writers began looking to the emergence of a distinctly South African "civilization" which had European roots but would take off in a rather different manner to the societies of the European metropolis.

The idea was frequently infused by a strong dose of Darwinian evolutionism. It became a driving force behind much political debate in South Africa in the years from Union up to World War Two. Thereafter, it entered a period of growing crisis as a number of writers and intellectuals tried to disconnect the notion of "civilization" from the apartheid policies of the South African state.

To many white English-speaking South Africans until comparatively recently the term "civilization" has remained important for showing the relative fragility of white power in the Southern African subcontinent and the need for strong political will to maintain it. As earlier chapters have shown, many of South Africa's English-speaking intellectuals had been educated in classics earlier in the century and there was the continual temptation of comparing the rise and possible fall of white rule with earlier civilizations that had risen and fallen in the past. This classical view was not shared by all opinion-formers in South Africa and indeed became steadily undermined in the course of the entrenchment of racial segregation. But it provided a focal point of reference for political argument through its theory of historical catastrophe. Political debate tended to take on some of the features of the prophetic as it became determined by what the literary critic Frank Kermode has termed a "sense of an ending" and the warning of a possible future "end-dominated crisis".[5]

The classical ideal of civilization embraced the notion of historical progress and the humanizing of the political sphere with an ethic of wholeness at a time when the society appeared to be polarizing into opposing fragments. It buttressed the notion of a movement towards greater modernity and this, by the inter-war years, became linked with a growing vogue for science and technological change. To this extent the ideal performed an important role in the evolution of white South African political thought in the first half of the twentieth century.

The Classical Model

The extension of English-language culture to South Africa as a result of the imperial connection did much to reinforce the idea that the emergent white society could be seen in terms of a model of classical "civilization". This ideal had been one that had been much favoured among the intellectual aristocracy of Victorian Britain where the classical curriculum known as *Literae Humaniores* and Greats had been established at Oxford in 1830. Classical culture provided an historical yardstick by which to evaluate the worth of British imperial objectives and this ideal progressively seeped through into the colonial setting. Cecil Rhodes, for example, took a fellow of All Souls, Rochfort Maguire, on an expedition to Lobengula in 1893 in the hope of teaching classics to "Matabele" Thompson on the way.[6] Rhodes's often quoted dictum, "Equal Rights For All Civilised Men", became an ideal that many English-speaking liberals would look back to in their efforts to contain the segregationist impulse in the course of the twentieth century.

In its late Victorian form, the idea of "civilization" was often closely linked to an expansionist British imperialism. The Boer republics were frequently depicted by British imperial ideologues as locked into a static form of life derived from the seventeenth century and standing in sharp contradiction to the modernizing forces of mining capitalism. Percy Fitzpatrick described Paul Kruger in the propagandist tract *The Transvaal From Within* (1896) as "the old Dopper President, hemmed in once more by the hurrying tide of civilisation, from which his people have fled for generations – trying to fight both fate and nature – standing up to them a tide as resistless as the eternal sea".[7]

Not all writers and opinion-formers shared Fitzpatrick's clear imperial commitment to force the Boer republics to submit to British imperial domination. The republics were not seen as necessarily opposing capitalist development. The travel writer and explorer Francis Younghusband considered that the Boer society of the Transvaal had the advantage of not having a class of hereditary rulers who would block social and economic change. Younghusband predicted that a process of amalgamation would occur between Boers and British settlers which would prevent the society remaining locked in the seventeenth century.[8] The traveller, naturalist and colonial official Harry Johnstone went even further. Inter-breeding between Boer and British populations appeared to provide the splendid opportunity for a "civilized" British race to fuse with a "savage" – but white – African one to produce a fit white African race that could continue the imperial enterprise in Southern Africa:

> The descendants of the continental branch of the Anglo-Saxon race have had the advantage over us of two hundred years' previous colonisation of the Southern extremity of Africa. Their physical constitutions have adapted to the climate; on the other hand, it must be frankly stated, that in the outlying districts these South African dutchmen have relapsed to some extent into the condition of magnificent white savages. . . . To their land have come the English – restless, active, highly intelligent, and civilised almost beyond any other nation except perhaps France. The fusion of the two races must surely result in the great white race which is to dominate Africa.[9]

Johnstone's emphasis upon racial engineering producing a new white African nationalism overlooked the other increasingly contentious issue of the period, that of inter-racial "miscegenation". Many English-speaking writers saw the emergence of a mixed race "Coloured" population as threatening this nationalist project. The novelist Olive Schreiner championed the inter-breeding of Boers and British settlers but wrote virulently against the emergence of a "half-caste" race in South Africa, which she linked to social danger and disruption, since "without nationality, traditions or racial ideals, his [the halfcaste's] position is even today not analogous in South Africa with that of any folk of any pure-bred race".[10]

Some imperial advocates such as the scholar and statesman James Bryce did see South African society eventually leading to a fusion of sorts between white and black races. Unlike Fitzpatrick and Johnstone, Bryce saw gold-mining in South Africa as only a temporary phenomenon and he looked in the long term to a future when the mines would be exhausted. The pattern of advance of civilization would, he considered, be slow, though he envisaged the power of tribal chiefs as vanishing within fifty years, and after a hundred years, or even longer, the society would be relatively free of inter-ethnic conflict. By that time it would be "filled by a large coloured population, tolerably homogeneous, using the same language, having forgotten its ancient tribal feuds, and not, like the people of India, divided by caste or by mutual hatred of Hindus and Mussulmans".[11] Bryce saw a process of racial separation developing which would delay this process, for there would be strong sanctions against "miscegenation" and the society would develop on the basis of a minimum pattern of inter-racial contact:

> Two races will be living on the same ground, in close and constant economic relations, both those of employment and those of competition, speaking the same language and obeying the same laws, differing no doubt, in strength of intelligence and will, yet with many members of the weaker race superior as individual men to many members of the stronger. And these two races, separated by the repulsion of physical differences, will have no social intercourse, no mixture of blood, but will each form a nation by itself for all purposes save those of industry and perhaps of politics.[12]

Bryce's vision did not necessarily entail the massive extension of authoritarian state power that was essential to the development of the apartheid system by the 1950s and 1960s. He saw an apparently "natural" aversion to racial inter-mingling in South Africa and a process of separation which would keep African societies on the land.[13] His view fed into a wider debate after the Anglo-Boer War of 1899–1902 on the nature of South African "native policy" which, as chapter 1 has shown, led to the emergence of the ideology of segregation.

The segregationist debate was partly defined by the growing popularity of Darwinian evolutionism in South African political discussion. It appeared biologically sound to assert that different races had evolved on varying lines and had attained different degrees of "civilization" or "barbarism". For some of the participants in the debate, the key question was not only how to release Africans as workers in the white-controlled economy but also to advance the cause of "civilization" in South Africa. Africans were seen as people inherently divested of "civilization" and a historical theory was generated to explain this in terms of the "savagery" of African society before contact with whites.

The discourse of "civilization" depended to a considerable degree on a set of historical mythologies to justify British imperial intrusion. The historian George McCall Theal did much in the years after 1902 to promote a view of history pivoted on the idea that a united white race in South Africa had to save the African people from irremediable savagery. Theal's extensive writings, including the eleven-volume *History of South Africa*, reinforced the idea that Africans welcomed the benefits of white rule and that the liberal missionaries of the early nineteenth century, such as the Reverend John Philip, had tried to undermine white land settlement.[14]

Another important mythology that was propagated at the time was that pre-colonial African societies in Southern Africa were completely lacking in any of the accoutrements of civilization. It became essential to emphasize that the archaeological ruins which did exist, such as those of Zimbabwe in Rhodesia, were the work of non-African peoples. The militantly racist ethnologist, A. H. Keane, for example, wrote in *The Gold of Ophir* in 1901 that the ruins were not the work of the surrounding Shona peoples but were constructed by a Semitic population. This people had merely used the local population as labour in order to work the small mines that had been the base of the old Monomotapa empire recorded by sixteenth-century Portuguese explorers. The work accorded with views that were then widely prevalent in archaeological circles that Africans could not have built the ruins and had always been subject to the influence of some form of higher "civilization".[15]

By the early years of the twentieth century the notion of "civilization" became a basic assumption behind the objective of "social control" which was one of the main aims of many of the English-speaking segregation theorists.[16] The amateur ethnologist

Dudley Kidd in his influential tract *Kafir Socialism* (1908) broadly reflected this concern. The book argued that in its pristine state African society was socialist rather than individual in nature, though it had now embarked on irreparable transformation through contact with the "white civilization" of South Africa. Kidd differed from "scientific racists" such as Keane by arguing that, if left alone, the African society of South Africa would have developed its own civilization, though this was now impossible with the disintegration of the clan system as a result of contact with the capitalist economy.[17] Furthermore, Kidd pointed out that since it was impossible to renounce a belief in the ethics of "white civilization" so these had in turn to be imparted by missionary education to Africans in order to uplift their society.[18] Kidd, though, shared Theal's mistrust of too rapid a programme of missionary proselytization but recognized that the cultural base of "civilization" was acquired and not inherited. He warned that "civilizations have waxed and waned because cultural atmospheres are easily destroyed".[19] It was not a utopian hope for a "Kafir renaissance" to occur because this was going to be essential to avoid the competing appeal of "Ethiopianism" and independent church sectarianism.[20] No less a parallel was provided by the ancient Greeks who were "to start with but a race of barbarians devoid of any special intellectual promise".[21] The success of all this would depend upon an educational strategy focusing both on individuals of the existing generation as well as a eugenic programme of improvement in the "stock" or "germ plasm" of the race as whole.[22]

Kidd's ideas fed into the debate on segregation and reinforced the commitment in a number of missionary circles to industrial training. His views were partly shared by Lord Selborne, who succeeded Alfred Milner as High Commissioner of South Africa in 1905. Selborne brought considerable prestige to bear as a politician, administrator and public servant. In January 1907 he issued the Selborne Memorandum on the question of Union and was strongly committed to enhancing the British imperial position in South Africa. He was anxious not to be put off course in this enterprise by the stirring of Afrikaner nationalism in the former Boer republics. Those who argued for delay in Union were, he wrote to the Kindergarten member Patrick Duncan, short-sighted for "while the general instability of South Africa continues, all real prosperity will be impossible and all expansion, and the Dutch will continue to preponderate at elections".[23]

Selborne was driven by a strong faith in the justness of the Union cause, which he saw as conducive to economic and industrial development. In an address at the University of the Cape of Good Hope in February 1909, he considered the issue in terms of white colonial trusteeship. Like Kidd he felt it possible that "the black man" if he "had never seen or heard of the white man ... might possibly in the course of ages have evolved a satisfactory civilisation on lines of his own". However, "having been brought into contact with the white, he must surely go dangerously astray unless the white man gives all the help he can in his evolution".[24] There was a need to continue the civilizing mission initiated by the missionaries and Selborne favoured maintaining the reserves under the control of tribal chiefs in order to prevent the possible spread of "Ethiopianism".[25]

Selborne was anxious to avoid as far as possible "miscegenation" between whites and blacks, which he considered to be an inherently "unnatural" phenomenon. This was less likely to happen, he argued, with the advance of "civilization" among Africans for "the more the Bantu is civilised, the fewer objectionable traits and unnatural traits there will be for the European to assimilate".[26] Broadly speaking, Selborne's address marked a general support for segregationist precepts in South African "native policy" by a senior member of the British imperial establishment. He argued for only a limited recognition of African political rights which he felt could best be expressed through tribal gatherings or local councils. He supported a limited African franchise with the test of civilization being performed not according to educational or property qualifications but by high court judges.[27]

Like Kidd's *Kafir Socialism*, Selborne's address linked segregation with a wider discourse on "civilization" and "evolution" that was strongly infused at that time with a Social Darwinism. It linked South African domestic debate on "native policy" with a wider British imperial self-confidence, which was to last until at least the 1920s before doubts began to set in over the capacity of South Africa to become a "white man's country".[28]

Given the centrality of the classical model of "civilization" in British imperial language before the First World War, it became that much harder for opponents of segregation to develop the ethical basis of their case. One notable exception was Olive Schreiner's pamphlet of 1909 on *The Native Question* in which she rejected the whole idea that South African white society could emulate the classical model. "We in South Africa," she wrote,

> can never hope exactly to repeat the records of the past. We can never hope, like Greece, to give to the world its noblest plastic art; we can never hope, like Rome, to shape the legal institutions of half the world.... But the great national parts are not exhausted; and there lies before us in South Africa a part as great and inspiring as any which any nation has ever been called upon to play.[29]

Olive Schreiner saw the success of the whole project of Union as hinging upon the ability of the polity to tackle the one dominating question in the society's politics, the "native question". Schreiner wrote in defence of a local patriotism rather than a more classically inspired imperialism. The "true wealth of a nation," she urged, "is the health, happiness, intelligence, and content of every man and woman born within its borders." She rejected the precepts of classical imperialism in favour of a more materialistic doctrine that was partly inspired by the ideals of social and eugenic reform of her lover Karl Pearson in England. This implied some sense of political obligation by the South African governing class for "the true crown of honour on the head of a dominant class is that it leads and teaches, not uses and crushes".[30]

Olive Schreiner considered this notion of political obligation to entail citizenship rights for the dispossessed black majority in South Africa. To do otherwise was merely to invite disaster in the context of an expanding capitalist system that threatened to break up African social organization. Schreiner felt less optimistic than contemporary liberals, such as Howard Pim and Maurice Evans, that segregation would be a means of maintaining social control over the African population during this industrialization. She feared the spectre of black working-class revolt, for

> if, uninstructed in the highest forms of labour, without the rights of citizenship, his social organisation broken up, without our having aided him to participate in our own; if, unbound to us by gratitude and sympathy, and alien to us in blood and colour, we reduce this vast mass to the condition of a great

seething, ignorant proletariat – then I would rather draw a veil over the future of this land.[31]

Olive Schreiner's bleak vision of a possible future trajectory of South African politics was, as two biographers have noted, "an ominous and prophetic vision which set her apart from her contemporaries".[32] She pointed out that the future of South African society lay in the centrality of citizenship for the black majority rather than the maintenance of a racially exclusive "white civilization". But her plea for a rethinking of racial segregation and the inclusion of Africans into the polity met with no major response at the time of Union.

The Native Question became a reference point for a number of later critics of segregation. In 1925, the poet Roy Campbell, who considered Olive Schreiner one of the few really significant South African writers, wrote to Edward Garnett bitterly attacking the Pact government's segregation policy. "It is obvious to everybody that the population will be eventually a coloured one," he declared:

There is no other standard by which one is entitled to judge races than that of efficiency. If we take it on ourselves to be their lords and masters because they are less civilized, we have no right to oppose their aspirations towards our civilisation.[33]

Campbell went further than most liberals at this time in supporting inter-racial "miscegenation". But his was a lone voice that was soon to be silenced by his departure from South Africa after his resignation from the literary magazine *Voorslag*. Though he had envisaged the flowering of a new and distinct South African culture in his poem *Flaming Terrapin* in 1924, his ideas were not well understood in South African literary and intellectual circles.[34] Campbell was not seen as particularly liberal either by many English-speaking intellectuals. By the 1930s he moved towards a romantic conservatism that condemned the bourgeois values of the nineteenth century and hoped, rather half-heartedly, to move South Africa back towards a more patrician society in which landed gentry looked after their black serfs and noble savages.[35]

Another important South African politician and thinker Jan Christian Smuts had a considerably different ideal, though he too recognized that the "white civilization" of South Africa could not look only to the classical models inherited from British imperial expansion. Smuts frequently took a gloomy view of South Africa's future, interspersed by periods of pronounced optimism that white-settler societies in Southern Africa might be able to expand further northward into the African continent. In the period before Union the "native question" seemed too massive even to think about. "When I consider the political future of the Native of South Africa," Smuts confessed to John X. Merriman, "I must say that I look into the shadows and darkness; and then I feel inclined to shift the intolerable burden of solving that sphinx problem to the ampler shoulders and stronger brains of the future."[36] Smuts favoured, in fact, the exclusion of Africans altogether from South African national politics.[37]

Over the years, however, Smuts's thinking evolved as he tried to keep abreast of the changing climate of international opinion on race issues. Despite being a former Boer politician and guerrilla leader, Smuts proved a crucial figure in English-speaking intellectual circles in South Africa in the years after Union. He addressed numerous academic and professional gatherings in the English-speaking community and acted as an opinion-leader as he gained their trust and confidence, especially through his links with the governing establishment in Britain. During the First World War he served in the Lloyd George war cabinet, though after the war he refused to support moves for closer imperial unity on the lines of an imperial federation.

Smuts realized, like Olive Schreiner, that the Victorian classical model of civilization had its limits. It was not essential to compare South Africa with Europe. In a speech on Union "native policy" at the Savoy Hotel in London in 1917, Smuts pointed to previous civilizations that had occurred elsewhere in Africa such as the "great Saracen civilization in Central Africa", the University of Timbuctoo and the archaeological remains at Great Zimbabwe which he also accepted had been built by Phoenicians or Arabs rather than the apparently backward local Shona peoples.

Where, asked Smuts, were all these previous African civilizations now? They had all disappeared, and Smuts went on to draw the moral that "barbarism once more rules over the land" making the "thoughtful man nervous about the white man's future in Southern Africa". The historical analogy with previous civilizations indicated a cyclical pattern in his thought in which it appeared likely that the emergent "white civilization" in South Africa was destined to go through a similar pattern of rise and fall. This was particularly likely to happen if the society allowed "miscegenation" between the races. Smuts attacked the notion of the British racist Houston Stewart Chamberlain that there could be complete "race purity", but was careful to endorse only inter-mixing between the white "races" of "British" and "Boers" in South Africa in order to create a new white South African race. A wider "inter-mixture of blood" would be reminiscent of the now dead African civilizations since it contained within it "the seeds of decay".[38]

To Smuts protection of the newly emergent white South African "civilization" depended on measures to protect white racial identity as well as an expansionist drive north to open up other parts of the African continent to white-settler society. "We have started by creating a new white base in South Africa," he declared, "and to-day we are in a position to move forward towards the North and the civilisation of the African continent."[39] The speech reflected a recognition in Smuts's mind that the white "civilization" in South Africa could not draw its strength in the long run entirely from the cultural resources of Europe but had, ultimately, to interact with the survivals of the civilizations elsewhere in Africa which it could in turn energize. He drew considerable inspiration from the idea of a "British Commonwealth of Nations" which he saw as both a new entity in international relations and a break with the older imperialisms of the past. He did not see the Commonwealth forming one single nation like the United States, for it was made up of a diversity of different states, including some like India which had ancient civilizations of their own. But unlike previous empires which had been based around a notion of "assimilation" and an attempt to "force human material into one mould," the British Commonwealth was based on the principle of self-government. It therefore did not stand for either "standardisation" or "denationalisation".[40]

Smuts saw that the one way of warding off the prophesied future crisis in South Africa was through the mobilization of national political will. The laws of biological evolution appeared to be working in harmony with this idea for, like earlier theorists such as Harry Johnstone, he considered it possible biologically to engineer a new white African race which would be fit enough to undertake this specific task. His book *Holism and Evolution* tried to rethink

Darwinian ideas of evolution in terms of what the French philosopher Emile Bergson termed "creative evolution".[41] Holism was in effect a modern doctrine of evolution that saw the world evolving towards ever larger wholes, though Smuts acknowledged that there could also be a degenerative process in this since wholes could also be "weak" and "inchoate".[42]

Smuts's doctrine of holism was an attempt to provide a philosophical base to South African statecraft in the inter-war years. It formed an intellectual justification for a policy of sub-regional imperialism by the South African state during a period when everything appeared still fluid. The present policies of the South African government might, Smuts wrote in 1928 to the former Milner Kindergarten member Philip Kerr, "very largely determine the lines of the future" and he warned of a danger of "want of vision and too keen a preoccupation with the immediate difficulties, instead of looking ahead and trying to catch the greater vision of future development".[43]

One of the main audiences that Smuts tried to impress with such ideas was the imperial establishment in Britain. It was at Oxford in 1929 that he gave his lectures *Africa and Some World Problems*. The same year the headquarters of the Rhodes Trust was opened at Oxford in the form of Rhodes House, a building designer by the architect Herbert Baker (who also designed the Union Buildings in Pretoria). Smuts hoped to mobilize interest in a city that was seen by some to have pretensions to being the intellectual capital of the British Empire-Commonwealth.[44]

Smuts expounded in the lectures an imperial doctrine of *Lebensraum* in which he saw the expansion of white settlement in Africa as crucial to the economic development of the continent. He paid attention to the new developments in anthropological research on African cultures, but his lectures were marked by the survival of an older pattern of race thinking based on the idea of distinct racial "types". "The negro and the negroid Bantu," he wrote, "form a distinct human type which the world would be poorer without." This African "type" had adapted to the African continent and its geographical and climatic differences over thousands of years. But it was now becoming possible for a white population to survive in the tropical and subtropical regions of the globe after a long period when this was thought to be physically impossible.[45] The lectures were partly directed against the "humanitarian feeling" in Britain represented by a figure such as Sydney Olivier, whom Smuts felt had undermined the drive for white emigration to Southern Africa.[46]

The lectures formed an impassioned plea for thinking of Africa as a continent of experiment where new races and social groupings could be established. "It is even possible," Smuts declared,

> that just as in the biological world new types are evolved in a new environment, so a new human type may in time arise under the unusual climactic conditions of Eastern Africa. The Transvaal Boer already seems to be evolving into a type very different from his Dutch Huguenot ancestors. The human laboratory of Africa may yet produce strange results, and time alone can show whether or not the experiment was worthwhile in the interests of humanity.[47]

The lectures reflect a belief in racial and eugenic engineering just before this started to become intellectually unfashionable with the rise of Nazism in Central Europe in the 1930s. Smuts viewed ethnic – or what he termed "racial" – categories not as fixed but subject to processes of change, evolution or amalgamation. He saw the African continent as requiring the guiding hand of imperial trusteeship, though he interpreted this doctrine not in terms of a benign rule from Whitehall but the entrenchment of white-settler power.

Africa and Some World Problems represented a last great statement of belief by a major international political figure of the Victorian ideal of an imperial *mission civilisatrice* in the Africa continent. The fact that this did not excite any major new spurt of interest in imperial development in Britain indicates that it was to a considerable degree the voice of another age. The main effect of the lectures was to stimulate interest in the idea of a major survey of the African continent and this led to a committee being formed under Round Table auspices that eventually led to the *Africa Survey* published by Malcolm Hailey in 1938.[48]

The tone of the lectures tended to jar on liberal ears. J. H. Oldham of the International Missionary Council published a rebuttal of the lectures in 1930 arguing that the main objectives of British policy should be not the active fostering of massive new white settlement schemes in Africa but the development of its colonial economies and the sale of its tropical products on the world market.[49]

Similar doubts were expressed in South Africa by Jan H. Hofmeyr. A child prodigy who came from a prominent family of Anglicized Afrikaners in the Cape, Hofmeyr had been briefly professor of classics at the University of Cape Town and later at the University of the Witwatersrand in the early 1920s before becoming Administrator of the Transvaal in 1924. In 1929 he had been elected to Parliament for the SAP as a believer in "co-operation" between South Africa and the British-controlled African colonies to the north. Hofmeyr was sceptical of Smuts's idealistic scheme for one great white dominion stretching up to Eastern and Central Africa.[50] He was rather more aware than Smuts of the strength of white, and especially Afrikaner, political feeling at the local level in the Transvaal. The Pact government of General Hertzog had won the 1929 election against Smuts's South Africa Party on a "Black Manifesto" that warned that Smuts's expansionist ideas threatened white rule in South Africa by being absorbed into a "Black kaffir state" to the north. Hofmeyr was anxious not to try and "pour oil on troubled waters" by defining too closely alternative principles to those of Afrikaner nationalism or indeed trying to set up a new centre party.[51]

Hofmeyr was cautious in his response to Smuts's expansionist dream of a "United States of Africa". He considered that it was by no means clear a white race could establish itself permanently in the climactic conditions of Africa; anyway, without avenues for employment as unskilled labourers, white settlement on any extensive scale in East and Central Africa would be on an uncertain basis.[52] Hofmeyr favoured a policy of informal imperialism by the South African state whereby the educational and scientific skills of South African engineers and scientists could be mobilized for African economic development. With a strong sense of classical history he saw this as a new form of imperial mission which was far more likely to succeed in African conditions that the older classical model:

> It is Science, which more than any other single factor, can define, determine, and guide the future of Africa. Perhaps previous failure helps to make the challenge more pressing. European culture has sought before now to bring Africa within its sphere. In the Mediterranean lands of Africa the Greco-Roman civilization won some of its greatest triumphs, and the evidences of these triumphs are even now being uncovered from the sands of what has been allowed to become the North

African desert. But in the end Rome failed to conquer Africa for civilization – failed because the solid mass of African barbarism, and the defiant resistance of African nature. Those who in the nineteenth and twentieth centuries have taken the place of Rome in the response to the challenge of Africa are still faced by the same enemies, but in taking up that challenge they are not alone. Partner with them in the enterprise is Science, vigorous, resourceful, purposeful, able to confront those foes with weapons of which Rome never dreamed.[53]

This was an attempt to redefine the expansionist dreams of Cecil Rhodes in a more modern terminology that caught the contemporary vogue for "science". It was a rather bland political ideology that was unlikely to have a huge political appeal. By the late 1930s as war increasingly loomed on the political horizon, Hofmeyr's leader Smuts began to abandon the scientific faith for religion, realizing that none of the achievements in science had been able to halt the "barbarism" of Nazism.[54]

Hofmeyr's faith in science disguised a more basic uncertainty over the course of South African "native policy". His book *South Africa* said little about the future nature of the South African domestic political system and avoided spelling out what African political rights should be; indeed Hofmeyr considered that they were of secondary importance to the economic development of African societies in South Africa.[55] In 1936, Hofmeyr did make a principled stand in opposition to the removal of the Cape African franchise, but this still left open the question of what was to be the alternative to the advancing tide of segregation.

In the late 1930s and 1940s Hofmeyr continued to try to infuse some form of principle into the policies of the United Party government. He urged that it should take a "firm stand" against the "reactionary propaganda" of D. F. Malan's Gesuiwerde Nasionale Party, though he remained in favour of the principles of segregationism provided they were justly implemented.[56]

Hofmeyr proved to be a flawed political leader for white English-speaking South Africans. Though a number of senior figures in the English establishment put a considerable amount of trust in him, much depended upon a Micawberish hope that something would turn up that would somehow lead to a realignment of political parties. "If some sudden turn of events should bring political readjustment into the foreground," the editor of the *Cape Times*, B. K. Long, wrote to Geoffrey Dawson, editor of *The Times* in London in 1930,

> he would have a magnificent chance of leading the movement, and might suddenly find himself on the crest of the wave. If that did happen public opinion in the country, which is more favourable to political readjustment than Parliamentary opinion, would certainly support him. But it is all a toss up at the moment, with the odds rather against anything of the kind happening.[57]

Hofmeyr was an enigmatic political figure whose career was checkered throughout by the dominating figure of his autocratic mother. He certainly spoke in strong terms for English-speakers to recognize the power and importance of Afrikaner nationalist assertion and for their "full and unequivocal acceptance" into political life.[58] But he proved a failure as a political bridge-builder as he became perceived in Afrikaner nationalist circles as a dangerous figure who threatened the survival of white rule.[59]

English-speaking liberals such as Edgar Brookes and J. D. Rheinallt Jones were rather over-optimistic in assuming that Hofmeyr was really willing to take over the reins of power from the towering figure of Smuts. Hofmeyr recognized his own limitations and confessed to his friend Leif Egeland while serving as Minister of Finance during World War Two that he really did not have the ambition to become Prime Minister. "Perhaps I am too near the job," he wrote in 1941

> + have too much of what it means, perhaps also I am too conscious of my limitations to desire it. If it never comes my way, I shall shed no tears. If it does, apart from a natural sense of mounting satisfaction, I shall accept it as a matter of duty, without exaltation, but with a heavy heart.[60]

Hofmeyr's sentiments indicated no really burning zeal to achieve any major new direction in South African politics. To this extent, his outlook was a reflection of a more deep-seated malaise within English-speaking South African liberalism which had not been overcome even by the optimism engendered by the outbreak of World War Two. As Phyllis Lewsen has recently argued, Hofmeyr failed to rise to the challenge presented by Hoernle of trying to think out the principles for a liberal political order in South Africa.[61] Though he was able to move some way towards the recognition of a common citizenship in South Africa by increasing expenditure on African education seven times and increasing welfare payments, Hofmeyr was to a considerable degree defeated by the weakness of the South African administrative machine. Wartime conditions made it impossible to effect any sort of major reorganization of the Civil service even if there had been the political will to do this. The large number of English-speakers who went off to fight in the war made it difficult to draw on any pool of talent. The consequence was that there was an increasing sense that the tide was running against making South Africa into a state that followed the same sort of general political principles as elsewhere in the West. The newspaperman B. K. Long wrote in a confidential memorandum of his growing anxiety at the state of the civil service as the age of entry and the standard of education had been lowered since Union. "South Africa today," he wrote sometime in the early 1940s,

> is suffering from the continuance in public life of old men, brought up in old controversies and "pasts" in all parties, beyond the age of initiative or even capacity for new thought or output of work. In the sunshine, sport, leisure and social ['Society' is the precise word] activities of South Africa, the more well-to-do classes have – unlike those in the time of Cecil Rhodes – abandoned interest in political and public life, and even despise socially those who do enter such forms of public service. Trusting in the past to outstanding leaders like Botha and Smuts, and to the wealth of the United Party machine, with its powerful and extensive press support, they imagine that "something will turn up" and show all to little consciousness of the new forces alive the world over.[62]

There was considerable truth in Long's criticisms of the government's administrative machinery. By the 1940s many civil servants appeared unclear of the direction of government policy. In the case of the Native Affairs Department, for example, lack of qualified personnel meant the promotion of Gordon Mears first as Under Secretary of State and then, with Douglas Smit's appointment as Chairman of the Native Affairs Commission in 1945, to Secretary of Native Affairs. Mears was not a man of any real ambition; his main aim had been to become Chief Magistrate of the Transkei. He was committed to the British Civil Service ideal of being a public servant free of party political ties. He had only a poor grasp by the post-war years of the degree to which "native affairs" had become politicized by the 1946 African mine strike.[63]

During the war years the ideology of segregation fell increasingly out of favour, especially after Smuts's important address to the SAIRR in 1942 declaring that it had "fallen on evil days". The speech, though, had been particularly directed to an overseas audience at a time when Smuts was developing a close political accord with the Churchill government. It was by no means clear that belief in the ideology had dried up in mainstream United Party circles: some wartime legislation extended segregation, and at the war's end the 1945 Natives (Urban Areas) Act consolidated previous legislation restricting African residence in urban areas.

The intellectual exponents of segregation, though, were increasingly on the defensive by the 1940s in English-speaking circles. In contrast to the 1920s when a broad range of white (as well as some black) liberal opinion had still favoured it as a practical solution to race relations, it had become an ideology that was increasingly difficult to legitimate.

In part this can be traced to the comparatively feeble nature of right-wing ideologies of elitism in English-speaking intellectual circles. As was pointed out in chapter 1, some intellectuals were prepared until the mid to late 1930s to support various "scientific" ideas of genetic differences between races, but these were generally not expanded into a more consistent racism of the kind found in European fascist ideology. For the most part, English-speaking intellectuals on the right justified white rule in terms of the notion of "trusteeship" then prevalent in the British Commonwealth.

One example of this tendency was the Natal sugar-planter and former Native Commissioner in Northern Rhodesia, George Heaton Nicholls. Largely self-educated, Nicholls had an intense distrust of intellectuals, despite becoming a prominent race theorist in South Africa in his own right. Before going into politics in Natal in the 1920s he wrote a clumsy novel, *Bayete: Hail to the King* which was published in 1923. It had preached a gospel of segregation as means of preventing the urbanization of the African peasantry, whom Nicholls depicted as liable to mount an insurrection against white rule if allowed to settle in the towns.[64] In the early 1920s, Nicholls did not consider that segregation could ever be more than "partial" and he recognized that it did not have any central direction. His solution to the dilemma was to view whites in South Africa as a benevolent aristocracy based on a "civilizing instinct" which was lacking in African society. Politics as they were practised in Europe would thus not apply in South Africa which would remain under the control of a white racial elite.[65]

However, in the late 1920s and early 1930s, Nicholls established a reputation on the Select Committee on the Native Bills and in 1937 was appointed to the Native Affairs Commission. He became an ardent campaigner for segregation as a means of economically reviving the African reserve economies and restoring tribal leadership. His language now changed to reflect the international discourse on race relations. The 1936 bills, he claimed, were the fulfilment of the ideals of trusteeship, though at the same time Africans in South Africa formed a separate race unlike American blacks who formed a "submerged class of a mixed population". The legislation was important for stressing the "national" rather than "class" features of African society, for it was "concerned with the maintenance of the Bantu ethos in the interests of the Natives themselves and in the interests of Western civilisation".[66] This was an idea that won grudging support from the Alfred Hoernle who preferred to see national symbols triumph over class ones.[67]

Nicholls also tried to defend the administrative apparatus from attacks by the liberals in the SAIRR whom he accused of viewing the issue of segregation in a detached manner and failing to understand the electoral limitations on political decision-makers.[68] But by the outbreak of the Second World War both Smuts and Hofmeyr appear to have recognized the increasing political liability of having Nicholls close to policy-making on "native affairs". In 1942 he was sidelined by being appointed Administrator in Natal and two years later he was sent to London as High Commissioner where his strongly pro-imperial sentiments won him a number of warm admirers.[69] This did not deter Smuts in 1943 from appointing the segregationist Piet Van der Byl as Minister of Native Affairs on the death of Deneys Reitz, but Nicholls's danger lay in his importance as a theorist of segregation when the doctrine appeared increasingly outmoded politically.

Nicholls's equation of "civilization" with race was one that liberals found hard to accept by the late 1930s. The word had become increasingly employed in the 1920s in support of the crude defence of the job colour bar in the form of the Pact Government's "civilized labour" policy. The centenary celebrations of the Great Trek in 1938 also resulted in two torches being carried by relays of runners to celebrate the light of "freedom" and "white civilisation".[70]

After World War Two, English-speaking liberals felt it increasingly necessary to reassert liberal values in the face of a new world order increasingly hostile to doctrines of racialism. A number were also concerned to try to link these values to a Christian message of hope in contrast to Hoernle's rather more pessimistic prognostications before the start of the war. Jan H. Hofmeyr's restatement of liberal principles in 1945 avoided the term "civilization" in his Hoernle memorial lecture that year to the SAIRR entitled *Christian Principles and Race Problems*. The lecture was a notable statement of belief in the Christian idea of the brotherhood of man in opposition to philosophies of racialism. Hofmeyr contrasted Christian belief to policies of repression: while the South African policy of "trusteeship" towards Africans could only be described as domination, Christian ethics addressed the question of whether the motive behind the policy was self-regarding or other-regarding.[71] He considered the issues in South Africa should be approached by liberals not with fear but with a Christian faith. His words "stand firm by principle, and go forward in faith" became a *credo* for those active in the SAIRR in subsequent years, though these were in essence the sentiments of an embattled and isolated liberalism that became faced with an increasingly repressive apartheid state.[72]

Hofmeyr's affirmation of Christian liberal principles avoided the more anxious sort of historical questioning that asked, "Where is South African civilization going?" The commitment to piecemeal reform based on good moral intentions appeared, at least for the time being, to be winning over a small number of African converts. There were important political reasons for this. Hofmeyr was in many ways an Afrikaner intellectual despite his close links with the English community and his university background in Cape Town and Oxford. He continually resisted appeals from English liberals after 1945 to lead a Liberal Party, not merely through lack of ambition but because he wished to keep open links with moderate sections of Afrikaner political opinion. Even after the defeat of Smuts's United Party government in 1948, therefore, he discussed with John Cope and

R. M. De Villiers the possibility of forming a political association with N. G. Havenga, head of the small Afrikaner Party that was in coalition with Malan's GNP. Havenga was widely believed not to be especially happy with the alliance with Malan, though Hofmeyr believed that the success of such a strategy would depend on his keeping the "centre" of the United Party behind him.[73] This clearly foreclosed any possibility at this stage of forming a Liberal Party.

The Model in Crisis

In the years before World War Two, many black political leaders had accepted the idea that one of the main objectives of black struggle was incorporation into a single South African "civilization". They saw the notion of "civilization" as contradicting racial segregation since its ethical precepts denied the white minority the right to rule by force. D. D. T. Jabavu, a professor of classics at the University College of Fort Hare, wrote a pamphlet in 1932 championing equal rights for blacks in South Africa, which drew upon the support of several prominent figures in Britain, such as H. G. Wells, Sydney Olivier and the Bishop of St Albans, Michael Furse. The reason for the policy in South Africa of excluding Africans from "civilization" lay, argued Jabavu, in fear, though this was "a perilous guide in human affairs". Such fear undermined the civilized basis of white rule by threatening to reduce it to a naked assertion of racial supremacy:

> It blinds men's eye to truth and justice. It puts its sponsors down as beyond the reach of reason, for if the European can only maintain his civilisation by keeping his foot on the neck of the African, then he has already surrendered his mental superiority. A mentality of this nature, if encouraged, will react in a demoralising fashion on a ruling race that puts it into practice; because it will deaden its conscience on all ideas of right and wrong where blacks are concerned inasmuch as it will regard them as being animals of a sub-human species.[74]

By the end of the Second World War the generation of inter-war African leaders in the ANC began to come under growing political challenge from a younger and more radical generation in the Congress Youth League. The liberalism of Jabavu's generation was seen as lacking sufficient radical and nationalist fire against white rule. It was also viewed as fatally flawed by its continuing dependence on the overseas connection with Britain as the former imperial power. This had continually failed to stop the general segregationist trend of government policy.

A newer language based on human rights entered into the vocabulary of African leaders after World War Two. In 1945 the ANC drew up a "Bill of Rights" that demanded the abolition of all racial discrimination. At the same time a younger group of Africanists were starting to influence ideas within the ANC by their stress on the values of a traditional African culture. One of the most important of this group was Anton Lembede who fused Africanism with Roman Catholicism. Lembede's stress on the ethical values of "traditional" African culture marked a rejection of any dependency upon the values of an extraneous "civilization". The point was for African society to evolve from a tribal stage to that of a new "African nation" that was free from the influences of "foreign ideologies".[75]

Lembede's thought helped shape the Africanist challenge to multi-racialism of Congress Alliance in the 1950s. While in many respects romantic in its return to an idealized pre-colonial past, it was typical of the Pan-Africanist spirit of the 1940s. Its emphasis upon African self-reliance had a long-term effect on the new generation of African leaders in the 1950s even if, like Nelson Mandela and Oliver Tambo, they moved away from Africanism towards a more Marxist-inspired socialism. To this extent, Africanism of the kind espoused by Lembede acted as a strong catalyst for a break by African leaders from dependency upon Western liberalism and the notion that the main goal of African struggle was mere inclusion in a Western-style civilization.

The break did not come uniformly and some leaders such as Alfred Xuma, President of the ANC, continued to speak of a "British tradition of fair play" that was "in danger in South Africa", and of the need for "civilization" to be "maintained" in the country, though not "at the expense of certain sections of the multi-racial population".[76] The arrival of the Nationalist government later the same year – 1948 – made this kind of language appear anachronistic.

The African National Congress and other black political organizations began to resort to methods of passive resistance following the 1949 Programme of Action. By the 1952 Defiance Campaign, some senior ANC figures, such as the Secretary, General Walter Sisulu, saw the movement as being involved in a national liberation struggle.

The movement began to move towards what Thomas Hodgkin has termed "revolutionary democratic theories" in the course of the 1950s, especially after the failure of the 1952 Defiance Campaign. There was now a strongly populist strain in African politics based on the collective mobilization of a whole people in pursuit of democratic demands, reminiscent of the impact of the revolutionary ideas of Jean-Jacques Rousseau on the French Jacobins in the late eighteenth century.[77] This radicalization in political thought left a note of increasing anxiety in the circles of the English-speaking liberals.

As many of the European imperial powers started to move towards decolonization in Africa, a number of liberals in the early 1950s recognized that it was no longer possible to view South Africa as an outpost of a monolithic and white "Western civilization", though this continued to be the basis of much of the conflict between the National Party government and the opposition United Party. The historian Arthur Keppel Jones pointed out in 1952 that "the rest of the world can well understand, as too few South Africans do, that civilisation is not defined by the colour bar". Unless a major change in policy occurred, "the verdict of history on the evanescent European civilization in Southern Africa would be that it was a flame that flickered for only a few generations, and then became a mere historical interlude between two Dark ages".[78]

A more sober view came the same year from the economist Herbert Frankel in a pamphlet warning against a catastrophic view of African history and the idea that there could be any sort of "final solution" to South Africa's problems. But Frankel was not especially optimistic either. "Civilization" should, he argued, be seen as a social *process* based upon social co-operation rather than a frozen state of social relations. Urbanization led to a mass uprooting of South African society. The "social soil of Africa" was "shallow" and "the roots of modern civilisation" would be unlikely to "penetrate deep to resist the storms of circumstance; the least disturbances, like the rain and the wind, create a dust bowl and a desert".[79]

Most of the English-speaking intellectuals involved in this "civilization" debate in the 1950s saw it as a cultural instrument in the hands of the white English minority in South Africa. In the early 1950s there was still a strong mood in many English-speaking circles that the Nationalists had no legitimate claim to speak for "white civilization" in South Africa since their ideology appeared to resemble the Nazism that had been fought against in World War

Two. The upsurge of support in 1951 for the War Veterans Action Committee, later known as the Torch Commando, reflected the views of many ex-South African servicemen who were concerned that many of the ideals for which they had fought were now being undermined by the South African government. One of the Commando's leaders, the fighter ace "Sailor" Malan asked a meeting of 25,000 in May 1951: "Who has the greater claim to talk about saving white civilisation? the moles who now pay lip service to it or the men who fought for it?"[80] The Torch Commando, though, lacked a clear programme, and the following year became absorbed into more constitutional opposition by becoming part of the United Democratic Front along with the United Party and Labour party in order to fight the 1953 election.

After the success of the Nationalists in the 1953 election a mood developed among many English-speaking intellectuals that as a group they had been divested of political power at the national level and were unlikely to regain it either quickly or easily. Some writers hoped English-speakers could play an intermediary role in the society's ethnic politics between Afrikaners and Africans. E. E. Harris in an SAIRR pamphlet in 1954 urged that "civilisation" had to be seen apart from the idea of "white civilisation" since it could not depend upon white racial domination. The aim had to be common citizenship in a multi-racial society while political rights could be defined by a "standard of civilisation" – an ideal which he hoped would be achieved by gradual means.[81]

This notion of English-speakers continuing to act as a "civilizing" force in South African politics as a result of their international connections and cultural links was one that became progressively undermined by the radicalization of black politics in the course of the 1950s. A loss of nerve began to emerge amongst the English-speaking intelligentsia as it became clear that its former hold on both the state and direction of political debate had irreparably passed and that a new era was emerging based upon mass demands for popular sovereignty and citizenship rights.

The Freedom Charter and Popular Sovereignty

By the early 1950s, the liberal notion of "civilization" began to appear to radical critics to be an apology for doing relatively little politically to challenge apartheid. It led either to a cultural pessimism and withdrawal from politics or else a restatement of a gradualist position centred upon a qualified franchise. The civilization ideal began therefore to be challenged by a more populist conception of building a "common society" based not only on common citizenship rights but equal rights of democratic political participation as well.

The 1955 Freedom Charter in particular marked a major ideological challenge to the older precepts of mainstream white liberalism. Its commitment to the principle that "South Africa belongs to all who live in it" represented a patriotic ideal of popular sovereignty that rejected cultural or ideological dependency upon norms derived from "Western civilization". It reflected a wider climate of non-European nationalism in the 1950s, symbolized by the meeting the same year at Bandung in Indonesia of the leaders of the newly emergent Non Aligned Movement of states. This reinforced a mood that was anxious to emulate Western ideas of democratic behaviour but rejected at the same time any Western tutelage or "trusteeship" in the attainment of this end.

A small minority of English-speaking South African liberals did try to meet this ideological challenge. Patrick Duncan wrote in a 1953 pamphlet, *The Road Through the Wilderness*, of the forces working against Nationalist rule in South Africa, including "world civilisation", the power of God, economic forces, love of liberty and world opinion. The English-speaking minority he saw as remaining in a state of subordination, and only an alliance of African power with the "white conscience" could break the stranglehold of Afrikaner nationalism.[82]

Duncan's pamphlet was a rather confused attempt to break away from some of the orthodoxies of white liberalism, especially through the commitment to passive resistance or *Satyagraha*. It did suggest a shift away by English-speaking liberals from the old strategy of trying to appeal to moderate sections of Afrikaner political opinion in favour of a closer alliance with the Congress movement. But Duncan was fearful of communist influences in the Congress of the People and did not attend the 1955 Kliptown meeting promulgating the Freedom Charter. His activities in the Liberal Party after 1955 helped to build up its African membership, especially after he became editor of *Contact* in 1958. But his liberalism lacked a clear philosophical base and remained a series of fits and starts. After he left South Africa in 1962 he increasingly drifted towards Pan-Africanism and a revolutionary position despite remaining a strong anti-communist.[83]

The ambiguities of Duncan's political position reflected the uncertainties of South African liberalism in the 1950s. Some attempts were made to try and develop some form of public philosophy that could underpin the philosophical critique of apartheid. It was apparent to some intellectuals by the mid 1950s that the traditional commitment to evolutionary change was no longer adequate to deal with the emerging crisis in South Africa. As chapter 4 pointed out, the period of the late 1950s was important for the development of the idea of a "common society" forming the basis for a democratic liberalism, though some intellectuals tried to go further by linking this to a public philosophy that could command the allegiance of all social and ethnic groups in South African society.

The idea of a new public philosophy based upon a revival of the natural law tradition was suggested by the American liberal Walter Lippmann in *The Public Philosophy* (1956). His book was cautiously received in the United States where it appeared to many liberals to fail to relate to specific issues of human rights and social justice and to be more concerned with maintaining a fixed moral code from an older era.[84] In South Africa, however, where the legal process was by no means so well embedded, the idea of a revival of natural law was attractive to those liberals anxious not to concede to the demands of a popular sovereignty that had no political or constitutional checks on its power. Natural law was part of a long tradition of legal thinking in the West and so could be appealed to as a means of reviving the ideals of a "Western civilization" that otherwise looked like conceding to the demands of a new totalitarianism.

One of the main figures associated with the revival of natural law thinking was the constitutional lawyer Denis Cowen, who was married to Patrick Duncan's sister Deborah. Like Edgar Brookes, Cowen turned to the thought of St Augustine for the idea of a natural law which stood above the actions of the sovereign state. As a liberal, Cowen was critical of the stand of the Progressive Party which had been formed in 1959 by a group of break-away United Party MPs. He refused to join the Party's Commission established under the chairmanship of Donald Molteno to investigate constitutional change. He also considered that the Party's commitment to a Bill of Rights was qualified by statements that still supported the separate but equal doctrine that had been outlawed in the 1954 Supreme Court judgment *Brown v Board of Education* in the United States. Cowen considered that it was essential for any new South African constitution to be colour-blind and he opposed any idea of a racially based federation.[85] Cowen's return to natural rights thinking was thus part of a wider project to return to the philosophical tenets of the Western liberal tradition in order to assert its basic incompatibility with the authoritarian state power of a white settler or the incipient totalitarianism of popularly elected governments that overruled or over-looked the rights and claims of minorities.

In *The Foundations of Sovereignty*, published in 1961, Cowen argued that it was essential for power to be reconciled with law since otherwise "unfettered power is despotism or tyranny; unfettered freedom is licence or anarchy".[86] The idea of natural law fed into the revival of international debate on human rights since World War Two, and was best symbolized by the Universal Declaration on Human Rights in 1948. Cowen saw natural law as providing a philosophical basis to constitutional government since it was rooted in the idea of right reason which stretched back to the Ancient Greeks: it is seen, for instance, in Sophocles' tragedy *Antigone* in which the edict of King Creon forbidding the burial of Antigone's brother is challenged by Antigone who claims that it is subordinate to the edict of Zeus in heaven. The idea was again taken up in more recent times and provides a check on arbitrary government. Cowen disputed the idea that a constitution can be valid simply because "the people" have ordained it. An independent criterion of morality is required to limit the unchecked popular sovereignty which otherwise threatens to be a revival of royalist absolutism in another form.[87]

Cowen's case for natural law thinking had some appeal to constitutionally minded liberals in South Africa. Edgar Brookes saw natural law as one way to restrict political power, though felt it needed to be reinforced by the power of Christian love as well.[88] The arguments, however, tended to be eclipsed in the course of the 1960s by the erosion of the rule of law in South Africa and the lurch towards armed struggle by the exile Congress movement and *Umkhonto we Size*, which was increasingly dominated by a Marxist ideology of national liberation struggle. A desperate mood began to set in amongst a number of liberals who were concerned to try to save what they could of Western values in the future South Africa. Randolph Vigne, who had been active on *Contact* but was distrustful of the enthusiasm for Pan-Africanist ideas among many liberals, exemplified this turn of mind. Writing to Alan Paton in October 1962 that civil liberties were just as much in peril from African political models as from communist ones, he continued:

The fact is ... many are becoming less and less anti communist (myself included, on an emotional plane) as Stalin recedes and as the West commits itself more and more to apartheid. *Not that the African-third front ideals are no alternative to Cold war partisanship, nor that our people will learn from Africa only preventive detention from politicians. But* while our people – Liberals, PAC and Congress – seek their principles in Africa *out of despair*, and turn their backs on the western alliance for the same reason, they are likely to feel increasingly cold towards the best things in the western way and to lose South Africa to the west when the change comes.[89]

Paton himself continued to take a rather more optimistic view. Liberalism was the one bulwark, he wrote to a correspondent in 1964, against a complete lapse into authoritarianism. Liberals had a duty not to let the existing liberties disappear otherwise "the present tyranny will last until it is overthrown by force, and I think this will mean many years, probably generations of chaos, which will be of advantage neither to our people nor to our friends abroad".[90] It was this sort of sentiment which kept the small groups of liberals active until the reassessment of its role began in the SPRO-CAS deliberations of the early 1970s. In the course of that decade the term "white civilization" became increasingly embarrassing to mainstream English-speaking opinion as it linked civilizing attributes to genetical inheritance rather than to culture.[91]

At the same time, though, the resurgence of African nationalism following the collapse of Portuguese colonial rule in Angola and Mozambique in 1974 led to a revival in some South African discourses of catastrophy-laden theories regarding the fortunes of Western culture. It was reflected in some of the fiction of the period – in Nadine Gordimer's 1974 novel *The Conservationist*, for example, where a storm from the Mozambique Channel reformed the South African landscape, including the farm of the English-speaking anti-hero, Mehring, who ignominiously disappears in an abyss of moral corruption having picked up a seedy prostitute.[92]

Another graphic depiction of this theme is J. M. Coetzee's novel *Waiting for the Barbarians* published in 1981. This explores the cultural consequences of the progressive collapse of imperial civilization in a nameless frontier town governed by a well-meaning liberal magistrate. The magistrate is the repository of law in a situation of direct confrontation with the "barbarians" who stand immediately outside the Empire's frontiers and resemble the brutish warriors in the original Western conception of barbarism.

The magistrate is a man who refuses to accept the ultimate logic of the civilizing process. "All my life I have believed in civilised behaviour," he records. "Where civilisation entailed the corruption of barbarian virtues and the creation of a dependent people, I decided, I was opposed to civilisation".[93] The magistrate collects the artefacts from previous civilizations that have existed in the region and he realizes that the present regime is but one phase of a longer historical timespan.

The government at the centre decides, rather like the South African regime after 1948, to consolidate its power by moving in "new men of Empire" – such as Colonel Joll who "believe in fresh starts, new chapters, clean pages".[94] Some of the barbarians are tortured and the magistrate finally decides to refuse to accept this as the price of keeping the Empire. He decides to return his faceless and nameless barbarian mistress to her own people, though in the process he comes to realize that the barbarians think of the colonizers as mere visitors and transients in the land. On his return the magistrate is imprisoned and he decides to make a moral protest against the torture of the barbarians by breaking out of prison. On his release he comes to realize the essential *unnaturalness* of empires:

> Empire has located its existence not in the smooth recurrent spinning time of the cycle of the seasons but in the jagged time of rise and fall, of beginning and end, of catastrophe. Empire dooms itself to live in history and plot against history. One thought alone preoccupies the submerged mind of Empire: how not to end, how not to die, how to prolong its era. By day it pursues its enemies. It is cunning and ruthless, it sends its bloodhounds everywhere. By night it feeds on images of disaster: the sack of cities, the rape of populations, pyramids, acres of desolation.[95]

Coetzee's novel is a powerful polemic against a tradition of discourse based upon the idea of a catastrophic theory of history, a tradition which has even now not entirely disappeared from South African political debate. The novel looks to a new political vocabulary emerging in South African politics free from such an obsession with catastrophe. The signs are that a new discourse is gradually replacing the older language in the English-speaking intelligentsia, especially as a result of the return of a number of exiles after the relegalization of the Congress movements. As the concluding chapter suggests, the impact this will have on future political debate is likely to be profound.

CONCLUSION

English-speaking intellectuals have not been successful in developing any major political philosophy in response to segregation and apartheid. In part this can be explained by the domination in political debate until at least the 1950s of a humanistic race relations. This led to a tendency to avoid examining broader issues of citizenship and political obligation and to be preoccupied with more immediate concerns centred on "inter-racial accommodation" whether with Afrikaner or African nationalism.[1]

English-speaking intellectuals have traditionally felt politically weak in the face of Boer/Afrikaner power. Many English writers sought an accommodation with the Boer republics before the Anglo-Boer War and it was only a minority of imperialist jingoes – men such as Percy Fitzpatrick – who looked to their complete submission to British imperial hegemony. Many English-speaking business leaders in the Transvaal Republic accepted imperial domination since they saw it as inevitable. Most of the leaders of the English community indeed were, in M.J. Bonn's words, "turning into 'new Afrikanders' and looked upon the subcontinent as their children's home".[2]

The English-speaking intelligentsia by the time of Union in South Africa was torn between keeping its links with Britain as the "imperial motherland" and the appeals to a South African nationalism that were being made by a number of Afrikaner nationalists. This divided set of loyalties would continue down the years until the advent of the republic in 1961 finally severed the ties with Britain. Some of the liberals who emerged by the 1920s – Edgar Brookes, for example – were influenced by the international climate of Wilsonian liberalism and tried to reconcile their liberal ideals with Afrikaner nationalism. Within a decade this came to be seen as conniving with the entrenchment of an unjust system of racial segregation.

To some English-speaking writers there appeared from the 1930s onwards to be a general loss of nerve and an unwillingness to confront what Edgar Brookes now termed the "lie in the soul" of segregation. Internationally missionary and liberal opinion elsewhere in the English-speaking world such as Britain and the United States was beginning to turn against segregationism by the early 1930s. English-speaking liberals came under growing pressure to meet the standards of international humanitarian opinion. For some liberals, such as Edgar Brookes and Alfred Hoernle, the issue became especially stark once they had visited the United States and examined the pattern of race relations there at first hand. The advancement of black Americans appeared confirmation that people of African origins could advance in an industrial society. This fortified the resistance to "scientific" ideas of racial differences even if debate continued on how far cultural differences between whites and blacks prevented integration into a common society.

An imperial outlook in many cases continued to govern a lot of the debate. Some English-speaking South African intellectuals had considerable difficulty in freeing themselves from the idea that white "civilization" was fundamentally at risk from an upsurge of the "barbarians" in its midst. Some Afrikaner writers, such as Laurens van der Post, who mostly wrote in English, championed the San in preference to black Africans as examples of noble savages. But there were clear limits to their association with whites. Van der Post's writing was one example of an internal emigration away from direct confrontation with South African political realities. He ended up adopting the genre of British imperial writers and as late as the 1950s hoped that the imperial mission could be put on a new and sounder footing that would free it from colour discrimination.

There was a deep political pessimism in many of the contributions of English-speaking writers and intellectuals to political debate, despite the tradition of Christianity that urged its believers not to lose hope. To theorists such as Edgar Brookes, political thinking as well as religious teaching about citizenship and its duties could only take place in South Africa "in the stormy light of this borderland between hope and despair".[3]

Many English-speaking intellectuals abandoned segregationist ideas with reluctance. The original formulation of racial segregation owed much in the years before and after Union to English-speaking race theorists. Segregation was developed as an ideology of white supremacy alongside Darwinian ideas of social evolutionism at a time when many Afrikaner intellectuals were still dominated by more static notions of white supremacy underpinned by a Calvinist belief in salvation of the elect.[4] English-speaking intellectuals attached these evolutionary ideas to older Victorian imperial notions of a white "civilizing mission" in the subcontinent. They also developed them in a "scientific" discourse which updated the old Victorian belief in racial typologies based on craniology. By the inter-war years a number of English-speaking race theorists were responsible for developing a newer mode of race classification centred upon intelligence-testing. This updating of language spilled over into Afrikaner political thinking. Theorists such as R. F. A. Hoernle strove to maintain links with the Afrikaner intelligentsia as part of an attempt at political bridge-building. In turn, Afrikaners such as W. W. M. Eiselen saw some of the roots of the apartheid ideal in Hoernle's liberal model of racial separation.

The importance of the liberalism in English-speaking circles in South Africa lay in the absence of any serious competition from an ideology of white supremacy. Segregationism did not become allied to a coherent ideology of political elitism on the continental fascist model, while few English-speakers became allied to neo-fascist movement such as the *Ossewa Brandwag* (unlike more recent far-right bodies like the Conservative Party). The Natal segregationist George Heaton Nicholls privately believed in the ideal of a white aristocracy but in public at least talked by the 1930s a language of trusteeship. The Commonwealth connection and the towering figure of Smuts had some importance in moderating the language of many English-speaking intellectuals and race theorists on the political right.

This phenomenon was illuminated by the Jewish writer Sarah Gertrude Millin, whose views on race were restrained while Smuts and Hofmeyr were still alive in the years before the 1950s. Millin shared some of the outlook of the white liberals in the inter-war years, though she wrote a number of novels that were fiercely hostile to inter-racial "miscegenation". Her biographies of *Cecil Rhodes*

(1933) and *General Smuts* (1936) underlined her belief in a white civilizing mission in South Africa allied to a strong commitment to the British Commonwealth connection.

Even before the 1948 Nationalist victory, though, Sarah Gertrude Millin feared for the worst. The onset of Indian independence filled her with forboding for a future filled with catastrophe. It appeared that "white civilization" would end within less than two generations in Africa, she wrote ruefully to Smuts in 1946. Giving in to the Indians was only the thin end of the wedge since "if the Indians, even the illiterates, get everything, why not the half-castes; and if every District Six half caste, why not a native + if a dignified native, why not any native".[5] Millin recognized that there was a certain inherent logic to the demands of non-Western nationalism. But she berated its apparent consequences in an hysterical manner rather than initiating some form of counter-ideology.

In the years after 1948, Sarah Gertrude Millin moved towards an increasingly reactionary position on race and drifted towards supporting apartheid. In an article in the journal *Foreign Affairs* in 1949 she linked the idea of racial separation espoused in Hoernle's 1939 formulation to a longer vision stretching back to Rhodes's 1894 Glen Grey Act. Underlining her argument was a sentiment based merely upon fear, for "to give the black man too much may mean his own submergence".[6] This hardly amounted to a new and creative vision of the white presence in South Africa. Millin moved into an entrenched intellectual *laager* over the following years, reflecting the progressive isolation of the society she lived in. After 1960 old friendships with writers such as Vera Brittain and Rebecca West in Britain became severed and in 1965 Millin ended up supporting aid to the rebel Smith regime in Rhodesia. Her edited collection, *White Africans Are Also People* (1966), could not find a publisher outside South Africa and suggested in the crudest of terms that the fate of whites in a black-run South Africa was cannibals' stew-pots.[7] Such racist propaganda appeared to embarrass even the government of John Vorster in South Africa and at her funeral in 1968 no government representative was present.

The general trend of thought on the right of the English-speaking intelligentsia tended to be both atavistic and reactionary. In essence it ended up in a fellow-travelling position to the Nationalists' ideology of apartheid. The main intellectual developments among English-speakers by the 1960s tended to gravitate towards either liberalism or Marxism.

These developments were encouraged by the continued professionalizing of English-speaking intellectuals into universities. This process had begun after the First World War and in the 1920s and 1930s a newer intelligentsia began to emerge based on the English-speaking universities. This updated much of the older missionary discourse as it became organized around research work in such subjects as anthropology, psychology, economics and history. There was a progressive modification in the idea that the white society in South Africa was the extension of "Western civilization" towards the notion, derived in part from Toynbee and Spengler, that a rather different branch of this "civilization" had to be built up in South Africa.

In the debates of the 1930s the philosophy of pragmatic accommodation to segregationism articulated by R. F. A. Hoernle tended to prevail in English-speaking liberal circles over the more classical liberalism of Edgar Brookes. Hoernle's emphasis upon the role of groups as well as individuals in South African society appeared to be a means of reconciling metropolitan liberal values to an apparently triumphant segregationism. This disconnected liberalism from its revolutionary roots in nineteenth-century European history. It also shifted attention away from the central preoccupation of political philosophy with theories of morality and focused instead on the more technical question of how South African society was to be organized. The result was that English-speaking liberalism in the critical years of the 1940s and 1950s was left ill-equipped to provide a coherent code of morality by which to evaluate the action of the central state, which had tended to recede into the background of their political thinking.[8]

Much of the thinking of English liberal writers after 1945 was burdened by a concern to work within Hoernle's pragmatic accord with the central state in order to try to humanize it from within. A small number also ruminated speculatively over the crisis of Western civilized values before the advances of tribal nationalism. The historian Arthur Keppel-Jones viewed Afrikaner nationalism as a revival of a totalitarian National Socialism in his influential book *When Smuts Goes* (1947). Keppel-Jones saw a return to barbarism in South Africa under Nationalist rule which by the late 1980s would have descended to a level on a par with South American military regimes, subject to *coups d'état*. He predicted an exodus of English-speakers from South Africa to the British colonies of Central

Africa which would continue to remain under "civilized rule". The book was a strong plea for the retention of parliamentary government.[9]

A good proportion of English-speakers found it possible to live under apartheid. Many continued to vote for the conservative opposition United Party. There was strong opposition mounted by the quarter-million-strong Torch Commando in the early 1950s but this movement refused to adopt a policy on the "native question". By this time Keppel-Jones began to see the role of the English-speaking community in South Africa as a moral force to lead Afrikanerdom out of its pre-industrial parochialism into the modern world of multi-party politics.[10]

This notion of the mediatory role of English-speakers became an item of faith during the increasingly bleak years of the 1950s and 1960s, as the community appeared to be increasingly losing its political influence with the decline of British imperial power in the region. As late as 1965, Edgar Brookes still considered that English-speakers could be "the binding cement between the granite blocks with which it seems the structure of our new state must be built and certainly we are one of the best and most natural links between South Africa and the outside world".[11]

More radical critics saw this as a rationalization of political weakness and a failure to mount a more sustained alliance with black political opposition to apartheid. The problem that continually confronted the English-speaking South African intelligentsia was that the moral core of their political position was frequently mounted by churchmen and vocal critics of apartheid in Britain and the US. This stand often made a strong impact on black leaders. As early as 1952, the Anglican black politician Z. K. Matthews wrote in the United States that there could be "no doubt the Michael Scotts and Trevor Huddlestons are few and far between in church circles today. The price which such persons might be called upon to pay for being *kafferboeties* ["nigger lovers"] . . . is greater than most would be willing to pay".[12]

Some South African English-speaking liberals did try to make a stand during the 1950s around a more democratic liberalism that stressed the need to create a common society. One of the most vocal of these was Patrick Duncan but other liberals from the Cape province such as Donald Molteno began also to link traditional liberalism with democratic demands. Further opposition to apartheid was made by some legal and philosophical opinion around the precepts of natural law, though this tended to get lost in the wave of state trials and judicial repression in the early 1960s.

In the years after Sharpeville, English-speaking liberals found it increasingly difficult to try and keep up with an international climate of opinion which was escalating in hostility to apartheid. Many radical democrats were forced into exile after the 1960s and this tended to intensify the conservative trend within the English-speaking community generally. A broad section of English opinion moved towards the Nationalists in the course of that decade, leaving a small minority of English intellectual opinion veering towards liberalism.

This liberalism was a set of intellectual attitudes that had little political embodiment once the Liberal Party went into voluntary liquidation in 1968. The SAIRR under the leadership of Quintin Whyte and later Frederick Van Wyk remained locked in the traditional formula spelt out by Hoernle of accommodating as far as possible to Afrikaner nationalism and trying to wean away moderate Afrikaners from the *volk*. There seemed to be little to impel any major changes in this strategy once South Africa became increasingly insular in the course of the 1960s.

Newer developments had begun to occur at the cultural level during the 1950s as some English-speaking novelists such as Nadine Gordimer gained contact with black writers and artists in the heady days of the *Drum* era.[13] By the mid 1960s these contacts too had declined following the state clamp-downs after Sharpeville and white English-speaking writers felt increasingly isolated.

There was a growing sense of internal exile among many English-speaking intellectuals from the early 1960s. Many felt there was a need to rethink the theoretical and moral base of liberalism in South Africa, especially as a number of younger *verligte* Afrikaner intellectuals were beginning to emerge from universities who were more amenable to the intellectual accord that many liberals since the era of Hoernle had been hoping for. Some of this occurred in the course of the SPRO-CAS deliberations in the early 1970s. These broadly reflected a compromise between the classical school of liberalism based on the rights of the individual and a more group-orientated liberalism that traced its intellectual roots back to the thinking of Alfred Hoernle. The latter tended to prevail as the more classical liberals remained silent, partly through demoralization following the collapse of the Liberal Party and partly because many of the most prominent spokesmen of this school had left the country or been banned.

This exemplified a process that was occurring in other Western societies – in the United States, for example – where a gradual decline of public intellectuals living chiefly by writing for a popular audience coincided with the emergence of a campus intelligentsia organized around the routines of professional closure in academic disciplines.[14] While the older generation of prominent English-speaking intellectuals such as W. M. Macmillan, Edgar Brookes and R. F. A. Hoernle had been based in universities for at least part of their careers, they had to a considerable degree worked alongside other non-academic bodies such as the SAIRR and missionary and church groups that kept them in touch with a wider audience. At the same time, novelists such as Alan Paton and Nadine Gordimer had been able to write even in the post-war years as independent public intellectuals, fostering and sustaining political debate and dialogue.

The phenomenon of the public intellectual in the United States began to be superseded by the rapid expansion of universities in the 1960s and 1970s, and the same process occurred in South Africa too. It was aided by the state clamp-downs in the 1960s which forced a number of public intellectuals into exile or silence, though one or two notable figures such as Nadine Gordimer managed, with difficulty, to survive. The growth of a university-based intelligentsia was clearly reflected by the academic domination of the SPRO-CAS deliberations in the early 1970s, signalling that a newer generation of social-science-trained intellectuals had arrived on the scene.

SPRO-CAS One indicated some of the limitations of academically inclined liberalism. To some critics its fascination with "top-down" models of political consociationalism suggested a reluctance to consult with black political opposition. SPRO-CAS Two, on the other hand, did indicate the revival of a more radical opposition, anxious to forge links with newer African political opinion emerging in the black-consciousness movement. The two schools clashed in 1973–74 within the SAIRR, though they reflected much wider social and educational trends amongst the English-speaking intelligentsia.

The more conservative strand of opinion tended to prevail in the Institute, though in the years since then the organization has endeavoured to make a number of changes so that its research work can reach a wider black audience. The tradition of group-orientated liberalism made considerable intellectual headway in SAIRR circles in the mid to late 1970s during a period of mounting crisis in South African politics. Some liberal critics counselled caution against becoming fixated with ethnicity, for there were, wrote Andrew Prior in 1978, "long term dangers in fabricating political arrangements which correspond to transient racial, class and interest categories".[15] But the group-based model of political accommodation appeared to meet the needs of an opposition that was determined to be pragmatic in its dealings with the apartheid state.

The dialogue with *verligte* Afrikaner intellectuals, who, like the English-speakers, were campus-orientated, began to indicate the emergence of a white intellectual establishment that to a degree transcended the older ethnic divide. This dialogue over group-orientated political models following SPRO-CAS encouraged a progressive loss of faith in Whiggish constitutional models of political evolution that had been held by many of the English-speaking liberals until at least the early 1960s. This reflected a period when intellectuals in the legal profession had been driven into silence by the nature of the state's use of political trials. There were no obvious successors to O. D. Schreiner by the 1970s, though a number of important legal academics continued to write during this period and outline the erosion of the rule of law in the country.[16] But it was not altogether surprising that the main focus of debate shifted to the social sciences since to many it appeared that the only way out of the political impasse was through a social-science-driven model of reform and political negotiation.

The effect of this shift was a revitalization of Hoernle's emphasis in the late 1930s of asserting group as well as individual rights in the political process in South Africa. This dictated the agenda of white political debate in SPRO-CAS in the early 1970s and became extended to debate within the ruling power bloc in the wake of the 1976 Soweto crisis. This process led in turn to the new constitution of 1983, introduced by Chris Heunis, which provided for three separate ethnic chambers of parliament: for whites, coloureds and Indians, though not for Africans. If this was the fruition of the Hoernlean vision, it was one which its founder would probably have viewed with horror.

The reform process succeeded in moving the South African system towards one of "neo-apartheid" in which a number of changes were made in order to incorporate a small black middle-class elite in a modified variant of separate development. Petty apartheid barriers were also progressively removed and trade unions given the right to strike. At the local level, new avenues of political expression were created in the form of black local councils, though these were widely seen as having only limited powers. But they did little to meet the most basic demands of the exiled political movements whose presence, by the very fact of their official absence from political debate and dialogue, became ever more palpable in South African politics.

The revolutionary upsurge of 1984–85, beginning in the Vaal Triangle and which led to two states of emergency in 1985 and 1986, had a major impact in transforming indelibly the South African political landscape. The conservative wing of the English-speaking intelligentsia had effectively allied itself to the "survival politics" of Afrikaner ethnic nationalism and had no new vision of the way South African society could be shifted out of apartheid. Some analysts began to point out that a nation-building process had to be created, though how this is to be achieved from a top-down level remained unexplained.[17] It became clear that a far more direct engagement had to take place between intellectuals in South Africa and the popular political movements, whose intelligentsia remained far less professionalized than their white counterparts.

To some of the more radically inclined English-speaking intellectuals this dilemma had been evident for at least two decades. Nadine Gordimer had recognized in *The Late Bourgeois World* (1966) that though an alliance between isolated white liberals and black radicals would tend to have an opportunist dimension on both sides, it at least sought an engagement with one of the central forces of South African politics. By contrast, the character of the conservative businessman, Mehring, in her novel *The Conservationist* (1974) simply disappears before the winds of popular revolt symbolized by a storm from the Mozambique Channel.[18]

To Gordimer, the issue confronting white English-speaking intellectuals is a clear one. The South African crisis demands a shift away from a Eurocentric mode of thinking towards an Afrocentrism. South Africa is, to this extent, a unique culture in Africa in that it was made by both white and black and its literary consciousness should in turn reflect this. She considers that South Africa had an indigenous cultural tradition to a far higher degree than other settler societies such as those of Latin America or Australia and this could in time form the nucleus for a post-apartheid culture. "It could provide,"

Gordimer has suggested, "one way in which whites could enter the blacks into the discovery of truly African ideas, related to this continent and away from ties with other continents".[19]

Some critics might see at the heart of Gordimer's argument a cultural despair induced by a profound sense of guilt by association with the ideology of apartheid. It is likely, though, that a progressive Africanization of both the English- and the Afrikaans-speaking intelligentsia will occur over the next few decades. By the year 2000 it is estimated that the Pretoria-Witwatersrand-Vereeniging area alone will consist of some 12 million blacks (half in informal housing), while a booming university-educated black population (at present there are 35,000 black graduates entering the job market each year) will lead to a significant black intelligentsia emerging in South African politics. Black intellectuals will be increasingly setting the agenda of debate in South African politics alongside some of their white counterparts.

The key question emerges of how far ethnicity will determine the nature and course of intellectual discussion in South Africa after apartheid. Radicals in South African politics have increasingly looked to a "non-racial" political future compared to the "multi-racial" ideals of the common society liberalism of the 1950s. This non-racial ideal will probably shape the post-apartheid *national* intelligentsia in South Africa that will be pivoted around a rapidly expanding core of urban black intellectuals with various sub-groupings of English, Afrikaans, Indian and Coloured intellectuals floating around its edges.

The challenge facing this new South African intelligentsia will be to spell out the moral basis of the new post-apartheid regime. While it may well seek an African complexion, it will be confronted by a wider ideological crisis in post-colonial and "third-world" states. Marxist ideas of "scientific socialism" became intellectually discredited even before the collapse of the Eastern European communist regimes in 1989. Closer to home, models of Afro-Marxism have been a disastrous failure, while elsewhere in the continent the hopes for rapid modernization by the "Bandung generation" of political leaders, who came to the fore in the 1950s, have not been successful.

The liberal tradition in South African politics has thus acquired an unforeseen relevance after years when most serious analysts wrote it off as an option for the country's political system. It was considered by Pierre van den Berghe in 1979, for example, to have missed its opportunity in the 1950s when a more moderate generation of African leaders held sway in the ANC and to be too narrowly based on educated whites to have much impact on white opinion generally.[20] Radical writers such as Martin Legassick considered its moral base to have been eroded before the advent of mass-based black working-class movement in the 1950s and 1960s, leaving it only as a mechanism for the mediation of escalating class conflict.[21] I myself, in a study of liberalism from 1921 to 1960, also considered that liberal values would be unlikely to achieve much political importance given the manner in which conservative liberals successfully marginalized more radical efforts to relate liberal values to a wider constituency at the local level.[22]

These assessments were rather premature. The fortunes of liberalism do not exactly follow any prescribed political and social pattern, though they are more likely to prevail in a society where there is a relatively high degree of education, some modern infrastructure and a reasonably cohesive and self-confident middle class. To this extent, liberal political orders tend to be most stable in advanced capitalist regimes, though liberal values have a capacity too to prevail among intelligentsias trying to promote modernization in authoritarian states.[23]

Utilitarian liberal values rooted in self-interest alone, however, lead to social atomization. There is a need for a teleological vision to work towards, otherwise liberalism is left with no sense of social direction. It is probable that in South Africa any vibrant liberalism will have to work in close accord with the African churches and talk a language of human rights. In so far as any post-apartheid social order will seek to be "non-racial" it will be affirming the rights of the individual over those of the racial group. The classical tradition of liberalism associated with a figure like Edgar Brookes will take on a new relevance, even if it emerges in a rather different language of political and theological "liberation".

The new challenge facing the South African liberal intelligentsia, whatever its language background, will be to rethink liberal ideals to reflect demands for democratic rights in South Africa. The new constitution of a post-apartheid society is likely to reflect both group and individual rights, though it will be a challenge to make these group rights not simply an instrument for the conservative defence of white privilege but also an active component of a new society. First-generation political rights too will probably be accompanied by second-generation economic and social rights, while third-generation rights will stress the rights of women, peace and a clean environment. Many of these latter issues are just beginning to be debated in South Africa.[24] There is a new and burgeoning educational role for English-speaking intellectuals to perform in the making of a genuinely national South African intellectual community.

NOTES

Introduction

1. Edward Shils, "The Intellectuals and the Powers" in *The Intellectuals and the Powers and Other Essays*, Chicago and London, The University of Chicago Press, 1972, p. 5.
2. H. L. Watts, "Portrait of English Speaking White South Africa" in Andre de Villiers (ed), *English Speaking South Africa Today*, Cape Town, OUP, 1976, p. 86.
3. For the growth of the *kholwa* in Natal see Norman Alan Etherington, "The Rise of the Kholwa in Southeast Africa: African Christian Communities in Natal, Pondoland and Zululand, 1835–1880", Ph.D Thesis, Yale University, 1971; for Luthuli see Albert Luthuli, *Let My People Go*, London Collins, 1962. See also Richard W. Hull, *American Enterprise in South Africa*, New York and London, New York University Press, 1990, pp. 42–51.
4. See, for example, Andre Odendaal, *Vukani Bantu!: The Beginnings of Black Protest Politics in South Africa to 1912*, Cape Town, David Philip, 1984.
5. Rodney Davenport, *The Afrikaner Bond*, Cape Town, OUP, 1966.
6. Andre Du Toit, "No Chosen People: The Myth of the Calvinist Origins of Afrikaner Nationalism and Racial Ideology", *American Historical Review*, 88, 4 (October 1983), pp. 920–957.
7. B. K. Murray, *Wits: The Early Years*, Johannesburg, Witwatersrand University Press, 1982.
8. Isaiah Berlin, "The Birth of the Russian Intelligentsia", in *Russian Thinkers*, Harmondsworth, Penguin Books, 1979, p. 117.
9. Aleksander Gella, "An Introduction to the Sociology of the Intelligentsia" in Aleksander Gella (ed), *The Intelligentsia and the*

Intellectuals, London and Beverley Hills, Sage Publications, 1976, pp. 9–34.
10. G. H. Calpin, *There Are No South Africans*, London and New York, Nelson, 1941; W. K. Hancock, *Are There South Africans?*, Johannesburg, SAIRR, 1966.
11. Randolph Starn, "Historians and 'Crisis'", *Past and Present*, 52 (August 1971), p. 17.
12. Galla, *op. cit.*, p. 15.
13. Karl Mannheim, *Ideology and Utopia*, London, Routledge and Kegan Paul, 1936. Mannheim's volume though is important for other reasons, especially the recognition that political thinking is by its nature a collective rather than an individual activity. See Richard Ashcraft, "Political Theory and Political Action in Karl Mannheim's Thought: Reflections upon *Ideology and Utopia* and its Critics", *Comparative Studies in Society and History*, 23 (1981), pp. 23–50.
14. Gertrude Himmelfarb, " 'History With the Politics Left Out' " in *The New History and the Old*, Cambridge, Harvard University Press, 1987, p. 18.
15. Dominick Lacapra, "Rethinking Intellectual History and Reading Texts", *History and Theory*, XIX (1980), p. 253. See though Felix Gilbert, "Intellectual History: Its Aims and Methods", *Daedalus*, 2 (Spring 1971), pp. 81–97 for a rather different conception stressing the complementary nature of intellectual and social history.
16. *Ibid.*, p. 164.
17. John Dunn, "The Identity of the History of Ideas", *Philosophy*, XLIII, 164 (April 1968), p. 92.
18. See, for example, John Higham, "Intellectual History and Its Neighbours", *Journal of the History of Ideas*, XV, 3 (June 1954), pp. 339–347.
19. Allister Sparks, *The Mind of South Africa*, London, Heinemann, 1990, p. 70.
20. F. G. Butler, "The Nature and Purpose of the Conference" in Andre de Villiers, *op. cit.*, p. 8.
21. N. G. Garson, "English-speaking South Africans and the British Connection, 1820–1961" in *ibid.*, p. 17.
22. David Welsh, *The Roots of Segregation*, Cape Town, OUP, 1971.
23. See, in particular, Leroy Vail "Introduction: Ethnicity in South African History" in Leroy Vail (ed), *The Creation of Tribalism in Southern Africa*, London, James Currey and Berkeley and Los Angeles, University of California Press, 1989, pp. 1–20.

1 Science and White Supremacy

1. See, for example, W. H. Vatcher, *White Laager: The Rise of Afrikaner Nationalism*, London, Pall Mall Press, 1965; T. Dunbar Moodie, *The Rise of Afrikanerdom: Power, Apartheid and the Afrikaner Civil Religion*, Berkeley, University of California Press, 1979; Dan O'Meara,

Volkskapitalisme: Class, Capital and Ideology in the Development of Afrikaner Nationalism, 1934–1948, Johannesburg, Ravan Press, 1983.
2. Leonard Thompson, *The Political Mythology of Apartheid*, New Haven and London, Yale University Press, 1986; see also Christopher Saunders, *The Making of the South African Past*, Cape Town and Johannesburg, David Philip, 1988.
3. Martin Legassick, "The Making of South African 'Native Policy' 1903–1923: The Origins of Segregation", London, Institute of Commonwealth Studies (mimeo), 1972, "British Hegemony and the Origins of Segregation, 1900–1914", *ibid.*, 1973.
4. Harold Wolpe, "Capitalism and Cheap Labour Power in South Africa: From Segregation To Apartheid", *Economy and Society*, XIV (1972), pp. 425–56.
5. Saul Dubow, *Racial Segregation and the Origins of Apartheid in South Africa, 1919–36*, London and Basingstoke, The Macmillan Press, 1989, p. 24.
6. M. Swanson, "The Sanitation Syndrome: Bubonic Plague and Urban Native Policy in the Cape Colony, 1900–1909", *Journal of African History*, XVIII, 3 (1977), pp. 387–410.
7. Dubow, pp. 77–127; "Holding a Just Balance Between White and Black: The Native Affairs Department in South Africa, 1920–33", *Journal of Southern African Studies*, XII, 2 (1986), pp. 217–239.
8. John W. Cell, *The Highest Stage of White Supremacy: The Origins of Segregation in South Africa and the American South*, Cambridge, Cambridge University Press, 1982.
9. Philip Curtin, *The Image of Africa*, Madison, University of Wisconsin Press, 1964, pp. 429–31.
10. C. T. Loram, *The Education of the South African Native*, London, Longmans, Green and Co, 1927, pp. 17–25.
11. John S. Haller, *Outcasts From Evolution: Scientific Attitudes to Racial Inferiority, 1859–1900*, New York, Columbia University Press, 1975, p. 209. One South African theorist of race, though, continued to believe as late as the 1890s that the "aborigines" of the continent would die out in the face of "Caucasian" advance. See F. S. Tatham, *The Race Conflict in South Africa*, Pietermaritzburg, 1894.
12. Paul B. Rich, "Milnerism and a Ripping Yarn: Transvaal Land Settlement and John Buchan's Novel *Prester John*, 1901–1910" in Belinda Bozzoli (ed), *Town and Countryside in the Transvaal*, Johannesburg, Ravan Press, 1983, pp. 412–33.
13. Colin Bundy, *The Rise and Fall of the South African Peasantry*, London, Heinemann, 1979, esp. pp. 134–140.
14. See the discussion in Cell, *op. cit.*, pp. 204–219.
15. Legassick, "British Hegemony", p. 3.
16. Ronald Hyam, *Elgin and Churchill at the Colonial Office*, London and New York, Macmillan, 1968, pp. 371–2.
17. *Godfrey Lagden Papers*, A951/A7 Diary entry for 16 March 1903. In a memorandum on the SANAC report, Lagden felt that it was "desirable to move steadily and quietly so as to avoid any unnecessary

disturbance of the native mind". He opposed African lands being scattered throughout the white population since this would "accentuate feelings of race prejudice and animosity with unhappy results", Archives of the Transvaal Secretary of Native Affairs, SNA 265, *Memorandum by the Commissioner for Native Affairs upon the Report of South African Native Affairs Commission in its Relation to the Transvaal*, 1905, pp. 1–4.

18. SNA 4/442/01 G. Lagden to R. Rose Innes 31 October 1901; *Lagden Papers*, Diary entry for 30 January 1905.
19. SNA 11/1300/1902 G. Lagden "Notes for Council – Taxation of Natives", n.d.
20. *The Transvaal Leader*, October 19 1904.
21. *J. Howard Pim Papers*, G. Lagden to H. Pim 29 November 1903, 6 and 24 April 1905.
22. Howard Pim, *The Native Question in South Africa*, Johannesburg, 1903.
23. Howard Pim, *The Native Problem in South Africa*, Johannesburg, 1905, p. 11. "To think that we can civilise the native is an idle dream", Pim wrote, "He must civilise himself or die", *ibid.*, p. 13. See also Howard Pim, *The Question of Race*, Johannesburg, 1906.
24. *The Native Problem in South Africa*.
25. John David Shingler, "Education and Political Order in South Africa, 1902–1961", Ph.D Dissertation, Yale University, 1973, p. 17; in Britain, though, many aspects of the old racial typology survived well into the 1940s, Paul B. Rich, *Race and Empire in British Politics*, Cambridge, CUP, 1986.
26. *Izwi Labantu*, March 20 1906. Some black papers had felt doubtful over Lagden's chairmanship of SANAC from the very beginning. "I do not think that the country will benefit under his chairmanship", wrote "a native". "He has not the training of a judge – a man who has studied impartially to perfection", *Koranta ea Becoana*, October 21 1903.
27. A. R. Colquhoun, *The Afrikaner Land*, London, John Murray, 1906.
28. *J. Howard Pim Papers*, Transvaal Native Affairs Society, *Constitution and Rules*, Johannesburg, 1908, para. 1.
29. *Ibid.*, Transvaal Native Affairs Society, Minute Book.
30. *Ibid.*
31. Legassick, "British Hegemony".
32. *Transvaal Leader*, November 4 1908 and July 8 1909.
33. *A. H. Haddon Papers*, 4071, A. H. Keane to A. C. Haddon, 27 January 1903 A. H. Keane, *Ethnology*, Cambridge, Cambridge University Press, 1896, p. 10.
34. *Transvaal Leader*, September 29 1909.
35. Howard Pim, *The Native Problem: Presidential Address Read at the Inaugural Meeting of the Native Affairs Society April 21, 1908*, Johannesburg, 1908, p. 1.
36. Fred W. Bell, *The South African Native Problem: The Solution of Segregation*, Johannesburg, Central News Agency, 1909, p. 13. Bell later reflected that the Native Affairs Society had come close to "being captured by those who may, I think, with reason be claimed as 'negrophilists' ", *F. W. Bell Papers*, handwritten ms, n.d.

37. Harry Johnstone, "The Native Problem and Sane Imperialism", *The Nineteenth Century*, August 1909, pp. 234–44.
38. Howard Pim, *A Plea For The Scientific Study of the Races Inhabiting South Africa*, Johannesburg, 1910.
39. H. J. Crocker, *The South African Race Problem*, Johannesburg, 1908.
40. Edward Dallas, *Notes on the South African Race Problem*, Johannesburg, 1909, p. 1. See also Trevor Fletcher, "The Native Problem: A Transcendental View", *The African Monthly* 4, 24 (November 1908), p. 585.
41. *The Star*, July 15 1910.
42. *F. W. Bell Papers*, F. W. Bell to J. B. M. Hertzog, 26 September 1911.
43. See, for example, the evidence of Edward Dower, Secretary of Native Affairs, to the Beaumont Commission, *Report of the Natives Lands Commission, Vol. 11, UG22–1916*, p. 230; Dubow, *op. cit.*, p. 80.
44. John X. Merriman to M. T. Steyn, October 18 1912 in Phyllis Lewsen (ed), *Selections from the Correspondence of John X. Merriman*, Cape Town, The Van Riebeeck Society, 1966, p. 225.
45. *F. W. Bell Papers*, F. W. Bell, *Farewell Address to the Transvaal Native Affairs Society*, Johannesburg, 1910.
46. Maurice Evans, *Studies in the Southern States from a South African Point of View*, Address to the Durban Native Affairs Reform Committee, (Durban, 1912?), p. 10.
47. *Ibid.*
48. Paul B. Rich, "The Appeals of Tuskegee: James Henderson, Lovedale and the Fortunes of South African Liberalism, 1906–1930", *The International Journal of African Historical Studies*, 20. 2 (1987), pp. 271–92.
49. Stephen Jay Gould, *The Mismeasure of Man*, Harmondsworth, 1984, Penguin Books, pp. 146–233.
50. Jan H. Hofmeyr, for example, declared when opening the 1929 meeting of the Association that the emergence of South African science could serve as a "Southern gateway ... effectively to permeate Africa", Jan H. Hofmeyr, *Africa and Science*, Cape Town, SAAAS, 1929, p. 11.
51. Stephen Gottheid Rich, "Binet Simon Tests in Zululand", *Report of the SAAAS*, Stellenbosch, 1917 (Cape Town, 1918), p. 482. For the importance of the First World War on the US military see Franz Samuelson, "World War I Intelligence Testing and the Development of Psychology", *Journal of the History of Behavioral Science*, 13 (1977), pp. 274–82; David Muschinske, "The Non white as Child: G. Stanley Hall on the Education of Nonwhite Peoples", *Journal of the History of the Behavioral Sciences*, 13 (1977), pp. 328–336. For an important recent study of mental testing in South Africa, see Saul Dubow, "Mental Testing and the Understanding of Race in Twentieth-Century South Africa", in T. Meade and M. Walker (eds), *Science, Medicine and Cultural Imperialism*, New York, St Martin's Press, 1991, pp. 148–177.
52. *The Education of the South African Native*, p. 127.
53. For the significance of Thorndike's work at the Columbia Teacher's

College see Hamilton Cravens, *The Triumph of Evolution: American Scientists and the Heredity-Environment Controversy, 1900–1941*, Pennsylvania, University of Pennsylvania Press, 1978, pp. 15–86.
54. Loram, *op. cit.*, p. 192.
55. *Ibid.*, pp. 224–5.
56. J. M. Coetzee, "Blood, Flaw, Taint, Degeneration: The Case of Sarah Gertrude Millin", *English Studies in Africa*, 23, 1 (1980), pp. 1–59, repr. in *White Writing*, New Haven, Yale University Press and Johannesburg, Ravan Press, 1988. The attack on "miscegenation" occurred in scientific circles at this time as well. At the 1917 meeting of the SAAAS Rev. Noel Roberts argued that there was a "native mentality" which missions had to train in the art of reasoning. This "mentality" was based upon the "arrested development" of African children whose "early promise" was checked by a wave of "sexualism" which in many cases took "entire" possession of their natures to the exclusion of every other desire". The 1913 *Report of the Commission To Inquire into Assaults on Women* was cited in support of this assertion. N. Roberts, *Report to The SAAAS*, (Cape Town, 1918), p. 99.
58. *H. B. Fantham File*, H. B. Fantham, lecture "Evolution and Mankind" delivered to the School of Mines, Johannesburg, July 9 1918.
59. H. B. Fantham, "Heredity in Man: Its Importance Both Biologically and Educationally", *South African Journal of Science*, XXI (1924), pp. 498–527; "Some Factors in Eugenics, Together With Notes on Some South African Cases", *South African Journal of Science*, XXII, (1925), pp. 400–12; "Some Thoughts on the Social Aspects of Eugenics, with notes on some further cases of human inheritance observed in South Africa", *South African Journal of Science*, XXIII, (1926), pp. 624–43; "Some Thoughts on Biology and Race", *South African Journal of Science*, XXIV, (1927), pp. 1–20.
60. J. E. Duerden, "Genetics and Eugenics in South Africa: Heredity and Environment", *South African Journal of Science*, XXII, (1925), p. 63.
61. *Ibid.*, p. 69.
62. C. T. Loram, "The Claims of the Native Question Upon Scientists", Presidential Address to Section E, SAAAS, 1921, *Proceedings of the SAAAS*, (Cape Town, 1921), p. 100.
63. The Cape liberal and amateur astronomer Alex Roberts, for example, claimed in 1922 that with the spread of education African physical features were changing "and in this direction it is interesting to state that the shape of the head of the outstanding Native leaders is quite different from that of the ordinary kraal native", A. W. Roberts, "Certain Aspects of the Native Question", *Report of the 20th Meeting of the SAAAS*, (Maputo, 1922), p. 98; *The Star*, July 15 1922; *The Cape Argus*, June 30 1922.
64. Peter Nielsen, *The Black Man's Place in South Africa*, Cape Town, Juta, 1922, p. 10.
65. *Ibid.*, pp. 20–35.
66. *Ibid.*, p. 57.
67. J. D. Rheinallt Jones, "The Need for a Scientific Basis for South African Native Policy", *South African Journal of Science*, XXIII, (1923).

68. *E. G. Malherbe Papers*, 425/1, R. F. A. Hoernle to EGM 20 and 24 March 1926.
69. *Ibid.*, 25 March 1926.
70. J. T. Dunstan, "Retarded and Defective Children: Native Mentality: Mental Testing", *Report of the SAAAS*, Bloemfontein, 1923, p. 155.
71. I. D. MacCrone, "Preliminary Results from the Porteus Maize Tests Applied to Native School Children", *South African Journal of Science*, XXV (1928), pp. 481–4.
72. *E. G. Malherbe Papers*, 619, C. T. Loram to E. G. Malherbe 3 and 29 November 1928. By the following year Loram wrote despondently that there did not appear to be anyone else for the NAC "brought up in our traditions", C. T. Loram to EGM, 4 March 1929.
73. *E. G. Malherbe Papers*, MSS 606 Fred Clarke to E. G. Malherbe February 26 1925. "Sometimes silence is the only possible form of support", Clarke wrote to Malherbe, "once you have given a clear statement of your position".
74. E. G. Malherbe, "Education and the Poor White", *South African Journal of Science*, XXVI (1929), pp. 883–903.
75. The Kallikak and Jukes family studies in the United States were recognized by a number of prominent South African psychologists at this time. See, for example, R. W. Wilcocks, "Intelligence, Environment and Heredity", *South African Journal of Science*, XXVIII (1931), pp. 63–76.
76. E. G. Malherbe, *Never a Dull Moment* (Cape Town, Juta 1981), p. 181.
77. M. L. Fick, "Intelligence Test Results of Poor White, Native (Zulu), Coloured and Indian school children and the educational and Social Implications", *South African Journal of Science*, XXVI (1929), p. 910.
78. *Ibid.*, p. 913.
79. The black newspaper *Ilanga lase Natal*, though, wondered whether the concept of "adaptation" was not simply "repression" in another guise. *Ilanga lase Natal*, September 9 1932.
80. D. D. T. Jabavu, "Higher Education and the Professional Training of the Bantu", *South African Journal of Science*, XXVI (1929), pp. 934–5.
81. Shingler, *op. cit.*, p. 29.
82. *Minute Book of the Gamma Sigma Club*, African Studies Institute, University of the Witwatersrand, 20 March 1931; *The Star*, 18 April 1931. R. F. A. Hoernle was in the chair.
83. *Z. K. Matthews Papers*, Z. K. Matthews to Tennyson Makiwane 18 September 1936.
84. See for example Rich, "The Appeals of Tuskegee".
85. Edgar Brookes, *Native Education in South Africa*, Pretoria, Van Schaik, 1930, p. 15.
86. *Report of the Interdepartmental Committee on Native Education, 1935–36*, U.G.29–1936, p. 86.
87. *Ibid.*, p. 87.
88. *Ibid.*, p. 89.
89. A. W. Hoernle, "New Aims and Methods in Social Anthropology", *South African Journal of Science*, XXX (October 1933), pp. 74–92.

90. I. D. MacCrone, "Psychology in Perspective" in *Our Changing World View*, Johannesburg, 1932, p. 16.
91. I. D. MacCrone, "The Problem of Race Differences", *South African Journal of Science*, XXXIII, (1936), pp. 92–107.
92. *The Natal Mercury*, 27 July 1936.
93. I. D. MacCrone, *Race Attitudes in South Africa*, Johannesburg, University of the Witwatersrand Press, 1937. See also Saunders, *The Making of the African Past*, p. 120.
94. E. G. Malherbe (ed), *Educational Adaptations in a Changing Society*, Cape Town, Juta 1937, p. 448.
95. *J. D. Rheinallt Jones Papers*, AD843.B.93.4. O. Black to J. D. R-J 26 March 1935.
96. W. Eiselen, "Foreword" in M. Laurence Fick, *The Education of the South African Native*, Pretoria, 1939. For the impact of Volkekunde on apartheid ideology see John Sharp, "The Roots and Development of Volkekunde in South Africa", *Journal of Southern African Studies*, 8, (1981), pp. 16–36; Adam Kuper, "Anthropology and Apartheid" in John Lonsdale (ed), *South Africa in Question*, London, J. Currey 1988, pp. 33–51.
97. *E. G. Malherbe Papers*, 565, EGM Notebook entry during WW2.
98. S. Biesheuvel, *African Intelligence*, Johannesburg, SAIRR, 1943, p. v.
99. *Ibid.*, p. 37.
100. *Ibid.*, p. 149.
101. *Ibid.*, p. 198.
102. *Ibid.*, pp. 206–7.
103. *Ibid.*, pp. 89–90 citing Ellen Hellman, "Life in a Johannesburg Slum Yard", *Africa*, VIII, 1 (1935), pp. 34–62.
104. I. D. MacCrone, "Race Attitudes" in Ellen Hellman (ed), *Handbook on Race Relations in South Africa*, Cape Town, OUP, 1949, pp. 669–705.
105. See chapter 4.
106. I. D. MacCrone, "Ethnocentric Ideology and Ethnocentrism", *Proc of the South African Psychological Assoc*, 4, 1953, p. 22.
107. I. D. MacCrone, "Human Relations in a Multi-Racial Society", *Race Relations*, XXXV, 1 & 2, (Jan–June 1958), p. 41.
108. S. Biesheuvel, "The Nation's Intelligence and its Measurement", *South African Journal of Science*, October–November 1952, pp. 120–138. Biesheuvel also tested African mineworkers for the Gold Producers Committee of the Chamber of Mines and tried to devise tests for "personnel selection" for African "boss boys". Though there was ethnic variation he put this down to the methods of sampling. He concluded that the "mass testing of primitive Africans for occupational purposes" to be both "feasible and worthwhile", S. Biesheuvel, "Personnel Selection tests for Africans", *South African Journal of Science*, August 1952, p. 12.

2   R. F. A. Hoernle and Liberal Idealism

1. Martin Legassick, "Race, Industrialisation and Social Change in South Africa: The case of R. F. A. Hoernle", *African Affairs*, LXXV, (1976), pp. 224–239.

2. Richard Elphick, "Mission Christianity and Interwar Liberalism" in Jeffrey Butler, Richard Elphick and David Welsh (eds), *Democratic Liberalism in South Africa*, Middletown (Conn), Wesleyan University Press and Cape Town and Johannesburg, David Philip, 1987, p. 79.
3. Jan H. Hofmeyr, "R. F. Alfred Hoernle: A Tribute", *Common Sense*, August 1943, p. 12; Louis F. Freed, "R. F. A. Hoernle: The Philosopher and the Man", address to the Annual General Meeting of Convocation of the University of the Witwatersrand, 12 April 1967, p. 7. I am grateful to Professor Bruce K. Murray for supplying me with the document.
4. Stefan Collini, "Hobhouse, Bosanquet and the State: Philosophical Idealism and Political Argument in England: 1880–1980", *Past and Present*, 72, (1976), pp. 86–111; *Liberalism and Sociology: L. T. Hobhouse and Political Argument in England, 1880–1915*, Cambridge, CUP, 1979. See also Reba Soffer, "The Revolution in English Social Thought, 1880–1914", *American Historical Review*, 75, 7 (December 1980), pp. 1938–1964.
5. Andrew Vincent and Raymond Plant, *Philosophy, Politics and Citizenship*, Oxford, Basil Blackwell, 1984, pp. 86–111; Michael Freeden, *The New Liberalism: An Ideology of Social Reform*, Oxford, OUP, 1976.
6. John Morrow, "Liberalism and British Idealistic Political Philosophy", *History of Political Thought*, V, 1 (Spring, 1984), pp. 97–98.
7. B. Bosanquet, "The Duties of Citizenship" in B. Bosanquet (ed), *Aspects of the Social Problem*, London, Macmillan, 1895, p. 12.
8. See, in particular, Stefan Collini, Donald Burrow and John Winch, *That Noble Science of Politics*, Cambridge, CUP, 1983.
9. Professor R. F. A. Hoernle, "Money and Its Influence on National and Individual Character", *Journal of the Institute of Bankers of South Africa*, V, 4 (July 1908), p. 105.
10. *Ibid.*, p. 109.
11. R. F. Alfred Hoernle, "Bernard Bosanquet's Philosophy of the State", *Political Science Quarterly*, XXXIV (1920), p. 630.
12. R. F. A. Hoernle, "A German Appreciation of South African Native Policy", *The State*, 1 (April 1909), p. 403.
13. R. F. A. Hoernle, "The Place of Classics in Modern Education", *Report of the Ninth Annual Meeting of the South African Association for the Advancement of Science, Bulawayo, 1911*, Cape Town, 1912, pp. 119–124.
14. David Nicholls, *The Pluralist State*, London and Basingstoke, The Macmillan Press, 1975.
15. R. F. Alfred Hoernle, "The Foundations of Sovereignty", *The South African Quarterly*, Sept–Nov 1923, pp. 10–13.
16. J. C. Smuts, *Holism and Evolution*, London, Macmillan, 1927.
17. R. F. A. Hoernle, *Matter, Life, Mind and God*, London, Methuen, 1923, p. 67.
18. *Ibid.*, p. 131.
19. A. N. Whitehead, *Science and the Modern World*, Cambridge, CUP, 1926, p. 64. Hoernle appears to have become increasingly moved by Whitehead's arguments in an anti-metaphysical direction. "the

scientist who believes" he noted in his edition of Alfred North Whitehead, *Adventures in Ideas*, London, 1933, "that the past conditions the future is a metaphysician", copy in *R. F. A. Hoernle Collection*.
20. *J. C. Smuts Corr*, R. F. A. Hoernle to J. C. Smuts, 27 July 1925.
21. *The Star*, 21 July 1943.
22. Deposited in the *R. F. A. Hoernle Collection*.
23. Lucien Levy-Bruhl, *How Natives Think*, London, Allen and Unwin, 1923.
24. R. F. A. Hoernle, "The Concept of the 'Primitive' ", *Bantu Studies*, 11 (1923–26), p. 232. See also R. F. A. Hoernle, "Prolegomena to the Study of the Black Man's Mind", *Journal of Philosophical Studies*, 11, 5 (1927) repr. in I. D. MacCrone (ed), *Race and Reason*, Johannesburg, Witwatersrand University, 1945, pp. 79–91.
25. Deposited in the *R. F. A. Hoernle Collection*.
26. ARSAIRR B43 (f), R. F. A. Hoernle, "Notes on Assimilation", n.d., pp. 4–5.
27. W. M. Macmillan, *Complex South Africa*, London, Faber, 1930. For a more detailed survey of the development of Macmillan's ideas and their impact on South African politics see Hugh Macmillan and Shula Marks (eds), *Africa and Empire: W. M. Macmillan, Historian and Social Critic*, London, Temple Smith, 1989.
28. *Minutebook of the Gamma Sigma Club*, 20 March 1931.
29. *Ibid.*, 17 April 1931; *The Star*, 18 April 1931.
30. Hoernle also voted to exclude Margaret Ballinger from teaching history at the University of the Witwatersrand on her marriage. *W. M. Macmillan Papers*, R. F. A. Hoernle to W. M. Macmillan, 11 April 1934.
31. ARSAIRR AD843 93.1.7 R. F. A. Hoernle, "Memorandum on the urgent need for developing the scientific study of social problems at the University", 1933.
32. *Ibid.*
33. Brian M. Du Toit, "Missionaries, Anthropologies and the Policies of the Dutch Reformed Church", *Journal of Modern African Studies*, 22, 4 (1984), pp. 624–625.
34. ARSAIRR B43 (f) pamphlet *Afrikanerbond Vir Rassestudie*, n.p. n.d., p. 4.
35. W. W. M. Eiselen, *Die Naturelle Vraagstuk*, Stellenbosch, 1929, p. 8.
36. John David Shingler, "Education and Political Order in South Africa, 1902–1961", Ph.D Diss. Yale University, 1973, p. 17.
37. Elphick, *op. cit.*
38. Leonard Thompson, *The Political Mythology of Apartheid*, New Haven and London, Yale University Press, 1985, p. 27.
39. ARSAIRR B43 (a) Agenda of Conference of *Rasseverhoudingsbond van Afrikaners*, Voortrekkergedenksaal, Pretoria, 19 and 20 June 1935; notes on conference in RFAH's handwriting, p. 4. The SAIRR initially hoped to co-operate with the body after its foundation ARSAIRR B97 (g) J. D. Rheinallt Jones to M. D. C. de Wet Nel, 18 July 1935.

40. ARSAIRR B43 (f) handwritten notes by R. F. A. Hoernle entitled "The Future of the Native in South Africa".
41. R. F. A. Hoernle, "Can SA Natives develop along their own lines?", *Journal of Secondary Education*, November 1935, p. 25.
42. *Ibid.*, p. 27.
43. ARSAIRR B43 (c) J. Rose Innes to R. F. A. Hoernle, 1 February 1936.
44. ARSAIRR B100 (a) R. F. A. Hoernle to J. D. Rheinallt Jones, 15 February 1936.
45. *Ibid.*, R. F. A. Hoernle to J. D. Rheinallt Jones, February 29 1936.
46. ARSAIRR AD 843 B97. 5 R. F. A. Hoernle, ms entitled "The Native Problem and Race Mixture", n.d. The article attacked an article of Peter Nielsen in *The Cape Times* of 28 May 1934.
47. R. F. A. Hoernle, "Race Mixture and Native Policy" in I. Schapera (ed), *Western Civilisation and the Natives of South Africa*, London, 1934 repr. in I. D. MacCrone (ed), *Race and Reason*, Johannesburg, Witwatersrand University Press, 1945, p. 58.
48. MacCrone, *op. cit.*, p. xvi.
49. ARSAIRR AD843 B97.5 R. F. A. Hoernle to I. J. M. Van Niekerk, July 8 1938; I. J. M. Van Niekerk to R. F. A. Hoernle, 29 July 1938. Eugen Fischer's work on the Bastars was completed before the First World War and saw them as a problem community. Eugen Fischer, *Die Rehebother Bastards und das Bastardierungsproblem beim menschen Anthropologische und ethnographische Studien an Rehebother Bastardvolk in Deutsch-Sudwest-Afrika*, Jena, 1913.
50. Paul B. Rich, *Race and Empire in British Politics* (2 edn), Cambridge, CUP, 1990, esp. pp. 120–144.
51. ARSAIRR AD 843 B.97.2.3–4 unpublished lecture notes, n.d.
52. *Alexander Kerr Papers*, R. F. A. Hoernle to A. Kerr, n.d.
53. ARSAIRR B43 (c) P. Duncan to R. F. A. Hoernle, 7 January 1936.
54. R. F. Alfred Hoernle, "Native Education At The Cross-Roads in South Africa", *Africa*, XI, 4 (October 1938), p. 399; Paul B. Rich, *White Power and the Liberal Conscience*, Manchester, Manchester University Press, 1984, pp. 66–67.
55. R. F. A. Hoernle, "A South African Tribute" in S. Radhakrishnan (ed), *Mahatma Gandhi*, London, Allen and Unwin, 1939, pp. 119–120.
56. ARSAIRR, Hoernle Coll., R. F. A. Hoernle to G. J. Ponsonby, 28 May 1938.
57. R. F. A. Hoernle, *South African Native Policy and the Liberal Spirit*, Cape Town, University of Cape Town for the Phelps Stokes Fund, 1939, pp. 42–51.
58. *Ibid.*, pp. 67–70.
59. *Ibid.*, pp. 109–110.
60. *Margery Perham Papers*, 367, R. F. A. Hoernle to M. Perham, 18 May 1942; M. Perham to R. F. A. Hoernle, 31 July 1942; R. F. A. Hoernle to M. Perham, 8 October 1942.
61. *Race and Empire in British Politics*, esp. pp. 169–204.

62. *White Power and the Liberal Conscience*, pp. 40–47.
63. R. F. A. Hoernle, "Native Opinion and the Transfer of the Protectorates", *The African Observer*, V, 2 (1934), p. 19.
64. *R. F. A. Hoernle Mss* AD1623 AB/623 Aa4.1 R. F. A. Hoernle to Lord Harlech, 22 August 1941. Hoernle suggested that the British government ask Tshekedi Khama of Bechuanaland to mediate in the dispute with Sobhuza, though this proposal was rejected by the three Resident Commissioners in Swaziland, *ibid.*, Hoernle to Harlech, 24 September 1941; Harlech to Hoernle, 24 October 1941.
65. Thomas Haskell, "Capitalism and the Origins of Humanitarian Sensibility", *American Historical Review*, 90, 2 (April 1985), pp. 339–361 and 90, 3 (June 1985), pp. 547–566.
66. R. F. Alfred Hoernle, "The Future of the British Commonwealth of Nations", *The South African Journal of Economics*, 6, 4 (December 1938), p. 377.
67. For an assessment of the work of De Kiewiet and Walker see Christopher Saunders, *The Making of the South African Past*, Cape Town and Johannesburg, David Philip, 1988.
68. *South African Native Policy and the Liberal Spirit*, p. 168.
69. *Ibid.*, p. 172.
70. Sheridan Johns, "The Comintern, South Africa and the Black Diaspora", *Review of Politics*, XXXVII (1975), p. 234.
71. ARSAIRR AD843 B1.1 G. Findley to J. D. Rheinallt Jones, 29 October 1934.
72. *Ibid.*, R. F. A. Hoernle to J. D. Rheinallt Jones, 2 October 1934.
73. *South African Native Policy and the Liberal Spirit*, p. 178.
74. ARSAIRR, AD1623 Aa3 R. F. A. Hoernle to E. Brookes, January 22 1940.
75. *Ibid.*, R. F. A. Hoernle to J. Harris, January 2 1940.
76. *Robert Shepherd Papers* MS16,362 (ii) R. F. A. Hoernle to R. Shepherd, 10 October 1940 and 30 April 1941.
77. *Race Relations*, VII, 2 (1940), pp. 33–34. See also *The Forum*, April 20 1940. One reviewer in the radical paper *The Guardian* attacked Hoernle's "caste" notion which implied that the interests of employers and workers were one and ignored class conflict. *The Guardian*, January 23 1941.
78. B. A. Farrell (ed), *Summary of Findings of Seminar on South African Native Policy and the Liberal Spirit*, n.p., n.d., deposited in the library, Institute of Commonwealth Studies, London, p. 3.
79. *Race Relations*, Second Quarter, 1940, p. 36.
80. R. F. Alfred Hoernle, "Present-Day Trends in South African Race Relations", *Race Relations*, First Quarter 1941, p. 13.
81. *Ibid.*
82. ARSAIRR *AD1623* Aa3 R. F. A. Hoernle to H. R. Raikes, 26 July 1940.
83. ARSAIRR AD843. B45.1 Minutes of Conference on Alexandra Township, 23 October 1942, p. 4.

84. ARSAIRR AD843 B64/5 R. F. A. Hoernle to SNA, 2 November 1942.
85. *J. Smuts Archive* A1/155 D. L. Smit, memo "The Future of Alexandra Township", 20 December 1943.
86. R. F. Alfred Hoernle, "Suggestions For The Improvement of the Economic Conditions of Urban African Workers" in *The Union's Burden of Poverty*, Johannesburg, SAIRR, 1942, p. 40.
87. "Present-Day Trends", p. 21.
88. *Douglas Smit Papers*, 25/41 R. F. A. Hoernle to D. Smit encl. memo "Reflections on the Racial Caste Society of the Union", n.d. (1943?).
89. *The Forum*, May 24 1941.
90. Alexander Campbell, *Smuts and Swastika*, London, V. Gollancz, 1943, p. 45.
91. Ellen Hellman, "A Liberal Looks at S.A. Native Policy: 'Heartbreak House' ", *Jewish Affairs*, April 1946, p. 10.
92. W. W. M. Eiselen, "The Meaning of Apartheid", *Race Relations*, XV (1948), pp. 77–78; see also the reply by A. W. Hoernle, "Alternatives to Apartheid", *ibid.*, XV (1948), pp. 90–91.
93. See Hugh Macmillan, " 'Paralysed Conservatives': W. M. Macmillan, the Social Scientists and the 'Common Society', 1923–1948", in Macmillan and Marks (eds), *op. cit.*, pp. 84–85.
94. Patrick Duncan, "Liberalism Renewed", *Indian Opinion*, 24 February 1956.
95. Donald Molteno, *Towards a Democratic South Africa*, Johannesburg, SAIRR, 1959, pp. 3–4.
96. H. J. Simons, "What is Apartheid?", *Liberation*, 35, (March 1959), pp. 16–17.

3 Edgar Brookes and the "Lie in the Soul" of Segregation

1. Richard Jenkyns, *The Victorians and Ancient Greece*, Oxford, Basil Blackwell, 1980; Frank M. Turner, *The Greek Heritage in Victorian Britain*, New Haven and London, Yale University Press, 1981; Raymond F. Betts, "The Allusion to Rome in British Imperialist Thought of the Late Nineteenth and Twentieth Centuries", *Victorian Studies*, XV, 2 (December 1971), pp. 149–159.
2. *The Christian Express*, 2 February 1915; *The Star*, 23 January 1915.
3. AD 1433 Cp9.4.1 *Minutebook of the Pretoria Joint Council*, entry dated 8 December 1921.
4. *Ibid.*, 27 August 1923.
5. E. H. Brookes, "Segregation as a Fundamental Plank of Native Policy; European and Bantu", Papers and Addresses read at the Conference on Native Affairs, Johannesburg, 27–29 September 1923. Published for the Federal Council of the D.R. Churches, n.d. (1923?), p. 35. See also *Rand Daily Mail*, 28 September 1923.
6. R. A. Lehfeldt, "Labour Conditions in South Africa", *South African*

Journal of Science, xvii, 1 (November 1920), p. 92; Bruce K. Murray, *Wits: The Early Years*, Johannesburg, Witwatersrand University Press, 1982, p. 142.

7. W. M. Macmillan, *The Land, The Native and Unemployment*, Johannesburg, 1924, p. 4; Paul B. Rich, "W. M. Macmillan, Segregation and Commonwealth Race Relations" in Hugh Macmillan and Shula Marks (eds), *Africa and Empire: W. M. Macmillan, Historian and Social Critic*, London, Temple Smith, 1989, pp. 192–211.
8. Edgar Brookes, *A South African Pilgrimage*, Johannesburg, Ravan Press, 1977, pp. 16–17.
9. *J. B. M. Hertzog Papers*, A32, Box 35 E. Brookes to J. B. M. Hertzog, 13 February 1924; J. B. M. Hertzog to E. Brookes, 17 and 18 March 1924; E. Brookes to J. B. M. Hertzog, 22 March 1924; *A South African Pilgrimage*, p. 22.
10. Edgar Brookes, *A History of South African Native Policy*, Pretoria, Die Nasionale Pers, 1924, p. 51.
11. *Ibid.*, p. 115.
12. *Ibid.*, pp. 310–311.
13. *Hertzog Papers*, A32 Box 35 J. B. M. Hertzog to E. Brookes, 23 March, 5 and 11 August 1924; E. Brookes to J. B. M. Hertzog, 14 August 1924.
14. *Rand Daily Mail*, 10 May 1924.
15. *Rand Daily Mail*, 7 May 1924. Msimang felt that Brookes's scheme for segregation was a "beautiful castle which came crumbling down after the fashion of the proverbial tower of Babel and left us speaking in many tongues", *Umteteli wa Bantu*, 3 November 1923.
16. Saul Dubow, "Holding a 'Just Balance Between White and Black': The Native Affairs Department in South Africa, c1920–1933", *Journal of South African Studies*, 12, 2 (April 1986), pp. 223–224.
17. NST 1696/36/276 T. W. C. Norton, memo entitled "Comments on Professor Brookes's suggestions for Native Administration" encl. in T. W. C. Norton, CNC to SNA, 29 December 1924, p. 2.
18. *Ibid.*, p. 8.
19. *J. B. M. Hertzog Papers*, A32 Box 45, T. Boydell to J. B. M. Hertzog, 27 February 1925; J. H. Conradie (Org Sec) to J. B. M. Hertzog, 30 January 1925.
20. *The Star*, 11 November 1925. The Head Committee of the National Party in the Transvaal appointed a sub committee on "native policy" too at this time and also opposed any extension of the Cape African franchise, *Rand Daily Mail*, 10 November 1925.
21. For details of the Johannesburg Joint Council's efforts to influence the Pact in the middle 1920s see Paul B. Rich, *White Power and the Liberal Conscience*, Manchester, Manchester University Press, 1984, pp. 24–25.
22. ARSAIRR, C. T. Loram to J. D. Rheinallt Jones, 22 September 1926.
23. Edgar Brookes, *A History of South African Native Policy*, 2nd edn, Cape Town, J. L. Van Schaik, 1927, p. 64.
24. *Ibid.*, p. 344.
25. Edgar H. Brookes, *The Political Future of South Africa*, Pretoria, Van Schaik, 1927, pp. 37–38.

26. *Ibid.*, p. 86.
27. *Ibid.*, p. 44.
28. *A South African Pilgrimage*, pp. 30–31.
29. Paul B. Rich, "The Appeals of Tuskegee: James Henderson, Lovedale and the Fortunes of South African Liberalism, 1906–1930", *International Journal of African Historical Studies*, 20, 1 (1987), pp. 271–292.
30. *A South African Pilgrimage*, p. 34.
31. Alain Locke, "The New Negro" in Alain Locke (ed), *The New Negro*, New York, A & C Bain, 1925, p. 9.
32. *The Cape Times*, 11 February 1929. See also *Report of the National European-Bantu Conference*, Cape Town, 6–9 February 1929, Lovedale, Lovedale Press, 1929.
33. *A South African Pilgrimage*, pp. 45–46.
34. Paul B. Rich, *Race and Empire in British Politics*, Cambridge, CUP, 1986, pp. 70–91.
35. R. V. Selope Thema, "Land, Industry and the Bantu: in *Christian Students and Modern South Africa: A Report of the Bantu-European Student Christian Conference*, Fort Hare, 27 June–3 July 1930, SCA/ Fort Hare, 1930, pp. 170–171.
36. *Alfred Xuma Papers*, ABX 300610 Max Yergan to A. B. Xuma, 10 June 1930.
37. Edgar H. Brookes, "The Racial Question in the Light of Christian Teaching" in *Christian Students and Modern South Africa*, pp. 186–187.
38. ARSAIRR B3 (L) E. Brookes to J. D. Rheinallt Jones, 14 October 1932.
39. Edgar H. Brookes, *Native Education in South Africa*, Pretoria, Van Schaik, 1930, pp. 53–54.
40. *Ibid.*, pp. 61–67.
41. Edgar H. Brookes, *The Colour Problems of South Africa*, Lovedale, Lovedale Press, 1934, p. 50. This "lie in the soul" Brookes saw as "the growth of a persistent dishonesty, all the more dangerous as it has become unconscious" which was "an undoubted phenomenon of South African life", *ibid.*, p. 166.
42. *Manchester Guardian*, 22 January 1935.
43. *Economica*, February 1935.
44. *Die Huisgenoot*, 1 February 1935.
45. *Colour Problems*, p. 13.
46. ARSAIRR B2 (a) C. T. Loram to J. D. Rheinallt Jones, 8 May 1934.
47. *Gilbert Murray Papers*, Mabel Palmer, "Memorandum on the need for special institute for the study of the economics of inter-racial contact' encl. in E. Lewis to G. Murray, 30 April 1928; Mabel Palmer, "Some Problems of the Transition From Subsistence to Money Economy", *South African Journal of Science*, XXVII (November 1930), pp. 1117–1125, C. T. Loram had also proposed, while he was a member of the Native Affairs Commission, the establishment of a chair "Bantu Studies" at the University of Natal. He urged this on the grounds that "... Natal perhaps today presents the most satisfactory relationship between black and white, because the growing industries

of Natal will be more and more dependent on the economics of the Bantu people, and because Natal is the province to which, by reason of the disparity of population, the Native question is a matter of life and death". *C. T. Loram Papers*, 11, Box 2, Folder 79, Memorandum by C. T. Loram on the Necessity For a Professional Chair of Bantu Studies at Natal University College, n.d.
48. *A. W. G. Champion Papers*, (Unisa), Mabel Palmer to A. Champion, February 13 1930; A. Champion to M. Palmer, 17 February 1930; M. Palmer to A. Champion, June 29 1930.
49. *M. Webb Papers* KCM 21994 (7) M. Webb to J. D. Rheinallt Jones, November 20 1940.
50. D. E. Burchell, "Adams College, Natal, c1920–1956: A Critical Assessment", *J. Univ. Durban-Westville*, New Ser, 1 (1984), pp. 151–159.
51. ARSAIRR B100 (a) E. Brookes to J. D. Rheinallt Jones, 14 October 1932.
52. ARSAIRR, B100 (a) Minutes of a meeting of the Executive Committee, Natal Technical College, 8 and 10 July 1935; R. F. A. Hoernle to D. Smit, 13 July 1935.
53. *Umteteli wa Bantu*, 1 June 1935.
54. ARSAIRR 100 (a) E. Brookes to J. D. Rheinallt Jones, 22 and 25 October 1935; Z. K. Matthews to E. Brookes, 22 October 1935.
55. *White Power and the Liberal Conscience*, p. 65.
56. Albert Luthuli, *Let My People Go*, London, Collins, 1962, p. 96.
57. ARSAIRR 100 (a) M. Webb to J. D. Rheinallt Jones, 12 December 1935.
58. ARSAIRR 100 (a) E. Brookes to L. Egeland, 24 February 1936.
59. ARSAIRR 100 (a) E. Brookes to J. D. Rheinallt Jones, 24 February 1936.
60. *A. W. G. Champion Papers*, C. Frost to A. Champion, 20 April 1936.
61. *A. W. G. Champion Papers*, (UCT) BC581 A1.177, L. J. Gobhozi to A. Champion, 6 April 1937.
62. Maynard Swanson, " 'The Fate of the Natives': Black Durban and African Ideology", *Journal of Natal and Zulu History*, 14 (December 1984), pp. 62–64.
63. *Ilanga lase Natal*, 22 February and 21 March 1936; *Umsebenzi*, 2 May 1936.
64. J. C. Smuts to M. C. Gillett, 30 November 1937 in Jan Van der Poel (ed), *Selections from the Smuts Papers*, Vol VI, Cambridge, CUP, p. 107.
65. *A. W. G. Champion Papers*, (UCT) BC 581 A1.128 E. Brookes to A. Champion, 16 August 1937.
66. *Ilanga lase Natal*, 29 June 1938.
67. *Zulu Society Papers* 111/9 C. Mpanza to E. Brookes, 25 May 1939.
68. *Champion Papers* (UCT), A1. 183 A. Champion to E. Brookes, 11 June 1942.
69. *Zulu Society Papers* 11/10 A. Champion to C. Mpanza, 4 February 1942.
70. *A. B. Xuma Papers* ABX 4211/C P. Mosaka to A. B. Xuma, 11

November 1942; ABX 4211266 Rev. J. Calata to A. B. Xuma, 26 November 1942; *Midland News*, 11 May 1943.
71. *E. Brookes Papers* MS BRO 4.049 E. Brookes, article "Solving the Native Problem: Do the Bills Succeed in Doing It?", n.d. (1936?).
72. Edgar Brookes, *The Bantu in South Africa*, Johannesburg, SAIRR, 1943, pp. 53–55.
73. Edgar Brookes, *The Natives Representatives Council and the Senate in the Political Representation of Africans in the Union*, Johannesburg, SAIRR, 1942; *The Forum*, 10 May 1941.
74. *Ilanga lase Natal*, 13 March 1943.
75. *Donald Molteno Papers* BC 579 C3.26 E. Brookes, Memorandum for Consideration by the Parliamentary Group, 17 April 1944.
76. *Margaret Ballinger Papers*, A410/B2 8.4 E. Brookes to D. Buchanan, February 10 1943.
77. *Jan H. Hofmeyr Papers*, E. Brookes to J. H. Hofmeyr, 9 September 1946.
78. *Douglas Smit Papers*, 29/46 E. Brookes to D. Smit, 2 September 1946 encl. memo to Native Affairs Commission.
79. *J. C. Smuts Archive*, A1/163/1 memo on Proposed Amendments to the Representation of Natives Act No. 12 of 1936 encl. in E. B. Young, SNA to Private Sec, PM, 16 October 1945.
80. *White Power and the Liberal Conscience*, pp. 107–10.
81. Social and Economic Planning Council, Report No 9, *The Native Reserves and Their Place in the Economy of the Union of South Africa*, Pretoria, 1946, p. 3.
82. *J. C. Smuts Archive*, A1 S171 Memorandum on report No 9 of Social and Economic Planning Council, 20 November 1947.
83. Edgar H. Brookes, "I see a seething pot . . ." in E. H. Brookes et al, *South Africa Faces UNO*, Johannesburg, SAIRR, 1947, p. 22.
84. *Ilanga lase Natal*, 3 January 1948. The author of this was probably Jordan Ngubane.
85. *Rheinallt Jones Papers*, E. Brookes to J. D. Rheinallt Jones, 15 November 1949.
86. Edgar H. Brookes, *We Come of Age*, Johannesburg, SAIRR, 1950, p. 6; "The Whale v the Elephant", *The Forum*, 23 October 1948.
87. *Patrick Duncan Papers*, P. Duncan to E. Brookes, 8 June and 15 August 1953; E. Brookes to P. Duncan, 16 September 1953. For the evolution of Duncan's ideas as a radically inclined liberal in South African politics, see Tom Lodge, "Patrick Duncan and Radical Liberalism", unpublished paper, University of Cape Town, 1976.
88. C. J. Driver, *Patrick Duncan: South African and Pan African*, London, Heinemann, 1980, pp. 62–63.
89. *A South African Pilgrimage*, p. 97.
90. Jacques Maritain, *Man and the State*, Chicago, University of Chicago Press, 1961, p. 7.
91. Edgar Brookes, "The Light of Liberalism in South Africa", *The Times*, November 5 1965.
92. Edgar H. Brookes, *South Africa In A Changing World*, Cape Town, CUP, 1953, p. 25.

93. *Ibid.*, pp. 105–106.
94. Gunnar Myrdal, *An American Dilemma*, (2 Vols), New York, Harper and Row, 1944.
95. *South Africa in a Changing World*, p. 108.
96. Edgar Brookes, "South Africa: the possibilities of an impossible situation", *African Affairs*, 55, 220 (July 1956), pp. 193–194.
97. *Z. K. Matthews Papers*, AD 1699 C.262 E. Brookes to Z. K. Matthews, 22 September 1956.
98. Edgar H. Brookes, *The City of God and the Politics of Crisis*, London, OUP, 1960, p. 51.
99. *Ibid.*, p. 12.
100. Carl Becker, *The Heavenly City of the Eighteenth Century Philosophers*, New Haven, Yale University Press, 1932. For Becker's rather ambiguous attitude towards the idea of progress see Richard Nelson, "Carl Becker Revisited: Irony and Progress Revisited", *Journal of the History of Ideas*, XLVIII, (April–June 1987), pp. 307–323. Ernest L. Fortier has argued that the appeal to Christians of Augustine's *City of God* was its "transendent" goal making it "wholly independent of any observable improvement in the political sphere", "Augustine's *City of God* and the Modern Historical Consciousness", *Review of Politics*, XLI (1979), p. 343.
101. Trevor Huddleston, *Naught For Your Comfort*, London, Collins, 1956, p. 239.
102. Edgar H. Brookes, *Power, Law, Right and Love: A Study in Political Values*, Durham, Duke University Press, 1963, p. 76.
103. *Ibid.*, p. 79.
104. Edgar Brookes, *Three Letters From Africa*, Pendle Hill, Lebanon (USA), Pendle Hill Pamphlet No 139, 1965, p. 33.
105. Edgar Brookes, *America In Travail*, Pendle Hill, Lebanon (USA), Pendle Hill Pamphlet No 159, 1968.
106. Edgar H. Brookes, *Apartheid: A Documentary study of Modern South Africa*, London, Routledge and Kegan Paul, 1968, p. xxvii.
107. H. I. E. Dhlomo, " 'The House of Bread': Poet Versus Politician", unpub. ms, n.d. repr. in *English in Africa*, 4, 2 (September 1977), pp. 73–76.
108. Allan Boesak, *Farewell to Innocence*, Johannesburg, Ravan Press, 1976, p. 10.

4 Liberals, Radicals and the Politics of Black Consciousness

1. Gwendolen Carter, *The Politics of Inequality*, London, Thames and Hudson, 1959, pp. 302–339; see also Janet Robertson, *Liberalism in South Africa, 1948–1963*, Oxford, Clarendon Press, 1971.
2. Robertson, *op. cit.*, pp. 110–111.
3. Alan Paton, "Evolution or Revolution? The Narrowing Gap", *Africa Today*, IV, 6 (November–December 1957), p. 10.

4. Peter Walshe, *The Rise of African Nationalism in South Africa*, London, C. Hurst and Co, 1970, p. 360.
5. Z. K. Matthews, "An African Policy for South Africa", *Race Relations*, XVI, 3 (1949), p. 80.
6. See in particular Z. K. Matthews, "Apartheid – Another View", *Journal of International Affairs*, 7, 2 (1953), p. 145.
7. Ambrose Reeves, *South Africa – Yesterday and Tomorrow*, London, Gollancz, 1962, p. 161.
8. Z. K. Matthews, "Political Arrangements in a Multi-Racial Society", paper presented to Multi Racial Conference, mimeo, 1957, pp. 1–4. For the impact of charterist thought see Raymond Suttner, *The Freedom Charter – The People's Charter in the Nineteen Eighties*, Cape Town, University of Cape Town, 1986.
9. Z. K. Matthews, "Political Arrangements", p. 150.
10. Govan Mbeki, "Economic Rights and Duties in a Multi Racial Society", paper presented to Multi Racial Conference.
11. Though these groups of Whites, Africans, Coloureds and Indians do not actually amount to a "four nation theory" which has never been adopted as ANC policy. Suttner, *op. cit.*, p. 17.
12. *James Rose Innes Corr.*, 767, J. H. Hofmeyr to J. Rose Innes, 1 January 1930.
13. Jeffrey Butler, Richard Elphick and David Welsh (eds), *Democratic Liberalism in South Africa*, Middletown (Conn), Wesleyan University Press and Cape Town and Johannesburg, David Philip, 1987, esp. pp. 1–17.
14. Martin Legassick, "The Rise of Modern South African Liberalism: Its Assumptions and Social Base", London, ICS (mimeo), 1972, p. 30; "Legislation, Ideology and Economy in Post 1948 South Africa", *JSAS*, 1, (1974), pp. 5–35.
15. South African Institute of Race Relations, *34th Annual Report, 1962–3*, Johannesburg, SAIRR, 1963, p. 1.
16. Leo Marquard, "Liberalism and the Institute", Johannesburg, SAIRR, unpub. memo RR 1/1963, p. 3.
17. South African Institute of Race Relations, *Go Forward In Faith: The Logic of Economic Integration*, Johannesburg, SAIRR, 1954.
18. Quintin Whyte, *Behind The Racial Tensions in South Africa*, Johannesburg, SAIRR, 1953, p. 14.
19. In 1957 Quintin Whyte began discussions with Professor L. J. Du Plessis and some other Afrikaner figures who were critical of some aspects of Government Policy, especially on the reserves, *Leo Marquard Papers*, BC587 E1.113 Q. Whyte to L. Marquard, 25 April 1957; *Fred Van Wyk Papers*, AD1752/33BO42 Lex Van Wyk to F. Van Wyk, 25 May 1960 encl. "Notes on thinking about race problems in the Ned Geref Kerk"; Ben Marais to F. Van Wyk, 31 October 1960 encl. "Further Notes by Ben Marais"; Paul B. Rich, "Doctrines of 'Change' in South Africa" in John D. Brewer (ed), *Can South Africa Survive*, London and Basingstoke, The Macmillan Press, 1989, pp. 281–311.

20. *Quintin Whyte Papers*, AD1502 Ba 4, "Notes On Interview with Bishop Reeves", 27 October 1958.
21. O. D. Schreiner, *Political Power in South Africa*, Johannesburg, SAIRR, 1964.
22. Quintin Whyte, "Techniques in Race Relations", unpub. memo RR 96/52, Johannesburg, SAIRR, 1952; "Human Relations in the United States", *Race Relations Journal*, LXIII (1951), pp. 16–26. Whyte at this time viewed the role of liberals as pivotal in African politics for it was "certain that for many years to come the advance of the Non European peoples will depend to a great extent upon the active collaboration and help which they will receive, not only from a European-dominated government but also from a sympathetic and liberal-minded European public on whose shoulders has so far lain the responsibility for the initiation of inter-racial cooperation", Quintin Whyte, "Inter-Racial Cooperation" in Ellen Hellman (ed), *Handbook on Race Relations in South Africa*, Cambridge, CUP, 1949, p. 659. Though Whyte was keen to see Africans appointed to the Institute's executive, he remained sceptical of their ability to contribute to the Institute's work in any substantial manner, complaining to W. M. Macmillan that there were "few Non-Europeans who can turn out work of the standard we now demand", *W. M. Macmillan Papers*, Q. Whyte to W. M. Macmillan, 1 February 1950.
23. *Quintin Whyte Papers* AD 1502 Bb 2.67 Quintin Whyte, "Notes on Potential Article", September 1963.
24. Quintin Whyte, "The Relevance of Transkeian Development To Race Relations In South Africa", Johannesburg, SAIRR, RR 94/63, 1963. See also "Social and Political Aspects of Separate Development in the Homelands Examined", unpub. mimeo, RR 6/66, Johannesburg, SAIRR, 12 January 1966.
25. *Quintin Whyte Papers*, AD1502 Ba5 Quintin Whyte memo dated 5 November encl. in Q. Whyte to H. E. Oppenheimer, 5 November 1963 (marked "By Hand and Confidential").
26. Robertson, *op. cit.*, pp. 222–225.
27. C. W. de Kiewiet, "Loneliness in the Beloved Country", *Foreign Affairs*, 42, 3 (April 1964), p. 421.
28. *Quintin Whyte Papers*, Ba 8, Quintin Whyte, "Some Notes on Trip to the United Kingdom and the United States of America", 1966, p. 6. Other liberals, though, took a different view and Leo Marquard had earlier found himself "moving towards a belief that what is called 'pressure' from overseas may be a vital element in our situation", *Leo Marquard Papers*, BC587 E1.155 L. Marquard to Q. Whyte, 20 May 1960.
29. *E. G. Malherbe Papers*.
30. *Die Vaderland*, 6, 7 and 8 May 1965.
31. SABC – Current Affairs, broadcast entitled "Realities Ignored", 24 February 1967.
32. *Quintin Whyte Papers*, Ba 1(5), Q. Whyte to C. W. de Kiewiet, 16 June 1969.

33. Heribert Adam, "The Rise of Black Consciousness in South Africa", *Race*, XV, 2 (October 1973), pp. 149–65; Robert Fatton Jr, *Black Consciousness in South Africa*, New York, State University of New York Press, 1986.
34. Gail Gerhart notes that though black consciousness was not a completely "imported" ideology "never had such a deliberate and thorough going effort been made to borrow and selectively adapt foreign ideas in order to influence mass thinking", Gail M. Gerhart, *Black Power in South Africa*, Berkeley, University of California Press, 1978, p. 273. For a more critical view see Baruch Hirson, *Year of Fire Year of Ash*, London, Zed Books, 1979, pp. 282–329.
35. John W. De Gruchy, "A Short History of the Christian Institute" in Charles Villa-Vicencio and John W. De Gruchy (eds), *Resistance and Hope: South African Essays in Honour of Beyers Naude*, Cape Town and Johannesburg, David Philip, 1985, p. 17. See also Peter Walshe, "Church Versus State in South Africa: The Christian Institute and the Resurgence of African Nationalism", *Journal of Church and State*, 19, 3 (1977), pp. 457–79; *Church Versus State in South Africa: The Case of the Christian Institute*, London, C. Hurst and Co, 1983; Colleen Ryan, *Beyers Naude: Pilgrimage of Faith*, Cape Town, David Philip, 1990.
36. *F. J. Van Wyk Papers*, AD1752 4Fb4 Interdenominational African Ministers Association of Southern Africa, Annual Report, 1963–1964.
37. *F. J. Van Wyk Papers*, 4Da3 memo "Evaluation of the Christian Institute of Southern Africa" (marked "confidential"), Johannesburg, August 1970.
38. *F. J. Van Wyk Papers*, 4Cb1 George J. H. Magqwashe to The Director, CI, 25 June 1966.
39. "Evaluation of the Christian Institute", p. 7.
40. *F. J. Van Wyk Papers*, 4Fa (7) Beyers Naude, "Memorandum on the Relationship Between AICA and the Christian Institute", (marked "confidential"), 1972. For details of the splits within AICA see *Black Review 1972*, Durban, Black Community Programmes, 1973, pp. 33–36.
41. *F. J. Van Wyk Papers*, 4Cc3 P. Randall to R. L. Barry, 28 August 1968.
42. *F. J. Van Wyk Papers*, 4Dc3 (h) Calvin Cook, "The Statement of the W.C.C. consultation on racism. By a member of the Executive of the S.A. Council of Churches", 1 August 1970 (marked "confidential"), p. 1.
43. *Quintin Whyte Papers* BC627 E7.1.5 Q. Whyte to P. Randall, 3 September 1969.
44. *SPRO-CAS Papers*, Background Paper Gen. 19, "Black Souls in White Skins?", 11 September 1970 repr. from *SASO*, August 1970.
45. It was also felt by some of those involved such as A. S. Mathews that the SPRO-CAS project "should not in my view invite African representation just for the sake of having them", *SPRO-CAS Papers*, 835/Ad6v A. S. Mathews to P. Randall, 10 August 1970.
46. *SPRO-CAS Papers*, 835/Ad6v A. Du Toit to P. Randall, 13 July 1970.

47. *Ibid.*, A. Paton to P. Randall, February 3 1970.
48. Richard Turner, "Black Consciousness and White Liberals", *Reality*, 4, 3 (July 1972), pp. 20–22.
49. *SPRO-CAS Papers*, 835/Ad6v R. Turner unpub. ms encl. in P. Randall to D. Welsh, September 5 1972. For John Rex's ideas see John Rex, "The Plural Society: The South African Case", *Race*, 12, 4 (1971), repr. in John Rex, *Race, Colonialism and The City*, London and Boston, Routledge and Kegan Paul, 1973, pp. 269–83.
50. *Ibid.*, R. Turner unpub. handwritten memo n.d.
51. Edgar Brookes, "Minority Report", *South Africa's Political Alternatives*, Johannesburg, SPRO-CAS, 1973, pp. 243–44. For Brookes's political shift away from segregationism see chapter 3 in this volume.
52. Denis Worrall, "Personal Statement", *South Africa's Political Alternatives*, pp. 245–48.
53. On 13 December 1973 Worrall met P. W. Botha in Cape Town to discuss joining the National Party, *B. J. Vorster Papers*, PV132 2/6/1/36 D. Worrall to B. J. Vorster, 7 January 1974. See also *The Times* (London), April 10 1974.
54. SPRO-CAS, *South Africa's Political Alternatives*, Johannesburg, SPRO-CAS, 1973, p. 87.
55. *Ibid.*, p. 102.
56. *Ibid.*, pp. 110, 209.
57. *Ibid.*, pp. 221–242.
58. *The Argus*, 18 December 1973.
59. *Quintin Whyte Papers*, BC627 D2.120 C. Eglin to Q. Whyte, 16 July 1973.
60. *South Africa's Political Alternatives*, pp. 247–248. See also Dennis Worrall, "English South Africa and the Political System" in Andre de Villiers (ed), *English Speaking South Africa Today*, Cape Town, OUP, 1976, pp. 194–215.
61. *SPRO-CAS Papers* A835/Ad6v R. Turner to P. Randall n.d. encl. notes on draft report; P. Randall to A. S. Matthews, February 28 1973.
62. W. A. de Klerk, "Christian neo marxism?", *Pro Veritate*, 15 September 1972, p. 12.
63. Stephen R. Clingman, *The Novels of Nadine Gordimer: History From The Inside*, Johannesburg, Ravan Press, 1986, pp. 90–134; see also chapter 5 in this volume.
64. Richard Turner, *The Eye of the Needle: Toward Participatory Democracy in South Africa*, Maryknoll (New York), Orbis Books, 1978 (1 ed. SPRO-CAS, Johannesburg, 1972), p. 94. There has been no general assessment of Rick Turner's thought for South African politics, but see M. A. Nupen, "Philosophy and the Crisis in South Africa", *Transformation*, 7 (1988), pp. 37–46.
65. The Eye of the Needle, pp. 96, 138.
66. *Ibid.*, pp. 122–23, 153.
67. *Ibid.*, p. ii.
68. *SPRO-CAS Papers*, A835/B10.11 P. Randall to The Editor, *The Cape Times*, June 21 1972. See also *Church Versus State*, p. 107.

69. *SPRO-CAS Papers*, A835/B11.iii, Report on a seminar on strategies for change held at the Ecumenical Centre, Stellenbosch, over the weekend 29 September to 1 October 1973. The convener was Neville Curtis, p. 7.
70. *Ibid.*, p. 11.
71. *Ibid.*, p. 18. Black Revolution was generally seen in the seminar as "non viable change", p. 19.
72. Black Community Programmes, *Year Report, 1972*.
73. *SPRO-CAS Papers*, A835/B4 Minutes of SPRO-CAS Staff Discussions, 27–28 January 1972.
74. *SPRO-CAS Papers* A835/B10iii B. Khoapa, "Memo from Mr Khoapa on Sponsorship of SPRO-CAS", n.d.; A835/133 P. Randall to B. Naude, December 18 1972. Khoapa saw SPRO-CAS's role as "co-ordinating current change rather than initiating new programmes – this is consistent with the broad view of SPRO-CAS as an enabling body", *ibid.*, Report of the First Meeting of the Joint Liaison Committee of SPRO-CAS Sponsors, 13 March 1972, p. 3.
75. *SPRO-CAS Papers*, A835/B10iii Minutes of Joint Meeting of Black Panels held in Johannesburg, 27 July 1972.
76. *Black Review 1972*, Durban, BCP, 1973, p. 48.
77. Heribert Adam, "The Rise of Black Consciousness in South Africa", p. 158.
78. See for example the Presidential Address by I. D. MacCrone, *The Price of Apartheid*, Johannesburg, SAIRR, 1970, for a restatement of this view.
79. *Leo Marquard Papers*, BC587 E1.288 L. Marquard to F. Van Wyk, 27 November 1972.
80. *Leo Marquard Papers*, BC587 E1.242 Q. Whyte to L. Marquard, 3 January 1969.
81. *Quintin Whyte Papers*, BC627 E2.112 F. Van Wyk to Q. Whyte, 4 June 1970.
82. "The Nature and Aims of the S.A. Institute of Race Relations", *Survey of Race Relations, 1972*.
83. F. J. Van Wyk, "Black Consciousness: The Institute's Position As I See It", Johannesburg, SAIRR, Memo R 120/72, January 1973.
84. Jaap Boekooi, "The Man in the Race Relations Hot Seat", *The Star*, 6 May 1972.
85. Ellen Hellman, "Culture Contacts and Social Change", *Race Relations Journal*, XV, 1–2 (1948), p. 35.
86. Ellen Hellman, *In Defence of a Shared Society*, Johannesburg, SAIRR, 1956, p. 3.
87. *Ellen Hellman Papers*, A1418/14 D. Grice to F. Van Wyk, 16 April 1973.
88. *Quintin Whyte Papers*, AB1502 Ba1(6) E. Hellman to Q. Whyte, 19 March 1973.
89. *Quintin Whyte Papers*, AD1502 Ba1 (6) E. Hellman to Q. Whyte, 12 April 1973. Alan Paton also opposed the Institute's decision, *The Star*, May 11 1973.

90. *The Sunday Times* (Johannesburg), 18 March 1973.
91. *The Star*, May 11 1973.
92. *The Star*, April 2 1973; A. Holiday, "The Sedate Liberals Show Their Teeth", *Rand Daily Mail*, May 22 1973.
93. *F. J. Van Wyk Papers*, BC587 E1.311 Clive Nettleton, memo "The Young Person's Guide To The Road Ahead", May 1973, p. 2. Nettleton also suggested "action research in which we may try to involve communities in research on problems affecting them", C. Nettleton to F. Van Wyk, Johannesburg, SAIRR, memo dated 5 June 1973, p. 2.
94. *White Power and the Liberal Conscience*, pp. 73–76.
95. *Ellen Hellman Papers*, AB1279/M2.1 E. Hellman to A. S. Mathews, 31 October 1973. See also Ellen Hellman, *The South African Institute of Race Relations, 1929–1979: A Short History*, Johannesburg, SAIRR, 1979, p. 20.
96. *F. J. Van Wyk Papers*, BC587 E1.311 H. Van Der Merwe to F. Van Wyk, May 28 1973 urging that the Institute's research committee "concentrate on research that will produce material relevant to the development of Black Consciousness, workers organisations and the development of responsible black leadership"; *Ellen Hellman Papers* AD1279/M2.2 A. S. Mathews, "The South African Institute of Race Relations – Future Policy", Johannesburg, SAIRR Memo R.R. 136/73 pointing out that "Both the activist and the non activist may wish to encourage the same response; but the activist's words are meant to be a trigger to action whereas those of the non activist are essentially a trigger to thought and reflection prior to action"; L. Schlemmer to the Director, SAIRR, 8 November 1973; A. S. Mathews to E. Hellman, 7 November 1973.
97. *Ellen Hellman Papers*, AD1279/M.2.2 F. O. Joseph, memo "The Future Role of the Institute", 25 July 1973.
98. South African Institute of Race Relations, *45th Annual Report 1973–1974*, p. 1.
99. South African Institute of Race Relations, *46th Annual Report 1974–1975*, p. 1.
100. Colin Legum, *Southern Africa: The Diplomacy of Detente*, London, Rex Collins, 1975, p. 16.
101. Andre Du Toit, "Anomalies in Our Political Structure", *Race Relations News*, 37, 3 (March 1975), pp. 4–6; see also Worrall, "English South Africa and the Political System".
102. Sam C. Nolutshungu, *Changing South Africa*, Manchester, Manchester University Press, 1982, p. 175.
103. Hirson, *op. cit.*, p. 295.
104. Njabulo Ndebele, "Black Development" in Njabulo Ndebele (ed), *Black Viewpoint*, Durban, SPRO-CAS Black Community Programme, 1972, p. 15.
105. *Ibid.*, p. 20.
106. Nigel Gibson, "Black Consciousness, 1976–87: The Dialectics of Liberation in South Africa", *Africa Today*, 1st Qtr, 1988, pp. 5–6.

107. For an account of the black consciousness trial see *The Testimony of Steve Biko*, London, Panther Books, 1979.
108. *White Power and the Liberal Conscience*, pp. 47–49; "Bernard Huss, Mariannhill and African Cooperatives" unpub. ms, University of Bristol, 1989.
109. Gerhart, *op. cit.*
110. C. M. C. Ndamse, "The New Day" in Ndebele, *op. cit.*, p. 37.
111. James H. Cone, "Black Consciousness and the Black Church" in Thoahlane Thoahlane (ed), *Black Renaissance: Papers From The Black Renaissance Convention*, Johannesburg, Ravan Press, 1975, p. 69. See also Fatton, *op. cit.*, pp. 107–119; David Bosch, "Currents and Crosscurrents in South African Black Theology", *Journal of Religion in Africa*, 11, 1 (1974), pp. 1–22.
112. Mafika Pascal Gwala, "Towards The Practical Manifestations of Black Consciousness" in Cone, *op. cit.*, p. 25.
113. Alan Brooks and Jeremy Brickhill, *Whirlwind Before the Storm*, London, International Defence and Aid, 1980, pp. 85–99; Hirson, *op. cit.*

5 Liberal Realism in South African Fiction

1. Nadine Gordimer, "English Language Literature and Politics in South Africa" in Christopher Heywood (ed), *Aspects of South African Literature*, London, Heinemann, 1976, p. 109.
2. Paul Rich, "Romance and the Development of the South African Novel" in Landeg White and Tim Couzens (eds), *Literature and Society in South Africa*, London, Longmans, 1984, pp. 120–137.
3. Michael Wade, "The Novels of Peter Abrahams", *Critique*, XI, 1 (December 1968), pp. 82–95; "South Africa's First Proletarian Writer" in Kenneth Parker (ed), *The South African Novel in English*, London and Basingstoke, The Macmillan Press, 1978, pp. 95–113.
4. Paul B. Rich, *White Power and the Liberal Conscience: Racial Segregation and South African Liberalism 1921–1960*, Manchester, Manchester University Press, 1984, pp. 92–97.
5. Nadine Gordimer, "The English Novel in South Africa" in NUSAS Winter School Conference, *The Novel and the Nation, 1959–1960*, Johannesburg, NUSAS, 1960, p. 16.
6. David Daiches, *The Novel and the Modern World*, Chicago and London, University of Chicago Press, 1960, p. 1.
7. Ian Watt, *The Rise of the Novel*, Harmondsworth, Penguin Books, 1970, pp. 7–35.
8. Timothy J. Reiss, *The Discourse of Modernism*, Ithaca and London, Cornell University Press, 1982, pp. 33–34.
9. Ioan Williams, *The Realist Novel in England: A Study in Development*, London and Basingstoke, The Macmillan Press, 1974, esp. pp. 3–11.
10. Julian Moynihan, "Pastoralism as Culture and Counter Culture in English Fiction, 1800–1928", *Novel*, Fall 1972, pp. 20–35.

11. William Plomer, *Turbott Wolfe*, London, The Hogarth Press, 1925; see also Michael Wade, "William Plomer, English Liberalism and the South African Novel", *The Journal of Commonwealth Literature*, VIII, 1 (June 1973), pp. 120–32; David Rabkin, "Race and Fiction: God's Stepchildren and Turbott Wolfe" in Kenneth Parker (ed), *The South African Novel in English*, London and Basingstoke, The Macmillan Press, 1978, pp. 77–94.
12. Plomer, *op. cit.*
13. Alan Paton, *Towards The Mountain: An Autobiography*, New York, Charles Scribners and Sons, 1981, p. 86.
14. David Rabkin, "Ways of Looking: Origins of the Novel in South Africa", *Journal of Commonwealth Literature*, XIII, (August 1978), p. 43.
15. Northrop Frye, *The Secular Scripture: A Study of the Structure of Romance*, Cambridge (Mass), Harvard University Press, 1976, p. 53.
16. Alan Paton, "Ha'penny" in *Debby Go Home*, Harmondsworth, Penguin Books.
17. Wulf Sachs, *Black Anger*, New York, Grove Press, 1947; see also V. A. February, *Mind Your Colour: The "Coloured" Stereotype in South African Literature*, London and Boston, Kegan Int., 1981, p. 84.
18. Alan Paton, *Cry The Beloved Country*, Harmondsworth, Penguin Books, 1960, p. 134.
19. Alan Paton, "Olive Schreiner – The Forerunner", *The Forum*, 4 (1955–56), pp. 26–29.
20. February, *op. cit.*, p. 69.
21. Alan Paton, *Too Late the Phalarope*, Harmondsworth, Penguin Books, 1971, p. 8.
22. *Ibid.*, p. 200.
23. Alan Paton, *Hofmeyr*, Oxford, Clarendon Press, 1964.
24. Phyllis Altman, *The Law of the Vultures*, London, Jonathan Cape, 1952.
25. For a similar view see Michael Wade, "The black looking glass in white South African literature", *African Affairs*, 82, 326 (January 1983), pp. 97–120.
26. Jack Cope, "A Turning Point in South African English Writing", *Crux*, Vol 4, June–Dec. 1970, p. 13.
27. Jack Cope, *The Fair House*, London, MacGibbon and Kee, 1955, p. 146.
28. *Ibid.*, p. 323.
29. *Ibid.*, p. 294.
30. *Ibid.*, p. 45.
31. *Ibid.*, p. 292.
32. *Ibid.*, p. 292.
33. Dan Jacobson, *A Dance in the Sun*, Harmondsworth, Penguin Books, 1956, pp. 155–156.
34. *Ibid.*, p. 205.
35. C. Baxter, "Political Symbolism in *A Dance in the Sun*", *English in Africa*, 5, 2 (September 1978), p. 50. Another way of reading Jacobson's work is through the notion of the "spoiled identity" of the

Jew who is forced, as a result of his stigmatization, to re-evaluate his own identity as a member of a minority group in relation to other social groups. See Marcia Leveson, "Power and Prejudice: Dan Jacobson's 'Jewish' fiction of the Fifties", unpub. paper, University of Witwatersrand. However, this re-evaluation can be seen as still failing to transcend more basic white colonial notions of "otherness" towards blacks.

36. Baxter, *op. cit.*, p. 120.
37. Anthony Sampson, *Drum*, London, Collins, 1956.
38. Nadine Gordimer, *A World of Strangers*, Harmondsworth, Penguin Books, 1958, p. 116.
39. *Ibid.*, p. 266.
40. Robert Green, "Nadine Gordimer's 'A World of Strangers': Studies in South African Liberalism", *English Studies in Africa*, 22, 1 (March 1979), p. 48.
41. "Liberal Conscience", *Contrast*, 3 (Winter 1960), p. 8.
42. *Ibid.*, p. 9.
43. Nadine Gordimer, "Where Do Whites Fit In?" in *The Essential Gesture: Writing, Politics and Places*, London, Jonathan Cape, 1988, p. 33; see also "How Not To Know the African", *Contrast*, 4, 3 (March 1967), pp. 44–49.
44. C. J. Driver, *Patrick Duncan*, London, Heinemann, 1980.
45. Nadine Gordimer, *The Late Bourgeois World*, London, Victor Gollancz, 1966, p. 114.
46. Ernst Fischer, *The Necessity of Art*, Harmondsworth, Penguin Books, 1963, p. 214.
47. *The Late Bourgeois World*, pp. 31–32.
48. *Ibid.*, p. 159.
49. *Ibid.*, p. 160.
50. "Where Do Whites Fit In?", pp. 34–35.

6 Laurens van der Post: The Noble Savage and the Romantic Image of Africa

1. Paul B. Rich, "Liberal Realism in South African Fiction, 1948–1966", *English in Africa*, 12, 1 (May 1985), pp. 47–81.
2. Harmondsworth, Penguin Books, 1988.
3. Donald Lammers, "Nevil Shute and the Decline of the 'Imperial Idea' in Literature", *The Journal of British Studies*, XVI, 2 (Spring 1977), pp. 121–52.
4. Laurens van der Post, *A Walk with a White Bushman*, Harmondsworth, Penguin Books, 1986, pp. 89–90.
5. David Maughan-Brown, "The Noble Savage in Anglo Saxon Colonial Ideology, 1950–1980" paper presented to the Conference on Anglo Saxon Racial Ideology, Birmingham, September 1982. Published as "The Image of the Crowd in South African Fiction", *English in Africa*, 14, 1 (May 1987), pp. 1–20.

6. Hoxie Neale Fairchild, *The Noble Savage: A Study in Romantic Naturalism*, New York, Oxford University Press, 1928, p. 2.
7. Katherine George, "The Civilised West Looks at Primitive Africa, 1400–1800", *ISIS*, XLIX, (March 1958), p. 72.
8. Hayden White, "The Noble Savage Theme as Fetish" in *Tropics of Discourse*, Boston and London, Johns Hopkins University Press, 1978, p. 191.
9. Peter J. Weston, "The Noble Primitive as Bourgeois Subject", *Literature and History*, 10, 1 (Spring 1984), p. 65.
10. *Ibid.*, p. 68.
11. J. M. Coetzee, "The Picturesque, The Sublime and the South African Landscape" in *White Writing*, New Haven and London, Yale University Press, 1988, pp. 36–62; Paul Rich, "Landscape, Social Darwinism and the Cultural Roots of Apartheid Theory", *Patterns of Prejudice*, 17, 3 (July 1983), pp. 1–15.
12. Paul B. Rich, "Milnerism and a Ripping Yarn: Transvaal Land Settlement and John Buchan's novel *Prester John*, 1901–1910" in Belinda Bozzoli (ed), *Town and Countryside in the Transvaal*, Johannesburg, Ravan Press, 1983, pp. 412–33.
13. J. M. Coetzee, "Idleness in South Africa" in *White Writing*, pp. 12–35.
14. Dudley Kidd, *The Essential Kaffir*, London, A and C Black, 1904; *Kaffir Socialism*, London, A and C Black, 1908.
15. See especially Saul Dubow, *Racial Segregation and the Origins of Apartheid in South Africa*, London and Basingstoke, The Macmillan Press, 1989.
16. G. Heaton Nicholls, *Bayete: Hail to the King!*, London, Allen and Unwin, 1923.
17. Charles van Onselen, "The Witches of Suburbia: Domestic Service on the Witwatersrand, 1890–1914" in *Studies in the Social and Economic History of the Witwatersrand, 1886–1914: 2 New Nineveh*, London, Longman, 1982, pp. 1–73.
18. Perceval Gibbon, *Margaret Harding*, (1 ed 1911), Cape Town and Johannesburg, David Philip, 1983.
19. J. M. Coetzee, "Blood, Taint, Flaw, Degeneration: The Novels of Sarah Gertrude Millin" in *White Writing*, pp. 136–62.
20. *A Walk with a White Bushman*, Harmondsworth, Penguin Books, 1987, p. 194.
21. David Trotter, "Modernism and Empire: reading *The Waste Land*", *Critical Quarterly*, 28, 1–2 (1986), pp. 143–53. Van der Post first read *The Waste Land* at school when it was given to him by his older brother studying at university. He recalled it as "the voice of my hour, it keeps my time", *A Walk with a White Bushman*, p. 181.
22. Laurens van der Post, *In a Province*, Harmondsworth, Penguin Books, 1983, p. 12.
23. *Ibid.*, p. 33.
24. *Ibid.*, p. 5.
25. Tim Couzens, *The New African: A Study of the Life and Work of H. I. E. Dhlomo*, Johannesburg, Ravan Press, 1985.

26. For Thaele's career in the Cape see Robert A. Hill and Gregory A. Pirio, "'Africa for the Africans'; the Garvey Movement in South Africa, 1920–1949" in Shula Marks and Stanley Trapido (eds), *The Politics of Race, Class and Nationalism in Twentieth Century South Africa*, London and New York, Longman, 1987, pp. 209–253.
27. *In a Province*, p. 113.
28. *Ibid.*, p. 122.
29. Max Gordan began as a full time union organizer on the Witwatersrand and had established seven African unions by the start of World War Two, Peter Walshe, *The Rise of African Nationalism in South Africa*, London, C. Hurst and Co, 1970, p. 309.
30. *In a Province*, p. 254.
31. *A Walk with a White Bushman*, pp. 224–5.
32. Laurens van der Post, *The Seed and the Sower*, Harmondsworth, Penguin Books, p. 101.
33. *Leif Egeland Papers*, Killie Campbell Library, Durban, L. van der Post to L. Egeland, 27 October 1947.
34. Ruth Benedict, *The Chrysanthemum and the Sword* (1 ed 1946), London, Routledge and Kegan Paul, 1977, pp. 220–1.
35. *The Seed and the Sower*, p. 25.
36. *A Walk with a White Bushman*, p. 228.
37. Gloria Young, "Quest and Discovery: Joseph Conrad's and Carl Jung's African Journeys", *Modern Fiction Studies*, 28, 4 (Winter 1982–83), pp. 583–589.
38. *Jung and the Story of Our Time*, Harmondsworth, Penguin Books, 1976, p. 51.
39. Farhad Dalal, "The Racism of Jung", *Race and Class*, XXIX, (1988), pp. 1–22.
40. L. Levy-Bruhl, *Primitive Mentality*, London, Allen and Unwin, 1923. The idea that African societies were governed by a pre-logical mode of thinking was attacked in the 1920s by some South African liberals. See, for example, J. D. Rheinallt Jones, "The Need for a Scientific Basis for South African Native Policy", *South African Journal of Science*, XXIII, (1926).
41. David Maughan-Brown, *Land, Freedom and Fiction: History and Ideology in Kenya*, London, Zed Books, 1985, pp. 47–48; J. C. Carothers, *The Psychology of Mau Mau*, Nairobi, Government Printer, 1954.
42. Laurens van der Post, *The Dark Eye in Africa*, London, The Hogarth Press, 1961 (1 edn 1955), p. 56.
43. *Ibid.*, p. 53.
44. Thomas Hodgkin, "n-Dimensional Africa", *Spectator*, December 16 1955.
45. *Leonard Woolf Papers*, University of Sussex, 111, L. van der Post to L. Woolf, 13 March 1956.
46. Thomas Hodgkin, "n-Dimensional Africa", *Spectator*, December 16 1955.
47. Laurens van der Post, *Flamingo Feather*, Harmondsworth, Penguin Books, 1983, p. 293.

48. *Ibid.*, p. 211.
49. *Ibid.*, p. 296.
50. James Stern, "Black-and-White-Africa", *Encounter*, IV, 6 (June 1955), pp. 81–2.
51. Lucy Mair, "Ritual and Rationality", *Encounter*, XLIII, 4 (October 1974), pp. 85–89.
52. *A Walk with a White Bushman*, pp. 89–90.
53. Laurens van der Post, *The Heart of the Hunter*, London, The Companion Book Club, 1961, p. 125.
54. *Ibid.*, p. 120.
55. *Ibid.*, p. 123.
56. W. H. I. Bleek and L. C. Lloyd, *Specimens of Bushman Folklore*, London, G. Allen and Co., 1911. See also R. J. Thornton, " 'This Dying Out Race': W. H. I. Bleek's Approaches to the Languages of Southern Africa", *Social Dynamics*, 9, 2 (1983), pp. 1–10.
57. George William Stow, *The Native Races of South Africa*, London, Swan Sonnenschein, 1905. See also A. E. Voss, "The Hero of *The Native Races*: The Making of a Myth", paper presented to the Conference on Literature and Society in Southern Africa, University of York, September 8–11 1981.
58. Geo McCall Theal, "Introduction" in *Specimens of Bushman Folklore*, p. xi.
59. *W. C. Scully Papers*, Bb1 W. C. Scully ms. "The Pygmy Cave Dwellers of South Africa", n.d.
60. *In a Province*, p. 102.
61. Laurens van der Post and Jane Taylor, *Testament to the Bushmen*, Harmondsworth Books, 1985, p. 28.
62. "The Hartebeest and the Eland" in W. H. I. Bleek and Lucy C. Lloyd, *The Mantis and His Friends*, Cape Town, Maskew Miller, pp. 10–12.
63. *The Heart of the Hunter*, p. 177.
64. Laurens van der Post, *A Far Off Place*, Harmondsworth, Penguin Books, 1987.
65. Laurens van der Post, *A Story Like the Wind*, Harmondsworth, Penguin Books, 1974, p. 27.
66. See, for example, Ronald Segal, *The Race War*, Harmondsworth, Penguin Books, 1966.
67. Laurens van der Post, *A Mantis Carol*, Harmondsworth, Penguin Books, 1989, p. 50.
68. *Ibid.*, p. 101.
69. *Ibid.*, p. 157.
70. Harmondsworth, Penguin Books, 1984.
71. Martin Green, *Dreams of Adventure, Deeds of Empire*, London, Routledge and Kegan Paul, 1980.
72. *A Walk with a White Bushman*, p. 109.
73. *Testament to the Bushman*, p. 123.
74. *New Statesman*, 27 October 1961.
75. George H. Szanto, "Geography, Private Property and the Western

Novel", *Canadian Review of Comparative Literature*, June 1983, pp. 167–81.

7 The Decline of the Idea of Civilization

1. W. R. James, "The 'Barbarians' in World Historical Perspective: Myth and Reality", *Cultures*, IV, 2 (1977), pp. 101–120. See also Philip Spencer, " 'Barbarian Assault': The Fortunes of a Phrase", *Journal of the History of Ideas*, XVI, 2 (April 1955), pp. 232–239.
2. Gerhard Masur, "Distinctive Traits of Western Civilisation Through The Eyes of Western Historians", *American Historical Review*, LXVII, 3 (April 1962), pp. 591–608.
3. Geoffrey Barraclough, "Metropolis and Macrocosm: Europe and the Wider World, 1492–1939" in *History in a Changing World*, Oxford, Basil Blackwell, 1957, pp. 135–153. For the impact of Arnold Toynbee and Oswald Spengler see James Joll, "Two Prophets of the Twentieth Century: Spengler and Toynbee", *Review of International Studies*, 11 (1985), pp. 91–104.
4. Paul B. Rich, *Race and Empire in British Politics*, (2nd edn), Cambridge, CUP, 1990, pp. 27–49.
5. Frank Kermode, *The Sense of An Ending*, London, OUP, 1966, p. 98.
6. Richard Jenkyns, *The Victorians and Ancient Greece*, Oxford, Basil Blackwell, 1980, pp. 332–333.
7. Percy Fitzpatrick, *The Transvaal From Within*, London, Heinemann, 1900. When the book was published the royalties were donated to the Imperial Light Horse suggesting that it was aimed at provoking hostilities, Andrew Duminy and Bill Guest, *Interfering in Politics: A biography of Percy Fitzpatrick*, Johannesburg, Lowry, 1987, pp. 79–80.
8. Captain Francis Younghusband, *South Africa Of Today*, London, Macmillan, 1896, pp. 115–117.
9. H. H. Johnstone, "The Boer Question", *The Fortnightly Review*, LVI, CCCXXXIII (August 1894), p. 163.
10. Olive Schreiner, "Stray Thoughts on South Africa", *The Fortnightly Review*, LX, CCCLV (July 1896), p. 17.
11. James Bryce, *Impressions of South Africa*, London, Macmillan, 1899, p. 363.
12. *Ibid.*, p. 465.
13. For the evolution of Bryce's thought see *Race and Empire in British Politics*, pp. 20–24; John Stone, "James Bryce and the Comparative Sociology of Race Relations", *Ethnic and Racial Studies*, 13, 3 (1973).
14. For an analysis of Theal's thought and its impact on early South African historiography see Christopher Saunders, *The Making of the South African Past*, Cape Town and Johannesburg, David Philip, 1988, pp. 9–29.
15. A. H. Keane, *The Gold of Ophir*, London, E. Stanford, 1901, p. 185. For an account of the first archaeological investigations at Zimbabwe see Peter S. Garlake, *Great Zimbabwe*, London, Thames and Hudson, 1973.

16. Saul Dubow, *Racial Segregation and the Origins of Apartheid*, London and Basingstoke, The Macmillan Press, 1989, p. 24.
17. Dudley Kidd, *Kafir Socialism and the Dawn of Individualism*, London, A & C Black, 1908, pp. 144–145.
18. *Ibid.*, p. 146.
19. *Ibid.*, p. 224.
20. *Ibid.*, pp. 227–229.
21. *Ibid.*, p. 229.
22. Though one critic strongly opposed Kidd's ideas on the eugenic improvement of the African "stock". "We may breed kafirs like prize oxen", wrote Trevor Fletcher, "and call it artificial selection, Eugenics, or any other name we like, but that there will be any advance in their mental and moral nature is purely a gratuitous assumption", "The Native Problem: A Transcendental View", *The African Monthly*, 24 (November 1908), p. 581.
23. *Patrick Duncan Papers* BC294 D6.3.6 Lord Selborne to P. Duncan, 30 November 1907.
24. Lord Selborne, *Address Delivered Before a Congregation of the University of the Cape of Good Hope*, 27 February 1909, Cape Town, 1909, p. 8.
25. *Ibid.*, p. 9.
26. *Ibid.*, p. 22.
27. *Ibid.*, p. 30.
28. Dean Inge, for example, considered in 1921 that the future of white South Africa was "problematical" for "it does not seem likely that it will ever be a white man's country like Canada or New Zealand", W. R. Inge, "The White Man and His Race", *The Quarterly Review*, 235, 467 (April 1921), p. 151.
29. Olive Schreiner, "The Native Question" in Uys Krige (ed), *Olive Schreiner: A Selection*, Cape Town, OUP, 1968, p. 186. The pamphlet was originally printed in *Review of Reviews* 39 (1909), pp. 138–141.
30. *Ibid.*, p. 188.
31. *Ibid.*, p. 189.
32. Ruth First and Ann Scott, *Olive Schreiner*, New York, Schocken Books, 1980, p. 258.
33. Roy Campbell to Edward Garnett, 20 November 1925 cited in Peter Alexander, *Roy Campbell*, Oxford, OUP, 1982, p. 65.
34. *Ibid.*, pp. 42–55.
35. See for example Roy Campbell, *Broken Record*, London, Boriswood, 1934, in which he wrote that "There is nothing really to prevent our country from becoming, with South America, the last citadel and tower of European culture, which we certainly possess and treasure more than European intellectuals do themselves", p. 51.
36. J. C. Smuts to J. X. Merriman, 13 March 1906 in K. Hancock and J. Van Der Poel (eds), *Selections From The Smuts Papers*, Vol. 11, Cambridge, CUP, 1966, p. 242.
37. J. C. Smuts to J. A. Hobson, 13 July 1908 in *ibid.*, p. 440; J. C. Smuts to J. X. Merriman, 2 October 1908 in *ibid.*, p. 526.
38. Reprinted as J. C. Smuts, "The White Man's Task" in *Greater South*

Africa: Plans For A Better World, Johannesburg, Truth Legion, 1940, pp. 14–15. By 1945 Smuts had come to believe that, while the basic work of the ruins was African "the direction and inspiring motifs must undoubtedly be sought elsewhere", *J. C. Smuts Archive*, A1/77 J. C. Smuts to W. K. Spenser, 12 October 1945.

39. Smuts: *Greater South Africa*, p. 15.
40. J. C. Smuts, "The Commonwealth Conception" in *Greater South Africa*, p. 27.
41. J. C. Smuts, *Holism and Evolution*, London, Macmillan, 1927, pp. 9, 96. See also Ronald Hyam, *The Failure of South African Expansion*, p. 76.
42. J. C. Smuts, "The Theory of Holism" in *Greater South Africa*, pp. 131–138.
43. *Lothian Papers*, Ed 40/17/31 J. C. Smuts to P. Kerr, 23 May 1928.
44. Frederick Madden and D. K. Fieldhouse (eds), *Oxford and the Idea of Commonwealth*, London and Canberra, Croom Helm, 1982.
45. J. C. Smuts, *Africa and Some World Problems*, Oxford, Clarendon Press, p. 74.
46. *Ibid.*, pp. 45–46.
47. *Ibid.*, p. 63.
48. See John W. Cell, "Lord Hailey and the Making of the African Survey", *African Affairs*, 88, 353 (October 1989), pp. 481–505.
49. J. H. Oldham, *White and Black in Africa: A Critical Examination of the Rhodes Lectures of General Smuts*, London, Longman, Green and Co, 1930.
50. See, for example, Jan H. Hofmeyr, "British Africa" in H. Clive Barnard (ed), *The Expansion of the Anglo-Saxon Nations*, London, Black, 1920, pp. 295–298.
51. *B. K. Long Papers* MS 6703 J. H. Hofmeyr to B. K. Long, 30 July 1929.
52. Jan H. Hofmeyr, *South Africa*, London, Ernest Benn, 1931, p. 269; "United States of Africa", *The Forum*, July 15 1939.
53. *Ibid.*, pp. 276–277.
54. J. C. Smuts to M. C. Gillett, 17 March 1939 in Van der Poel, *op. cit.*, Vol VI, p. 155. Similar doubts were expressed by T. M. Forsyth, "The Crisis in Our Present Civilisation", *South African Journal of Science*, XXVII (November 1930), p. 607.
55. *South Africa*, p. 323.
56. *The Forum*, January 7 1939.
57. *B. K. Long Papers*, MS6693 B. K. Long to G. Dawson, March 29 1930.
58. J. H. Hofmeyr, "The Essentials of National Unity", *The Forum*, October 31 1938.
59. See p. 82.
60. *Leif Egeland Papers*, J. H. Hofmeyr to L. Egeland, 28 November 1941. Smuts also doubted Hofmeyr's fitness to be prime minister. "Hofmeyr with all his great gifts", he wrote, "has no sense and often behaves like a grown-up boy and not a sensible grown up with a due sense of

proportion", J. C. Smuts to M. C. Gillett, 27 May 1939 in Jean Van Der Poel (ed), *Selections from the Smuts Papers, Vol VI*, Cambridge, CUP, 1976, p. 167.
61. Phyllis Lewsen, "Liberals in Politics and Administration, 1936–1948" in Jeffrey Butler, Richard Elphick and David Welsh (eds), *Democratic Liberalism in South Africa*, Middletown (Conn), Wesleyan University Press and Cape Town and Johannesburg, David Philip, 1987, pp. 111–112.
62. *B. K. Long Papers*, MS 6697 B. K. Long, "Some Notes on Union Internal Problems" (marked "very confidential"), n.d., p. 12.
63. Interview with Gordon Mears, Cape Town, July 15 1977; *White Power and the Liberal Conscience*, pp. 108–109.
64. G. Heaton Nicholls, *Bayete: Hail to the King*, London, Allen and Unwin, 1923.
65. *G. Heaton Nicholls Papers*, G. Heaton Nicholls to Warmington, 29 October 1923.
66. *G. Heaton Nicholls Papers*, KCM 13237 G. Heaton Nicholls, *The Native Bills: An Address*, September 1935, p. 5.
67. *Heaton Nicholls Papers*, KCM 3362 e R. F. A. Hoernle to G. Heaton Nicholls, July 26 1937.
68. ARSAIRR B100 (e) G. Heaton Nicholls to J. D. Rheinallt Jones, 11 November 1935.
69. The suggestion for a diplomatic appointment came originally from Margaret Ballinger to Jan H. Hofmeyr. See Margaret Ballinger, *From Union To Apartheid*, Cape Town, Juta, 1969, pp. 102–105.
70. Allister Sparks, *The Mind of South Africa*, London, Heinemann, 1990, p. 170.
71. Jan H. Hofmeyr, *Christian Principles and Race Problems*, Johannesburg, SAIRR, 1945, p. 15.
72. *Ibid.*, p. 16. See also chapter 4 in this volume.
73. *J. P. Cope Papers*, JPL/A/10 Minutes of Discussion between J. H. Hofmeyr, J. P. Cope and R. M. De Villiers, Pretoria, July 17 1948.
74. D. D. T. Jabavu, *Native Disabilities in South Africa*, Lovedale, 1932, repr. in Thomas Karis and Gwendolen Carter (eds), *From Protest To Challenge, Vol. 1*, Stanford, Hoover Institute Press, 1972, p. 288.
75. A. Lembede, "Some Basic Principles of African Nationalism", *Ilanga Lase Natal*, February 24, September 22, October 6 and November 24 1945. See also Gail M. Gerhart, *Black Power in South Africa: The Evolution of an Ideology*, Berkeley, University of California Press, 1978, esp. pp. 45–82.
76. *Ernest Stubbs Papers*, A. B. Xuma to E. Stubbs, 27 January 1948.
77. Thomas Hodgkin, "A Note On The Language of African Nationalism" in K. Kirkwood (ed), *African Affairs*, No 1, London, Chatto and Windus, 1961, p. 39.
78. Arthur Keppel Jones, *What Is Destroying Civilisation in South Africa*, Johannesburg, SAIRR, n.d., p. 12.
79. S. Herbert Frankel, *Some Reflections on Civilisation in Africa*, Johannesburg, SAIRR, 1952, p. 26.

80. Quoted in Michael Fridjon, "The Torch Commando & the Politics of White Opposition in South Africa, 1951–1953", unpub. seminar paper, University of the Witwatersrand, March 1976, p. 3.
81. E. E. Harris, *"White" Civilisation: How It Is Threatened and How It Can Be Preserved in South Africa*, Johannesburg, SAIRR, 1954.
82. Patrick Duncan, *The Road Through the Wilderness*, Johannesburg, Hygrade Pub., May 1953. Duncan felt by 1953 that "the centre of political gravity is shifting outside the boundaries of the white group, and our future is going to be decided largely by non-whites". *Leo Marquard Papers*, BC 587.E2.44, P. Duncan to L. Marquard, 31 August 1953.
83. C. J. Driver, *Patrick Duncan*, London, Heinemann, 1980.
84. Walter Lippmann, *The Public Philosophy*, Boston, Little, Brown and Cop, 1956. See also Ronald Street, *Walter Lippmann and the American Century*, London, The Bodley Head, 1980, pp. 491–496.
85. *Z. K. Matthews Papers*, D. V. Cowen to Z. K. Matthews, 8 February 1960.
86. D. V. Cowen, *The Foundations of Sovereignty*, London, OUP, 1961, p. 197.
87. *Ibid.*, p. 233.
88. Edgar Brookes, *Power, Law, Right and Love*, Durham, Duke University Press, 1963, pp. 12–13.
89. *Alan Paton Papers*, M865 R. Vigne to A. Paton, 30 October 1962.
90. *Ibid.*, M865 A. Paton to Herr Holtzen, 2 July 1964.
91. "We should drop that 'White' civilisation tag", *The Star*, February 10 1975.
92. Nadine Gordimer, *The Conservationist*, London, Jonathan Cape, 1974.
93. J. M. Coetzee, *Waiting For the Barbarians*, Johannesburg, Ravan Press, 1981, p. 24.
94. *Ibid.*, p. 38.
95. *Ibid.*, p. 133.

Conclusion

1. Dennis Worrall, "English South Africa and the Political System" in Andre de Villiers (ed), *English Speaking South Africa Today*, Cape Town, OUP, 1976, p. 206.
2. M. J. Bonn, *Wandering Scholar*, London, Cohen and West, 1949, p. 123.
3. Edgar Brookes, *The Commonwealth Today*, Pietermaritzburg, University of Natal Press, 1959, p. 44.
4. J. Alton Templin, *Ideology on a Frontier: The Theological Foundation of Afrikaner Nationalism, 1652–1910*, Westport (Conn), Greenwood Press, 1984.
5. *J. C. Smuts Archive*, A1/269 S. G. Millin to J. C. Smuts, 21 December 1946.
6. Sarah Gertrude Millin, "Fear in Africa", *Foreign Affairs*, 28, 1 (October 1949), p. 108.

7. Sarah Gertrude Millin, *White Africans Are Also People*, Cape Town, Timmins, 1966; see also Martin Rubin, *Sarah Gertrude Millin*, Johannesburg, AD Donker, 1977, esp. pp. 165–274.
8. Melody Anne Prince, "Watchman, What of the Night?: The Political Ideas of R. F. A. Hoernle and E. H. Brookes and Their Contribution to the Theory and Practice of South African Liberalism", M. Phil Thesis, University of Leicester, 1983, p. 99.
9. Arthur Keppel Jones, *When Smuts Goes*, Pietermaritzburg, Shuter and Shooter, 1947.
10. Arthur Keppel Jones, "Afrikaner Nationalism", *The Forum*, July 1952, pp. 14–15.
11. Edgar Brookes, *Three Letters From Africa*, Pendle Hill (USA), Pendle Hill Pamphlet No 139, 1965, p. 25.
12. Z. K. Matthews, "The Crisis in Southern Africa", *Christianity and Crisis*, 10 and 24 (1952).
13. See for example Nadine Gordimer's recollection of the black writer Nat Nakasa in 'One Man Living Through It' in Stephen Clingman (ed), *The Essential Gesture*, London, Jonathan Cape, 1988, pp. 79–86. For a more general account, see Anthony Sampson, *Drum*, London, Collins, 1956.
14. Russell Jacoby, *The Last Intellectuals: American Culture in the Age of Academe*, New York, Basic Books, 1987.
15. Andrew Prior, "Is Democracy Possible in South Africa", *The South African Outlook*, 103, 1281 (March 1978), p. 36.
16. See for instance A. S. Mathews, *Law, Order and Liberty in South Africa*, Cape Town, Juta, 1971, and 'Human Rights and the Rule of Law, II' in Jeffrey Butler *et al.*, *Democratic Liberalism in South Africa*, Middletown, CT, Wesleyan University Press, 1987, pp. 281–7; Albie Sachs, *Justice in South Africa*, Berkeley, University of California Press, 1973; J. Dugard, *Human Rights and the South African Legal Order*, Princeton, Princeton University Press, 1978, and 'Human Rights and the Rule of Law, I' in Butler, *op. cit.*, pp. 271–80.
17. Hermann Giliomee and Lawrence Schlemmer, *From Apartheid To Nation Building*, Cape Town, OUP, 1989.
18. Nadine Gordimer, *The Conservationist*, London, Jonathan Cape, 1974.
19. Nadine Gordimer, "From Apartheid to Afrocentrism", *English in Africa*, 7, 1 (March 1980), p. 47.
20. Pierre L. van den Berghe, "The Impossibility of a Liberal Solution in South Africa" in Pierre L. van den Berghe (ed), *The Liberal Dilemma in South Africa*, London, Croom Helm, 1979, pp. 58–67.
21. Martin Legassick, "Liberalism, Social Control and Liberation in South Africa", unpublished seminar paper, University of Warwick, 1977.
22. Paul B. Rich, *White Power and the Liberal Conscience: Racial Segregation and South African Liberalism*, Manchester, Manchester University Press, 1984.
23. John A. Hall, *Liberalism*, London, Paladin Books, 1988, esp. pp. 193–231.
24. Albie Sachs, "Towards a Bill of Rights For A Democratic South Africa", *The Hastings International and Comparative Law Review*, 12, 2 (Winter 1989), pp. 289–324.

SELECT BIBLIOGRAPHY

Manuscript Sources

1 Official Papers

Files, Reports and Minutes of the Secretary of Native Affairs, 1901–1910, Transvaal Archives Depot, Pretoria (prefix SNA).
Files, Reports and Minutes of the Union Native Affairs Department, Union Archives, Pretoria, (prefix NST).

Papers of Private Individuals

Margaret Ballinger Papers, Church of the Province Archives, University of the Witwatersrand.
F. W. Bell Papers, Church of the Province Archives, University of the Witwatersrand, Johannesburg.
E. Brookes Papers, Killie Campbell, Durban (this is only a file mostly of articles).
A. W. G. Champion Papers, Church of the Province Archives, University of the Witwatersrand, Johannesburg (prefix UW).
A. W. G. Champion Papers, Jagger Library, University of Cape Town (prefix UCT).
A. W. G. Champion Papers, University of South Africa, Pretoria, (prefix UNISA).
J. P. Cope Papers, Institute of Commonwealth Studies Library, London.
Patrick Duncan Papers, Jagger Library, University of Cape Town (these are of Patrick Duncan senior) (prefix S).
Patrick Duncan Papers, University of York Library (these are of Patrick Duncan junior) (prefix J).

Leif Egeland Papers, Killie Campbell Library, Durban.
H. B. Fantham File, Church of the Province Archives, University of the Witwatersrand, Johannesburg.
Alfred Court Haddon Papers, Cambridge University Library.
G. Heaton Nicholls Papers, Killie Campbell Library, Durban.
Ellen Hellman Papers, Church of the Province Archives, University of the Witwatersrand, Johannesburg.
J. B. M. Hertzog Papers, Union Archives, Pretoria.
R. F. A. Hoernle Collection, Wartenweiler Library, University of the Witwatersrand, Johannesburg.
Jan H. Hofmeyr, Church of the Province Archives, University of the Witwatersrand, Johannesburg.
Alexander Kerr Papers, Cory Library, Rhodes University, Grahamstown.
B. K. Long Papers, Cory Library, Grahamstown.
C. T. Loram Papers, Yale University Library, New Haven (Conn).
Lothian Papers (Philip Kerr), Scottish Public Record, Edinburgh.
E. G. Malherbe Papers, Killie Campbell, Durban.
W. M. Macmillan Papers, in the private possession of Mrs Mona Macmillan.
Leo Marquard Papers, Jagger Library, University of Cape Town.
Z. K. Matthews Papers, microfilm, Institute of Commonwealth Studies, London.
Donald Molteno Papers, Jagger Library, University of Cape Town.
Gilbert Murray Papers, Bodleian Library, Oxford.
Alan Paton Papers, Church of the Province Archives, University of the Witwatersrand, Johannesburg.
Margery Perham Papers, Rhodes House Library, Oxford.
J. Howard Pim Papers, Church of the Province Archives, University of the Witwatersrand, Johannesburg.
J. D. Rheinallt Jones Papers, Church of the Province Archives, University of the Witwatersrand.
Robert Shepherd Papers, Cory Library, Rhodes University, Grahamstown.
Douglas Smit Papers, Albany Museum, Grahamstown.
J. C. Smuts Archive, Union Archives, Pretoria.
J. C. Smuts Correspondence, Library of the South African Institute of International Affairs, Jan Smuts House, University of the Witwatersrand.
Ernest Stubbs Papers, Church of the Province Archives, University of the Witwatersrand, Johannesburg.
B. J. Vorster Papers, Institute of Contemporary History, University of the Orange Free State, Bloemfontein.
Maurice Webb Papers, Killie Campbell Library, Durban.
Quintin Whyte Papers, Church of the Province Archives, University of the Witwatersrand, Johannesburg.
Leonard Woolf Papers, University of Sussex Library.
F. J. Van Wyk Papers, Church of the Province Archives, University of the Witwatersrand, Johannesburg.
Alfred Xuma Papers, Church of the Province Archives, University of the Witwatersrand, Johannesburg.

SELECT BIBLIOGRAPHY   251

Papers of Organizations

Gamma Sigma Club, Minute Book deposited in the African Studies Institute, University of the Witwatersrand, Johannesburg.
Pretoria Joint Council, minute book, Church of the Province Archives, University of the Witwatersrand, Johannesburg.
SPRO-CAS, files, reports and minutes, Church of the Province Archives, University of the Witwatersrand, Johannesburg.
South African Institute of Race Relations, files, reports and minutes, Church of the Province Archives, University of the Witwatersrand, Johannesburg (prefix ARSAIRR).
Transvaal Native Affairs Society, Church of the Province Archives, University of the Witwatersrand, Johannesburg.
Zulu Society, files, reports and minutes, Natal Archives, Pietermaritzburg.

Published Sources

Official Publications

Report of the Native Lands Commission, UG22–1916.
Report of the Interdepartmental Committee on Native Education, 1935–36, UG29–1936.
Social and Economic Planning Council, Report No 9, *The Native Reserves and Their Place in the Economy of the Union of South Africa*, Pretoria, 1946.

Newspapers, Journals and Magazines

The African Monthly
The Christian Express
Common Sense
Contrast
Encounter
The Fortnightly Review
The Forum
Ilanga lase Natal
Indian Opinion
Izwi Labantu
Koranta ea Becoana
The Nineteenth Century
Proceedings of the South African Association for the Advancement of Science
Spectator
Pro Veritate
Race Relations
Race Relations Journal
Race Relations News
Rand Daily Mail
Reality
South African Journal of Science

The Star
The Transvaal Leader
Umsebenzi
Umteteli wa Bantu

Pamphlets

Bell, F. W., *The Native as a Political Factor in the Franchise*, Johannesburg, Addington and Co, 1908.
Bell, F. W., *The South African Native Problem: The Solution of Segregation*, Johannesburg, Central News Agency, 1909.
Bell, F. W., *Farewell Address to the South African Native Affairs Society*, Johannesburg, 1910.
Brookes, Edgar, *The Bantu in South Africa*, Johannesburg, SAIRR, 1943.
Brookes, Edgar et al, *South Africa faces UNO*, Johannesburg, SAIRR, 1947.
Brookes, Edgar, *The Natives Representative Council and the Senate in the Political Representation of Africans in the Union*, Johannesburg, SAIRR, 1943.
Brookes, Edgar, *We Come of Age*, Johannesburg, SAIRR, 1950.
Crocker, H. J., *The South African Race Problem*, Johannesburg, 1908.
Dallas, Edward, *Notes on the South African Race Problem*, Johannesburg, 1909.
Duncan, Patrick, *The Road Through the Wilderness*, Johannesburg, Hygrade Pub., 1953.
Eiselen, W. W. M., *Die Naturelle Vraagstuk*, Stellenbosch, 1929.
Evans, Maurice, *Studies in the Southern States from a South African Point of View*, Durban, 1912?
Federal Council of the D.R. Churches, *European and Bantu*, Johannesburg, DRC, 1923?
Frankel, S. Herbert, *Some Reflections on Civilisation in Africa*, Johannesburg, SAIRR, 1952.
Harris, E. E., *"White" Civilisation: How It is Threatened and How It Can be Preserved in South Africa*, Johannesburg, SAIRR, 1954.
Hellman, Ellen, *In Defence of a Shared Society*, Johannesburg, SAIRR, 1956.
Hellman, Ellen, *The South African Institute of Race Relations, 1929–1979: A Short History*, Johannesburg, SAIRR, 1979.
Jabavu, D. D. T., *Native Disabilities in South Africa*, Lovedale, Lovedale Press, 1932.
Keppel Jones, Arthur, *What is destroying civilisation in South Africa?*, Johannesburg, n.d., SAIRR, (1953?).
Macmillan, W. M., *The Land, The Native and Unemployment*, Witwatersrand, Council of Education, 1924.
Molteno, Donald, *Toward a Democratic South Africa*, Johannesburg, SAIRR, 1959.
Pim, Howard, *The Native Question in South Africa*, Johannesburg, 1903.
Pim, Howard, *The Native Problem of South Africa*, Johannesburg, 1905.
Pim, Howard, *The Question of Race*, Johannesburg, 1906.
Pim, Howard, *A Plea For the Scientific Study of the Races Inhabiting South Africa*, Johannesburg, 1910.

Schreiner, Oliver, *Political Power in South Africa*, Johannesburg, SAIRR, 1964.
Selborne, Lord, *Address Delivered Before a Congregation of the University of the Cape of Good Hope*, Cape Town, 1909.
South African Institute of Race Relations, *Go Forward in Faith: The Logic of Economic Integration*, Johannesburg, SAIRR, 1954.
Suttner, Raymond, *The Freedom Charter – The People's Charter in the Nineteen Eighties*, Cape Town, University of Cape Town, 1986.
Tatham, F. S., *The Race Conflict in South Africa*, Pietermaritzburg, 1894.
Whyte, Quintin, *Behind the Racial Tensions in South Africa*, Johannesburg, SAIRR, 1953.

Books and Excerpts

Alexander, Peter, *Roy Campbell*, Oxford, Oxford University Press, 1982.
Alexander, Peter, *William Plomer*, Oxford, Oxford University Press, 1989.
Altman, Phyllis, *The Law of the Vultures*, London, Jonathan Cape, 1952.
Biesheuvel, Simon, *African Intelligence*, Johannesburg, SAIRR, 1943.
Biko, Steve, *The Testimony of Steve Biko*, London, Panther Books, 1979.
Black Community Programme, *Black Review 1972*, Durban BCP, 1973.
Bleek, W. H. I. and L. C. Lloyd, *Specimens of Bushman Folklore*, London, G. Allen and Co., 1911.
Bleek, W. H. I. and Lucy C. Lloyd, *The Mantis and His Friends*, Cape Town, Maskew Miller, 1924.
Boesak, Allan, *Farewell to Innocence*, Johannesburg, Ravan Press, 1976.
Brookes, Edgar, *Apartheid: A Documentary Study of Modern South Africa*, London, Routledge and Kegan Paul, 1968.
Brookes, Edgar, *The City of God and the Politics of Crisis*, London, OUP, 1960.
Brookes, Edgar, *The Colour Problems of South Africa*, Lovedale, Lovedale Press, 1934.
Brooks, Edgar, *The Commonwealth Today*, Pietermaritzburg, University of Natal Press, 1959.
Brookes, Edgar, *A History of South African Native Policy*, (1 edn), Pretoria, Die Nasionale Pers, 1924 and (2 edn), Cape Town, Juta, 1927.
Brookes, Edgar H., *The Political Future of South Africa*, Pretoria, Van Schaik, 1927.
Brookes, Edgar, *Power, Law, Right and Love: A Study in Political Values*, Durham, Duke University Press, 1963.
Brookes, Edgar, *South Africa in a Changing World*, Cape Town, CUP, 1953.
Brookes, Edgar, *A South African Pilgrimage*, Johannesburg, Ravan Press, 1977.
Brooks, Alan and Brickhill, Jeremy, *Whirlwind Before the Storm*, London, International Defence and Aid, 1980.
Bryce, James, *Impressions of South Africa*, London, Macmillan, 1899.
Bundy, Colin, *The Rise and Fall of the South African Peasantry*, London, Heinemann, 1979.

Butler, Jeffrey, Elphick, Richard and Welsh, David (eds), *Democratic Liberalism in South Africa*, Middleton (Conn), Wesleyan University Press and Cape Town, David Philip, 1987.

Calpin, G. H., *There Are No South Africans*, London, Nelson, 1942.

Campbell, Alexander, *Smuts and Swastika*, London, V. Gollancz, 1943.

Campbell, Roy, *Broken Record*, London, Boriswood, 1934.

Carter, Gwendolem, *The Politics of Inequality*, London, Thames and Hudson, 1959.

Cell, John, *The Highest Stage of White Supremacy: The Origins of Segregation in South Africa and the United States*, Cambridge, Cambridge University Press, 1982.

Clingman, Stephen, *The Novels of Nadine Gordimer: History From The Inside*, Johannesburg, Ravan Press, 1986.

Coetzee, J. M., *Waiting For the Barbarians*, Johannesburg, Ravan Press, 1981.

Coetzee, J. M., *White Writing*, New Haven, Yale University Press and Johannesburg, Ravan Press, 1988.

Collini, Stefan, *Liberalism and Sociology: L. T. Hobhouse and Political Argument in England, 1880–1915*, Cambridge, CUP, 1979.

Cope, Jack, *The Fair House*, London, MacGibbon and Kee, 1955.

Couzens, Tim, *The New Africa: A Study of the Life and Work of H. I. E. Dhlomo*, Johannesburg, Ravan Press, 1985.

Cowen, D. V., *The Foundations of Sovereignty*, London, Oxford University Press, 1961.

Cravens, Hamilton, *The Triumph of Evolution: American Scientists and the Heredity-Environment Controversy, 1900–1941*, Pennsylvania, University of Pennsylvania Press, 1978.

Curtin, Philip, *The Image of Africa*, Madison, University of Wisconsin Press, 1964.

De Gruchy, John W. (ed), *Resistance and Hope: South African Essays in Honour of Beyers Naude*, Cape Town and Johannesburg, David Philip, 1985.

De Villiers, Andre (ed), *English Speaking South Africa Today*, Cape Town, Oxford University Press, 1976.

Driver, C. J., *Patrick Duncan: South African and Pan African*, London, Heinemann, 1980.

Dubow, Saul, *Racial Segregation and the Origins of Apartheid in South Africa, 1919–1936*, London and Basingstoke, The Macmillan Press, 1989.

Dubow, Saul, "Race, civilisation and culture: the elaboration of segregationist discourse in the inter-war years" in Shula Marks and Stanley Trapido (eds), *The Politics of Race, Class and Nationalism in Twentieth Century South Africa*, London and New York, Longman, 1987, pp. 71–94.

Evans, Ifor L., *Native Policy in Southern Africa*, Cambridge, Cambridge University Press, 1934.

Fairchild, Hoxie Neale, *The Noble Savage: A Study in Romantic Naturalism*, New York, OUP, 1928.

Fatton, Robert, *Black Consciousness in South Africa*, New York, State University of New York Press, 1986.

February, V. A., *Mind Your Colour: The 'Coloured' Stereotype in South African Literature*, London and Boston, Kegan Int., 1981.

Fick, M. Laurence, *The Education of the South African Native*, Pretoria, South African Council for Educational and Social Research, 1939.
First, Ruth and Ann Scott, *Olive Schreiner*, New York, Schocken Books, 1980.
Fischer, Ernst, *The Necessity of Art*, Harmondsworth, Penguin Books, 1963.
Fitzpatrick, Percy, *The Transvaal From Within*, London, Heinemann, 1900.
Gella, Alexander (ed), *The Intelligentsia and the Intellectuals*, London and Beverley Hills, Sage Publications, 1976.
Gerhart, Gail M., *Black Power in South Africa*, Berkeley, University of California Press, 1978.
Gibbon, Perceval, *Margaret Harding*, Cape Town and Johannesburg, David Philip, 1983.
Giliomee, Hermann and Lawrence Schlemmer, *From Apartheid To Nation Building*, Cape Town, Oxford University Press, 1989.
Gordimer, Nadine, *The Conservationist*, London, Jonathan Cape, 1974.
Gordimer, Nadine, *The Essential Gesture*, London, Jonathan Cape, 1988.
Gordimer, Nadine, *A World of Strangers*, Harmondsworth, Penguin Books, 1958.
Gordimer, Nadine, *The Late Bourgeois World*, London, Gollancz, 1966.
Gould, Stephen Jay, *The Mismeasure of Man*, Harmondsworth, Penguin Books, 1984.
Green, Martin, *Dreams of Adventure, Deeds of Empire*, London, Routledge and Kegan Paul, 1980.
Hall, John A., *Liberalism*, London, Paladin Books, 1988.
Haller, John S., *Outcasts From Evolution: Scientific Attitudes to Racial Inferiority, 1859–1900*, New York, Columbia University Press, 1975.
Hellman, Ellen, *Handbook on Race Relations in South Africa*, Cape Town and New York, Oxford University Press, 1949.
Heywood, Christopher (ed), *Aspects of South African Literature*, London, Heinemann, 1976.
Himmelfarb, Gertrude, *The New History and the Old*, Cambridge (Mass), Harvard University Press, 1987.
Hirson, Baruch, *Year of Fire, Year of Ash*, London, Zed Books, 1979.
Hoernle, R. F. A., *Matter, Life, Mind and God*, London, Methuen, 1923.
Hoernle, R. F. A., *South African Native Policy and the Liberal Spirit*, Cape Town, University of Cape Town for the Phelps Stokes Fund, 1939.
Hoernle, R. F. A., *Race and Reason*, Johannesburg, Witwatersrand University Press, 1945.
Hofmeyr, J. H., *South Africa*, London, Ernest Benn, 1931.
Huddleston, Trevor, *Naught For Your Comfort*, London, Collins, 1956.
Hyam, Ronald, *Elgin and Churchill at the Colonial Office*, London and New York, Macmillan, 1968.
Jacobson, Dan, *A Dance in the Sun*, Harmondsworth, Penguin Books, 1956.
Jacoby, Russell, *The Last Intellectuals: American Culture in the Age of Academe*, New York, Basic Books, 1987.
Jenkyns, Richard, *The Victorians and Ancient Greece*, Oxford, Basil Blackwell, 1980.
Keane, A. H., *Ethnology*, Cambridge, CUP, 1896.

Keane, A. H., *The Gold of Ophir*, London, Stanford, 1901.
Keppel Jones, Arthur, *When Smuts Goes*, Pietermaritzburg, Shuter and Shooter, 1947.
Kidd, Dudley, *The Essential Kaffir*, London, A & C Black, 1904.
Kidd, Dudley, *Kaffir Socialism and the Dawn of Individualism*, London, A & C Black, 1908.
Krige, Uys (ed), *Olive Schreiner: A Selection*, Cape Town, Oxford University Press, 1968.
Kuper, Adam, "Anthropology and Apartheid" in J. Lonsdale (ed), *South Africa in Question*, London, J. Currey, 1988, pp. 33–51.
Levy-Bruhl, Lucien, *How Natives Think*, London, Allen and Unwin, 1923.
Lewsen, Phyllis (ed), *Selections From the Correspondence of John X. Merriman*, Cape Town, Van Riebeeck Society, 1966.
Lippmann, Walter, *The Public Philosophy*, Boston, Little, Brown and Co, 1956.
Lonsdale, John (ed), *South Africa in Question*, London, J. Currey, 1988.
Loram, C. T., *The Education of the South African Native*, London, 1917.
Luthuli, Albert, *Let My People Go*, London, Collins, 1962.
Macmillan, Hugh and Marks, Shula (eds), *Africa and Empire: W. M. Macmillan, Historian and Social Critic*, London, Temple Smith, 1989.
Macmillan, W. M., *Complex South Africa*, London, Faber, 1930.
MacCrone, I. D., *Race Attitudes in South Africa*, Johannesburg, University of the Witwatersrand Press, 1937.
Madden, Frederick and D. K. Fieldhouse (eds), *Oxford and the Idea of Commonwealth*, London and Canberra, Croom Helm, 1982.
Malherbe, E. G. (ed), *Educational Adaptations in a Changing Society*, Cape Town and Johannesburg, Juta, 1937.
Malherbe, E. G., *Never A Dull Moment*, Cape Town, Juta, 1981.
Maritain, Jacques, *Man and the State*, Chicago, University of Chicago Press, 1961.
Maughan-Brown, David, *Land, Freedom and Fiction: History and Ideology in Kenya*, London, Zed Books, 1986.
Millin, Sarah Gertrude, *White Africans Are Also People*, Cape Town, Timmins, 1966.
Murray, B. K., *Wits: The Early Years*, Johannesburg, Witwatersrand University Press, 1982.
Ndebele, Njabulo (ed), *Black Viewpoint*, Durban, SPRO-CAS Black Community Programme, 1972.
Nicholls, G. Heaton, *Bayete: Hail to the King!*, London, Allen and Unwin, 1923.
Nielsen, Peter, *The Black Man's Place in South Africa*, Cape Town, Juta, 1922.
Nolutshungu, Sam C., *Changing South Africa*, Manchester, Manchester University Press, 1982.
Nielsen, Peter, *The Black Man's Place in South Africa*, Cape Town, Juta, 1922.
NUSAS, *The Novel and the Nation, 1959–1960*, Johannesburg, NUSAS, 1969.
Odendaal, Andre, *Vukani Bantu!: The Beginnings of Black Protest Politics in South Africa to 1912*, Cape Town, David Philip, 1984.

SELECT BIBLIOGRAPHY

Oldham, J. H., *White and Black in Africa: A Critical Examination of the Rhodes Lectures of General Smuts*, London, Longman, Green and Co., 1930.

Parker, Kenneth (ed), *The South African Novel in English*, London and Basingstoke, The Macmillan Press, 1978.

Paton, *Cry the Beloved Country*, Harmondsworth, Penguin Books, 1960.

Paton, *Debby Go Home*, Harmondsworth, Penguin Books, 1960.

Paton, Alan, *Hofmeyr*, Oxford, Clarendon Press, 1964.

Paton, Alan, *Toward the Mountain: An Autobiography*, New York, Charles Scribners and Sons, 1981.

Plomer, William, *Turbott Wolfe*, London, The Hogarth Press, 1925.

Reeves, Ambrose, *South Africa – Yesterday and Tomorrow*, London, Gollancz, 1962.

Rich, Paul B., "Doctrines of Change" in J. Brewer (ed), *Can South Africa Survive*, London and Basingstoke, The Macmillan Press, 1989, pp. 281–311.

Rich, Paul B., "Milnerism and a Ripping Yarn: Transvaal Land Settlement and John Buchan's novel *Prester John*, 1901–1910" in Belinda Bozzoli (ed), *Town and Countryside in the Transvaal*, Johannesburg, Ravan Press, 1983, pp. 412–433.

Rich, Paul B., *Race and Empire in British Politics* (2 edn), Cambridge, CUP, 1990.

Rich, Paul B., "Romance and the Development of the South African Novel" in Landeg White and Tim Couzens (eds), *Literature and Society in South Africa*, London, Longmans, 1984, pp. 120–137.

Rich, Paul B., "W. M. Macmillan, South African Segregation and Commonwealth Race Relations, 1919–1938" in Hugh Macmillan and Shula Marks (eds), *Africa and Empire: W. M. Macmillan, Historian and Social Critic*, London, Temple Smith, 1989, pp. 192–211.

Rich, Paul B., *White Power and the Liberal Conscience*, Manchester, Manchester University Press and Johannesburg, Ravan Press, 1984.

Robertson, Janet, *Liberalism in South Africa, 1948–1963*, Oxford, Clarendon Press, 1971.

Rubin, Martin, *Sarah Gertrude Millin*, Johannesburg, AD Donker, 1977.

Ryan, Colleen, *Beyers Naude: Pilgrimage of Faith*, Cape Town, David Philip, 1990.

Sampson, Anthony, *Drum*, London, Collins, 1956.

Saunders, Christopher, *The Making of the South African Past*, Cape Town and Johannesburg, David Philip, 1988.

Schapera, Isaac (ed), *Western Civilisation and the Natives of South Africa*, London, Routledge and Kegan Paul, 1934.

Smuts, J. C., *Africa and Some World Problems*, Oxford, Clarendon Press, 1930.

Smuts, J. C., *Greater South Africa: Plans for a Better World*, Johannesburg, Truth Legion, 1940.

Smuts, J. C., *Holism and Evolution*, London, Macmillan, 1927.

Sparks, Allister, *The Mind of South Africa*, London, Heinemann, 1990.

SPRO-CAS, *South Africa's Political Alternatives*, Johannesburg, SPRO-CAS, 1973.

Stow, George William, *The Native Races of South Africa*, London, Swan Sonnenschein, 1905.
Student Christian Association, *Christian Students and Modern South Africa: A Report of the Bantu–European Student Christian Conference, Fort Hare, 27 June–3 July 1930*, Lovedale, Lovedale Press, 1930.
Thoahlane, Thoahlane (ed), *Black Renaissance: Papers From the Black Renaissance Convention*, Johannesburg, Ravan Press, 1975.
Thompson, Leonard, *The Political Mythology of Apartheid*, New Haven and London, Yale University Press, 1986.
Turner, Richard, *The Eye of the Needle: Towards Participatory Democracy in South Africa*, Maryknoll (NY), Orbis Books 1978 (1 ed Johannesburg, 1972).
Vail, Leroy (ed), *The Creation of Tribalism in South Africa*, London, James Currey and Los Angeles, University of California Press, 1989.
Van den Berghe, Pierre (ed), *The Liberal Dilemma in South Africa*, London, Croom Helm, 1979.
Van der Post, Laurens, *The Dark Eye of Africa*, London, The Hogarth Press, 1966.
Van der Post, Laurens, *A Far Off Place*, Harmondsworth, Penguin Books, 1987.
Van der Post, Laurens, *Flamingo Feather*, Harmondsworth, Penguin Books, 1983.
Van der Post, Laurens, *In a Province*, Harmondsworth, Penguin Books, 1983.
Van der Post, Laurens, *Jung and the Story of Our Time*, Harmondsworth, Penguin Books, 1976.
Van der Post, Laurens, *A Mantis Carol*, Harmondsworth, Penguin Books, 1989.
Van der Post, Laurens, *The Seed and the Sower*, Harmondsworth, Penguin Books, 1966.
Van der Post, Laurens, *A Story Like the Wind*, Harmondsworth, Penguin Books, 1974.
Van der Post, Laurens and Jane Taylor, *Testament to the Bushmen*, Harmondsworth, Penguin Books, 1985.
Van der Post, Laurens, *A Walk with a White Bushman*, Harmondsworth, Penguin Books, 1986.
Walshe, Peter, *Church versus State in South Africa: The Case of the Christian Institute*, London, Hurst and Co., 1983.
Walshe, Peter, *The Rise of African Nationalism in South Africa*, London, Hurst and Co., 1970.
Watts, H. L. (ed), *English Speaking South Africa Today*, Cape Town, Oxford University Press, 1976.
Welsh, David, *The Roots of Segregation*, Cape Town, Oxford University Press, 1971.
Villa-Vicencio, Charles and de Gruchy, Charles (eds), *Resistance and Hope: South African Essays in Honour of Beyers Naude*, Cape Town and Johannesburg, David Philip, 1985.
White, Hayden, *Tropics of Discourse*, Boston and London, Johns Hopkins University Press, 1978.
Younghusband, Captain Francis, *South Africa of Today*, London, Macmillan, 1896.

Articles

Adam, Heribert, "The Rise of Black Consciousness in South Africa", *Race*, XV, 2 (October 1973), pp. 149–165.

Brookes, Edgar, "South Africa: The Possibilities of an Impossible Situation", *African Affairs*, 55, 220 (July 1956), pp. 191–197.

Burchell, D. E., "Adams College, Natal, c1920–1956: A Critical Assessment", *Journal of Durban-Westville*, New Ser., 1 (1984), pp. 151–159.

Collini, Stefan, "Hobhouse, Bosanquet and the State: Philosophical Idealism and Political Argument in England, 1880–1980", *Past and Present*, 72, (1976), pp. 86–111.

Dalal, Farhad, "The Racism of Jung", *Race and Class*, XXIX (1988), pp. 1–22.

Dubow, Saul, "Holding 'A Just Balance Between White and Black': The Native Affairs Department in South Africa, 1920–33", *Journal of Southern African Studies*, XII, 2 (1986), pp. 217–239.

Du Toit, Andre, "No Chosen People: the Myth of the Calvinist Origins of Afrikaner Nationalism and Racial Ideology", *American Historical Review*, 88, 4 (October 1983), pp. 920–957.

George, Katherine, "The Civilised West Looks at Primitive Africa, 1400–1800", *ISIS*, XLIX, (March 1958).

Gordimer, Nadine, "From Apartheid to Afrocentrism", *English in Africa*, 7, 1 (1980).

Haskell, Thomas, "Capitalism and the Origins of Humanitarian Sensibility", *American Historical Review*, 90, 2 (April 1985), pp. 339–361 and 90, 3 (June 1985), pp. 547–566.

James, W. R., "The 'Barbarians' in World Historical Perspective: Myth and Reality", *Cultures*, IV, 2 (1977), pp. 101–120.

Johns, Sheridan, "The Comintern, South Africa and the Black Diaspora", *Review of Politics*, XXXVII (1975), pp. 200–234.

Lacapra, Dominick, "Rethinking Intellectual History and Reading Texts", *History and Theory*, XIX (1980).

Legassick, Martin, "Race, Industrialisation and Social Change in South Africa: The Case of R. F. A. Hoernle", *African Affairs*, LXXV (1976), pp. 224–239.

Morrow, John, "Liberalism and British Idealistic Political Philosophy", *History of Political Thought*, V, 1 (Spring 1984), pp. 91–108.

Rich, Paul B., "The Appeals of Tuskegee: James Henderson, Lovedale and the Fortunes of South African Liberalism, 1906–1930", *International Journal of African Historical Studies*, 20, 2 (1987), pp. 271–292.

Sachs, Albie, "Towards a Bill of Rights for a Democratic South Africa", *The Hastings International and Comparative Law Review*, 12, 2 (Winter 1989), pp. 289–324.

Sharp, John, "The Roots of *Volkekunde* on Apartheid Ideology in South Africa", *Journal of Southern African Studies*, 8 (1981), pp. 16–36.

Simons, H. J., "What is Apartheid?", *Liberation*, 35, (March 1959), pp. 12–17 and 36 (May 1959), pp. 16–25.

Wade, Michael, "The Black looking glass in white South African literature", *African Affairs*, 82, 326 (January 1983), pp. 97–120.

Wade, Michael, "William Plomer, English Liberalism and the South African Novel", *The Journal of Commonwealth Literature*, VIII, 1 (June 1973), pp. 120–132.

Walshe, Peter, "Church Versus State in South Africa: The Christian Institute and the Resurgence of African Nationalism", *Journal of Church and State*, 19, 3 (1977), pp. 457–479.

Wolpe, Harold, "Capitalism and Cheap Labour Power: From Segregation to Apartheid", *Economy and Society*, XIV, (1972), pp. 425–456.

Theses and unpublished papers

Dubow, Saul, "Outline of Provisional paper on racial Ideology in early Twentieth Century South Africa", London, ICS, n.d.

Legassick, Martin, "Liberalism, Social Control and Liberation in South Africa", seminar paper, University of Warwick, 1977.

Legassick, Martin, "The Making of South African 'native policy': 1903–1923", London, 1972.

Legassick, Martin, "The Rise of South African Liberalism: Its Assumptions and Social Base", London, ICS, seminar paper, 1972.

Lodge, Tom, "Patrick Duncan and Radical Liberalism", seminar paper, University of Cape Town, 1976.

Prince, Melody Anne, "Watchman, What of the Night? The Political Ideas of R. F. A. Hoernle and E. H. Brookes and their contribution to the theory and practice of South African liberalism", M. Phil Thesis, University of Leicester, 1983.

Shingler, John David, "Education and Political Order in South Africa, 1902–1961", Ph.D Diss., Yale University, 1973.

INDEX

Abrahams, Peter 120
Adam, Heribert 111
Adams College 77
adaptation, racial 31
Africa Survey (1938) 182
African Resistance Movement (ARM) 95, 140
African National Congress 83, 91, 95, 138, 140, 144, 190–1, 197, 211
   Defiance Campaign 84, 93, 140, 191–2
   Programme of Action 83, 93, 191
Afrikanerbond vir Rassestudie see *Rasserverhoudingsbond van Afrikaners*
Alexandra Health Committee 61–2
Altman, Phyllis 120, 130, 133
   The Law of the Vultures 120, 130, 133
American Board of Missions 48, 77, 78
Anglo American Corporation 144
anthropology 15, 46, 181
   Malinowski school of social anthropology 33

apartheid 13, 85, 88, 92, 94, 103, 111, 115, 123, 147, 173, 193, 195, 200, 203, 206, 209–10
   neo-apartheid 208
   petty apartheid 208
   post-apartheid culture 209
arrested development, concept of 25, 27, 28, 35, 218*n*
assimilation, racial 16, 25, 51, 53, 54, 55, 58, 64, 70, 92, 180
Augustine, St 66, 86, 195
Azanian Peoples Organization (AZAPO) 116

Baldwin, James 87
Ballinger, Margaret 57, 81, 91, 246*n*
Ballinger, Willam 57
Bantu Men's Social Centre, Durban 80
Barlow, Arthur 71
Basner, Hyman 80, 81
BC *see* Black Consciousness
BCP *see* Black Community Programme
Becker, Carl 86

Bell, F. W. 20, 22
Benedict, Ruth 155
Berlin, Isaiah 4
Biesheuvel, Simon 36, 37, 38, 220*n*
  African Intelligence 36
Biko, Steve 109, 113, 115, 118
Black Community Programme (BCP) 109–10, 117–18
Black Consciousness 11, 100, 102, 103, 105, 107, 108, 110–11, 115, 117–18, 207, 233*n*, 236*n*
Black theology 116
Black Peoples Convention (BPC) 115, 117
Black Power 88
Black Renaissance Convention (1974) 117
Bleek, H. I. E. 148, 162–3
  The Mantis and his Friends 163
  Specimens of Bushman Folklore 162, 165
Boesak, Alan 88
Boraine, Alex 114
Bosanquet, Bernard 41–5
Boydell, Thomas 71
BPC *see* Black Peoples Convention
British Association for the Advancement of Science 18
Brookes, Edgar vii, 2, 9, 11, 15, 28, 32, 59, 65–90, 95, 104–5, 185, 195–6, 201, 207, 211
  City of God and the Politics of Crisis 86
  Colour Problems of South Africa 75
  History of Native Policy in South Africa 69–72
  The Political Future of South Africa 72
  Power, Law, Right and Love 87
  South Africa in a Changing World 85
Brown, Peter 87, 95

Bryce, James 18, 173
Buchan, John 10, 16, 120, 126, 133, 150–1, 164
  Prester John 16, 133, 150–1
Budlender, Geoff 108
Bushman, The *see* San, The
Buthelezi, Chief Gatsha 110
Butler, Guy 9

Campbell, Killie 77
Campbell, Roy 123, 146–7, 178, 244*n*
Cape African franchise 17, 19, 52, 71, 72, 78, 79, 184
Cape Coloured franchise 85
Cape liberalism 52, 73, 89
catastrophic theory of history 198
Cell, John 14
Chamberlain, Houston Stewart 180
Champion, A. W. G. 77, 79, 80, 83, 84
Christian Institute (CI) 100–1, 111, 118
Church of the Province 97
CI *see* Christian Institute
citizenship 43, 44, 72, 94, 112, 186, 200–1
  citizenship rights 63, 177, 193–4
Clarke, Fred 29, 219n
Coetzee, J. M. 120, 150, 197–8
  Waiting for the Barbarians 197
common society liberalism 93, 94, 104–6, 115, 194–5, 201, 210
Commonwealth, British 180, 202–3
Communist Party, South African (SACP) 91–2
Community of the Resurrection 78
Congress of Democrats 91, 140
Congress Movement 194, 199
Congress of the People 91, 93, 194
  see also Freedom Charter
Congress Youth League 80, 83, 92, 93, 117, 190
Conrad, Joseph 123, 156

INDEX   263

consociational democracy 106, 118, 207
Contact 91, 194, 196
Contrast 138
Cope, Jack 4, 131–3, 147
   The Fair House 131–2
Cope, John 189
Cottesloe Consultation (1960) 97, 100
Cowen, Dennis 195–6
   The Foundations of Sovereignty 196
Crocker, H. J. 21
Curtin, Philip 15
Curtis, Neville 109

Darwinism 17, 20, 45, 170, 174, 181, 202
   see also Social Darwinism
De Kiewiet, C. W. 58, 98–9
Department of Justice 70
Dhlomo, H. I. E. 88
Dinuzulu, Chief Mskiyeni ka 79–80
DRC *see* Dutch Reformed Church
Drum 136–7, 206
Dube, Rev. John 78
Dubow, Saul 14
Duerden, J. E. 26–7
Duncan, Patrick 44, 54, 64, 83, 91, 140, 175, 194–5, 247*n*
Durban Native Affairs Reform Club 22
Dutch Reformed Church 50, 93, 97, 99
   Federal Council of 67
Du Toit, Andre 103, 105, 108–9, 115

Egeland, Leif 79, 155, 185
Eglin, Colin 106
Eiselen, Prof. W. W. M. 35, 49, 50, 63, 76, 202
Eliot, T. S. 151, 167
   The Waste Land 152

Elphick, Richard 40, 50
Ethiopianism 175–6
eugenics 25–6, 39, 177, 182, 244*n*
Evans, Maurice 22, 23, 68, 177

Fairchild, Hoxie Neale 149
Fantham, H. B. 25–6, 35, 38
Faye, Carl 78
February, V. A. 128
Federal Theological Seminary 100
Fick, M. L. 30–2, 35, 36
   The Educability of the South African Native 35, 36
Findlay, George 59–60
Fischer, Bram 140
Fischer, Ernst 141–2
Fitzpatrick, Percy 171–3, 200
   The Transvaal From Within 171
Ford Foundation 98–9, 114
Frankel, Herbert 192
Freedom Charter 91, 93–4, 107, 137, 194
   see also Congress of the People
Friedman, Bernard 91
frontier thesis 34, 37
Frye, Northrop 126, 150
Furse, Bishop Michael 19, 67, 190

Gamma Sigma Club 48
General Law Amendment Act (1963) 140
Gesuiwerde Nasionale Party (GNP) 184, 190
   see also Malan, Dr D. F.
Gibbon, Perceval 151
   Margaret Harding 151
Glen Grey Act (1894) 44, 203
Gobhozi, W. J. 79
Gordimer, Nadine 107, 119, 121, 136, 138–9, 141–2, 144, 197, 206–7, 209–10
   Burger's Daughter 142
   The Conservationist 107, 197, 209

The Late Bourgeois World 107, 120, 139–42, 209
A World of Strangers 136–9, 142
Gould, Stephen Jay 23
Green, T. H. 41, 42, 43
Grice, Duchesne 112

Haggard, Rider 9, 120, 126, 131, 150
  King Solomon's Mines 150

Harris, E. E. 193
Harris, John 140
Havenga, N. G. 190
Hemming, Douglas 84
Hellman, Ellen 37, 63, 112–14
Henderson, Rev. James 32
Hertzog, General J. B. M. 21, 22, 31, 50, 52, 69, 70, 71, 183
  and 'Black manifesto' election (1929) 183
Heunis, Chris 208
Himmelfarb, Gertrude 6
Hodgkin, Thomas 192
Hoernle, R. F. A. 9, 11, 15, 28, 32–4, 36, 39–49, 50–66, 73, 75, 78, 84, 90, 93, 98, 105–6, 112, 127, 186, 188, 201–3, 206–8, 224*n*
  South African Native Policy and the Liberal Spirit 54–5, 59, 98
Hoernle Memorial Lecture 83
Hoernle, Winifred 33, 42
Hofmeyr, Jan H. 42, 78–9, 82, 94, 128, 130, 183–6, 188–90, 202, 245*n*, 246*n*
  Christian Principles and the Race Problem 189
  South Africa 184
Hofmeyr, 'Onze Jan' 2
Holism 181
Holloway, John 48
Horner, Dudley 109

Huddleston, Trevor 87
Human rights 196, 211

idealism, liberal 41, 43, 45, 58
  see also Green, T. H.
Immorality Act (1927) 25, 53, 128
Imvo Zabantsundu 2
Inge, Dean 244*n*
integration, racial 92, 96, 102
intelligence testing 9, 22, 28, 30, 39, 46, 75, 202
Interdenominational African Ministers Association of Southern Africa (IDAMASA) 100–1
Interdenominational African Ministers Federation (IDAMF) 93
International and Commercial Workers Union 153
Izwi Labantu 19

Jabavu, D. D. T. 2, 31–2, 78, 190
Jabavu, John Tengo 2
Jacobson, Dan 134
  A Dance in the Sun 134
Johnstone, Sir Harry 20, 172–3, 180
Joint Councils 28, 67, 71, 90, 154
  Durban 77, 79
  Johannesburg 74
Jung, Carl Gustav 148, 156–7, 164

Keane, A. H. 20, 174
Keppel-Jones, Arthur 83, 192
Kermode, Frank 171
Kerr, Alexander 54
Kerr, Philip *see* Lord Lothian
Khoapa, Bennie 109–10, 113, 235*n*
Kidd, Dudley 150, 175–6, 244*n*
Kipling, Rudyard 122, 152
Kirk, John 77
Kleinschmidt, Horst 113
Krige, Uys 147

INDEX 265

Kruger, Paul 171

Lagden, Godfrey 16–19, 215–16n
Lamarckism 23, 26–7
Laski, Harold 45, 73
Leftwich, Adrian 95
Legassick, Martin 13–14, 17, 40, 211
Lehfeldt, Prof. R. A. 69
Lembede, Anton 191
Levy Bruhl, Lucien 28, 47, 157, 160
Lewis Ethelreda 136
Lewsen, Phyllis 185
Liberal Party 72, 87, 90–2, 95–6, 99, 111, 118, 140, 189–90, 194, 206
liberation theology 86
Lippmann, Walter 195
Locke, Alain 47, 73
Long, B. K. 185–6
Loram, C. T. 16, 24–5, 27, 29, 30, 35, 72, 75–7, 219n, 227n
Lothian, Lord 44, 181
Lovedale 2, 51, 54, 78

MacBride, Rev Clive 110, 113–14
MacCrone, I. D. 29, 33–4, 37, 38, 53
Macmillan, W. M. 30, 48–9, 69, 75, 207, 232n
Mafuna, Bokwe James 109
Malan, Dr D. F. 50, 128, 184, 190
  and Gesuiwerde Nasionale Party 184
Malan, 'Sailor' 193
Malherbe, E. G. 2–3, 29–30, 34–5, 84, 99, 219n
  see also National Bureau for Education and Social Research
Makgatho, S. R. 67
Mandela, Nelson 91, 140, 191
Maritain, Jacques 84
Marquard, Leo 96, 111, 232n

Matthews, Z. K. 2, 32, 60, 78, 80, 86, 92–4
Mau Mau 157–8
Maughan Brown, David 148
Mbeki, Govan 93–4
Mbelle, I. Bud 67
Mears, Gordon 81, 186–7
Merriman, John X. 22, 179
Millin, Sarah Gertrude 25, 123, 151, 202–3
  Cecil Rhodes 202
  Dark Water 151
  General Smuts 203
  God's Stepchildren 123, 151
  White Africans Are Also People 203
Milner, Alfred 9, 175
  Milner Kindergarten 16, 20, 54, 175, 181
  Milnerites 43
Miscegenation, racial 25, 53, 123, 151, 172–3, 176, 178, 180, 202
Molteno, Donald 64, 195
  Molteno Commission 195
Moral Disarmament 74
Moroka, James 81
Mosaka, Paul 80
Mpanza, Charles 80
Msimang, Selby 70, 226n
Multi Racial Conference (1957) 93
Myrdal, Gunnar 85

NAC see Native Affairs Commission
NAD see Native Affairs Department
NRC see Natives Representative Council
Nasionale Pers, Die 69
National Bureau for Education and Social Research 29, 30
National Institute for Personnel Research 38–9
National Forum 115
national liberation, doctrine of 191, 196
National Party 9, 13, 93, 105, 226n

Nationalist Government 86, 191–2, 194
Nationalists 192–3
1948 election victory 83, 128, 189, 203
National Union of South African Students (NUSAS) 95, 100, 112–13
Native Administration Act (1927) 14, 70, 82
Native Advisory Boards 92
Native Affairs Act (1920) 27, 71
Native Affairs Commission 16, 27, 29, 54, 67, 70, 71, 72, 83, 186, 188, 219*n*, 227*n*
Native Affairs Department, Union 14, 21, 70, 71, 78, 81, 186
  Cape Native Affairs Department 21–2
Native Affairs Society *see* Transvaal Native Affairs Society
Native Bills (1936) 52, 72, 78, 79, 188
Native Economic Commission, Report of (1932) 31, 32, 33, 76
Natives Land Act (1913) 94
natives representation, boycott of 6
natives representatives 80, 81
Natives Representative Council 78, 79, 80, 81, 92
natural law 195–6, 206
natural rights 42
Naude, Dr Beyers 100–1, 118
Ndamse, C. M. C. 117
Ndebele, Njabulo 116
Nettleton, Clive 109, 113–14, 236*n*
Ngubane, Jordan 83
Nicholls, G. Heaton 54, 151, 187–8, 202
Nielsen, Peter 27, 28, 34, 53, 75

Nkomo, William 112
Noble savage, myth of the 145–6, 148–50, 167, 178, 201
Norton, T. C. 71
NRC *see* Natives Representative Council
NUSAS *see* National Union of South African Students

Oldham, J. H. 182
Olivier, Sydney 182, 190
Oppenheimer, Harry 9, 98, 114
Oxford Group *see* Moral Disarmament

Pact Government 70, 71, 189
Palmer, Mabel 77
Pan Africanism 191, 194, 196
Pan African Congress (PAC) 95, 138, 143, 197
Paton, Alan 4, 91, 103, 108, 119, 125–8, 147, 196–7, 207
  Cry the Beloved Country 119, 125–8, 152
  Ha'penny 126
  Too Late the Phalarope 128–30, 132
Paton, Jonathan 113
Perham, Margery 56
Petrie, Alexander 66
Phillips, Rev. Ray 48
Pim, Howard 18–20, 22, 42, 44, 68, 177, 216*n*
Pirow, Oswald 79
Plomer, William 123, 127, 146, 151
  Turbott Wolfe 123–4, 151
pluralism, theory of 45, 56, 103–5
Pretoria Native Welfare Association 67
Prior, Andrew 208
Progressive Party 87, 98, 106, 111, 114, 195

psychology 33, 34, 37–8, 46
  group psychology 37
  see also MacCrone, I. D.
public philosophy, idea of 195

Randall, Peter 102–3, 105, 108–9, 113
Rasserverhoudingsbond van Afrikaners 50–1, 65
Reeves, Bishop Ambrose 93, 97
Reitz, Deneys 188
Rex, John 104
Rheinallt Jones, J. D. 28, 34, 53, 59, 76, 77, 80, 83, 98, 185
Rhodes, Cecil 9, 171, 184, 186, 203
  see also Glen Grey Act
Rhodes Trust 181
Rose Innes, James 52, 94
Rose Innes, Richard 44

SAAAS see South African Association for the Advancement of Science
SACP see Communist Party, South African
SAIRR see South African Institute of Race Relations
San, The 148, 150, 161–6, 164, 167–8, 201
SASM see South African Students Movement
SASO see South African Students Organisation
SANAC see South African Native Affairs Commission
Schlebusch Commission 112
Schreiner, Olive 120, 125, 128, 172, 176–9
  The Native Question 176, 178
Schreiner, Justice O. D. 97, 208
Scully, W. C. 127, 136, 163
Segregation vi, 10, 13–15, 17, 20–22, 24, 31–2, 48–51, 54–8, 60, 62, 66, 67–70, 76, 78, 81, 85, 95, 98, 105, 143, 150, 170–1, 173, 176, 178, 184, 186–7, 190, 201–2
  liberal 94
  philanthropic 50
  possessory 70
  scientific vocabulary of 15
  separate but equal doctrine 195
  territorial segregation 16, 72
  theorists of 174
  university 86
Selborne, Lord 19, 20, 175–6
Selope Thema, Victor 74
Seme, Pixley 48, 78, 79
Shepstone, Douglas 79
Shepstone, Theophilus 9, 70
Shils, Edward 1
Simons, Jack 64–5
Sisulu, Walter 91, 191
Slabbert, Frederick Van Zyl 108
Smit, Douglas 61, 81, 82, 186
Smuts, General Jan 19, 21, 45, 46, 50, 58, 67, 80, 82, 83, 178–89, 202–3, 245*n*
  Address to SAIRR (1942) 187
  Africa and Some World Problems 181–2
  Holism and Evolution 180
  Savoy Hotel Speech (1917) 179
Smuts government 81, 82, 93, 128
Social and Economic Planning Council, Report No 9 (1946) 82
Social Darwinism 16, 37, 131–2, 150, 176
South Africa Party (SAP) 183
South African Association for the Advancement of Science 23–7, 28, 29, 31, 32, 33, 35
South African Bureau of Racial Affairs 65
South African Council of Churches 102

South African Institute of Race Relations 6, 30, 32, 34, 42, 49–50, 51, 59, 60, 73–8, 83, 90, 92, 96–102, 109–15, 187–9, 193, 206–7, 232n, 236n
Go Forward in Faith (1954) 96
South African Native Affairs Commission, Report of (1903–5) 16
South African Native Trust 79
South African Students Movement (SASM) 117
South African Students Organization 100–2, 115–18
Soweto crisis (1976) 208
Soweto Students Representative Council 118
Springbok Legion 90
SPRO-CAS 89, 102–4, 107, 110, 112–3, 197, 206–8, 235n
  SPRO-CAS TWO 109, 113, 207
  South Africa's Political Alternatives 103, 105, 108, 115
  see also Black Community Programme
Stow, George William 162
Suzman, Helen 113

Tambo Oliver 91, 191
Teachers College, Columbia University 24, 29
Thatcher, Margaret 148
Theal, George McCall 162, 174–5
Thompson, Leonard 13, 50
Tillich, Paul 87
Torch Commando 90, 193
Transvaal African Congress 67
Transvaal Leader 17
Transvaal Native Affairs Society 19–20, 216n
Transvaal Philosophical Society 18
Transvaal University College *see* University of Pretoria
Treason Trial 93

Trusteeship, doctrine of 55, 56, 57, 117, 176, 182, 187–8, 202
  South African policy of 60, 189
Turner, Rick 103–9
  The Eye of the Needle 107–8
Tuskegee Institute 20, 51, 73

Umkhonto we Sizwe 95, 196
Umteteli wa Bantu 78
United Party 50, 82, 90, 93, 186–7, 189–90, 192–3, 195
Universal Declaration of Human Rights 196
University College of Fort Hare 31–2, 74, 78, 83
University of Cape Town 29, 41, 176, 183
  Centre for Inter-Group Studies 114
University of Natal 77, 84, 227
  Chair of African Studies at 77, 227n
  Institute for Social Research 114
University of Pretoria 67, 69, 74
University of Stellenbosch 35, 76, 103
University of the Witwatersrand 28, 33, 42, 45, 49, 60–1, 69, 93, 183

Vaal Triangle uprising (1984) 209
Van den Berghe, Pierre 210
Van der Byl, Piet 188
Van der Post, Laurens 2, 3, 9, 10, 47, 122–4, 136, 144, 146–8, 152–68, 201
  And Yet Being Someone Other 166
  The Dark Eye in Africa 147, 157
  A Far Off Place 148, 163–4
  Flamingo Feather 158–9, 163–5
  The Heart of the Hunter 162
  Jung and the Story of Our Time 148
  In a Province 124, 146–7, 152–4, 161, 163, 167

The Lost World of the Kalahari 162
A Mantis Carol 148, 163, 166
The Seed and the Sower 147, 155–6
A Story Like the Wind 148, 163–4
Venture to the Interior 148
A Walk With a White Bushman 148
Van Wyk, Fred 97, 101, 109, 111–12, 206
verligtes 206, 208
Verwoerd, Dr. Hendrik 35, 82
Vigne, Randolph 91, 196
Volkekunde 35, 49–50, 65, 76
Voorslag 123–4, 146, 178
Vorster, John 99, 115, 203

Wallas, Graham 43, 46
Washington, Booker T. 20, 55, 73
Weisman, August 26
Whitehead, A. N. 45

Whyte, Quintin 97–9, 101–2, 106, 111–2, 206, 231n, 232n
Wilson, Woodrow 55
Wilsonian liberalism 201
Wolpe, Harold 14
Woolf, Leonard 158
World Council of Churches 97, 100, 102
Worrall, Dennis 105–6

Xuma, Alfred 2, 48, 113, 191

Yergan, Max 74
Young, E. B. 81
Younghusband, Francis 172

Zimbabwe ruins, origins of 174, 179, 245n
Zulu Society 80